lobal justice move-
o transformational
ry that beckons the
g so, be drawn nearer
instructs, is the very

ANG, Director of the
ustice Mission's (IJM)
e for Biblical Justice

Deeply grounded in theol-
nd orient our generation's
rist in anticipation of the

Mike Yankoski, Author of
Under the Overpass

eats, and then compelling the
ustice should be a concern for
he megachurch leaders and the
moms and soccer dads in the
g right what is wrong, so we are
der.

enreider, Author of One Bite
a Time, Blogger, and Creative
tor of SimpleLivingMedia.com

ma's Pursuing Justice avoids all the
eep and accurate understanding of
ate call to obey and imitate God by
d by scripture, rich in personal expe-
shy of acknowledging that the pursuit
though joyful nonetheless. I have no
o be an eye–opener.

lterstorff, Noah Porter Professor
us of Philosophical Theology, Yale
nior Research Fellow, Institute for
s in Culture, University of Virginia

Ken helped me draw nearer to God's heart and the people He loves. This isn't a book about doing more justice; it's a book about being just. Ken refuses to indulge the debates that ask the wrong questions—debates that force either/or positions on justification and justice, atonement and action, faith and works. Ken doesn't waste time lifting up cause celebrities or dictating God's pet issues for your time and place. *Pursuing Justice* is, at its heart, about right relationships. Ken's stories will thrill your heart and break your pride. And if you take this book seriously, it might just change your life!

JEREMY COURTNEY, FOUNDER
AND EXECUTIVE DIRECTOR OF
PREEMPTIVE LOVE COALITION

Ken Wytsma's courageous quest to understand the world around him through a deep commitment to God's ways shines through each page of this personal and thoughtful book. That world is both complicated and deeply unjust, so his writing calls us to face uncomfortable questions about our lives, and to reexamine the part we play in the different communities to which we all belong. It is my prayer that Ken's work will be rewarded by a true renewal of our love of mercy, of our doing justice, and of our walking humbly with God.

PETER HARRIS, CO-FOUNDER
AND PRESIDENT, A ROCHA
INTERNATIONAL

In this Kairos moment, the Holy Spirit is creating a wave of interest in justice throughout the church, including churches which have ignored it for many years. However, the wave often breaks on the shore of superficial concepts that neither result in changed lives nor changed communities. Thank you, Ken Wytsma, for taking the risk of telling the whole, rich, and deep truth about God's call to justice. I hope and trust that this book will fulfill its divine purpose—awakening and equipping the body of Christ to change the world.

ALEXIA SALVATIERRA, DIRECTOR OF
JUSTICE MINISTRIES, SOUTHWEST
CALIFORNIA SYNOD, EVANGELICAL
LUTHERAN CHURCH IN AMERICA

In *Pursuing Justice*, Ken is at the cutting edge of where God's heart is. This book is timely and needs to be read by everyone in the church.

JOHN M. PERKINS, CIVIL RIGHTS LEADER,
FOUNDER OF THE CHRISTIAN COMMUNITY
DEVELOPMENT ASSOCIATION (CCDA), AND
FOUNDER OF THE JOHN PERKINS FOUNDATION
FOR RECONCILIATION AND DEVELOPMENT

As a pastor, educator, entrepreneur, visionary, and father, Ken Wytsma brings a voice to the conversation on justice that is thoroughly and distinctly his own. A voice with the passion to captivate your heart, and the intellect to engage your mind. *Pursuing Justice* is a must-read for anyone desiring to live a life of purpose.

MELISSA MCCREERY, VICE PRESIDENT
OF DEVELOPMENT, KILNS COLLEGE

I'm grateful Ken Wytsma is helping shape the conversation about justice. Ken's multiple callings—teacher, pastor, strategic advisor, entrepreneur, thought leader—have situated him perfectly to refine and clarify biblical justice for a variety of audiences. He is a fresh voice of balance, humility, and collaboration. His enthusiasm is contagious and his challenge to the church to not only do justice, but to learn to do it well, is commendable. This book will bless, challenge, and stimulate your thinking.

KEITH WRIGHT, INTERNATIONAL
PRESIDENT OF FOOD FOR THE
HUNGRY

No matter what faith tradition you subscribe to—or reject altogether—Ken Wytsma's *Pursuing Justice* will rattle you. Not since C. S. Lewis put down his pen have readers been so provoked to think. Read *Pursuing Justice* with caution because it will change the way you approach others.

KAREN SPEARS ZACHARIAS, AUTHOR
OF *A SILENCE OF MOCKINGBIRDS* AND
WILL JESUS BUY ME A DOUBLE-WIDE?

For those of us stumbling to follow Jesus from the traditions of white evangelicalism, no question is more important today than how to pursue justice. Ken Wytsma is an honest, earnest disciple who has given himself to this pursuit without reservation. Like a first century Peter, he's engaged in a no-holds-barred pursuit of Jesus AND justice. Witnessing his passion, I can almost hear Jesus saying again, "On this rock I'll build my church."

JONATHAN WILSON-HARTGROVE,
AUTHOR OF *THE AWAKENING OF HOPE*

Inside all of us is the understanding that the world is not the way it should be. There is also a deep sounding somewhere inside that tells us our lives should be about making the world right. In *Pursuing Justice* Ken Wytsma taps into that inner calling and helps us not only understand Justice, but gives us the handles to become participants in making just communities, neighborhoods, and nations. Ken is a friend who is making a significant contribution to the conversation of Justice in his roles as a pastor, teacher, and leader, and now he has given us something more in this book. You need to read it.

RICK MCKINLEY, LEAD PASTOR OF IMAGO
DEI COMMUNITY, AUTHOR OF *KINGDOM
CALLED DESIRE* AND *THIS BEAUTIFUL MESS*

Justice is a buzzword in today's discourse, but Ken Wytsma brings to the conversation a comprehensive biblical understanding of how justice is closely related to grace, forgiveness, and mercy. *Pursuing Justice* eloquently demonstrates how shalom is only possible when the source of justice is Christ, the just judge and restorer of brokenness.

DR. CÉLESTIN MUSEKURA, PRESIDENT AND
FOUNDER OF AFRICAN LEADERSHIP AND
RECONCILIATION MINISTRIES, INC. (ALARM)

A must-read! Ken Wytsma shows us that we need the pursuit of justice just as much as it needs us by challenging us to live a life that embraces the bigger things God is doing in this world.

JAMES PEDRICK, WORLD VISION'S
ACT:S ACTIVISM NETWORK

Climbers use a specialized rope to navigate harsh and wild places. Ken Wytsma has made just such a rope in *Pursuing Justice*, a book that can help the church explore the uncharted terrain of global faith in the twenty-first century. Ken weaves together a prophetic and yet practical theology by plaiting ideas of worship and piety, history and education, social movement and self-sacrifice—all around the core idea of justice. This book is BIG theology.

PETER ILLYN, FOUNDER OF
RESTORING EDEN

Justice is not a new fad to attract the disenchanted, nor an optional component to the message of Jesus. It is central to who God is and must therefore radiate from all that his people do. As a pastor, prophetic voice, and entrepreneurial pragmatist, Ken Wytsma does a superb job of outlining why and how we, the people of God, must reflect his self-giving love and pursue justice.

NATHAN GEORGE, FOUNDER OF
TRADE AS ONE

Justice is an everywhere word these days, but all too often it is a word without biblical meaning. Ken Wytsma, a whole-life disciple of Jesus, helps us see that salvation must always include community shalom, that Jesus and justice can never be separated, that Ephesians 2:8–9 always goes on to 2:10. With insightful biblical exposition, rigorous analysis, and powerful stories, he helps us become Jesus followers.

GERRY BRESHEARS, PhD, PROFESSOR OF
THEOLOGY, WESTERN SEMINARY, PORTLAND, OR

Ken Wytsma was "doing" justice when justice wasn't cool. For Ken, justice isn't a trendy issue—it's about theology and an ethical imperative rooted in the character and heart of God. This book is for Christians of every generation and background who have heard a radical invitation to obey the command Jesus issues in response to the Parable of the Good Samaritan: "Go and do the same" (Luke 10:37).

ED UNDERWOOD, PASTOR OF CHURCH OF THE
OPEN DOOR, AUTHOR OF *REBORN TO BE WILD*
AND *WHEN GOD BREAKS YOUR HEART*

Pursuing justice is often a difficult task for many Christians in the United States—specifically as the tangles of our busy lives, or the self-doubt of whether we can actually make a difference, prevent us from taking action. This book offers not only critical insights into a theology of justice but also concrete and practical ways of how to act justly. Ken weaves poignant historical stories of justice with striking insights of current day issues, inspiring readers to believe and be equipped to make a difference here and now. *Pursuing Justice* is a prime starter for how Christians are to respond to injustice and is a powerful equipping tool every Christian should read!

JENNY YANG, DIRECTOR OF ADVOCACY AND POLICY, WORLD RELIEF, CO-AUTHOR OF *WELCOMING THE STRANGER: JUSTICE, COMPASSION AND TRUTH IN THE IMMIGRATION DEBATE*

From the vantage point of a president of a theologically conservative seminary, it appears that many of my fellow conservative evangelicals tend to have a flawed and narrow view of the word "justice." Using sound theology, compelling reasoning, and an accessible style, Ken Wytsma not only brings us back to a biblical understanding of justice, but also humbly calls us to pursue it in practice. After reading this book, I was both enlightened and motivated, and I trust you will be as well.

RANDAL ROBERTS, PRESIDENT OF WESTERN SEMINARY, PORTLAND, OR

This book explains love through a lens of justice and anchors justice to something foundational and sustainable: the love of a big God.

LINDA VAN VOORST, EXECUTIVE DIRECTOR OF MISSION KIDS

Pursuing Justice is far more than words for Ken Wytsma. These words go to the heart of his life and mission. You will find a sustained and holistic argument for seeking justice that is shaped by biblical wisdom and fleshed out with practical insights. Wytsma prophetically calls the American church to be consumed by Christ and His just love and not by our hedonistic and consumeristic culture. You dare not read this book if you want to play life safe and live the illusion that one can pursue Jesus or righteousness without pressing on toward justice. But read *Pursuing Justice* if you want to experience the reality of Jesus' fullness as you give your life away for Him and His just ways that will liberate a world in desperate need. Why settle for lesser things? Pick up, read, and live it out.

PAUL LOUIS METZGER, PHD, PROFESSOR
OF CHRISTIAN THEOLOGY & THEOLOGY OF
CULTURE, MULTNOMAH BIBLICAL SEMINARY/
MULTNOMAH UNIVERSITY, AUTHOR OF
*CONSUMING JESUS: BEYOND RACE AND CLASS
DIVISIONS IN A CONSUMER CHURCH*

Anytime I read a book on justice I brace myself for a slap on the wrist over not caring enough for the marginalized. What sets Ken Wytsma's *Pursuing Justice* apart is the balance he takes, which is needed to accurately articulate the subject matter well. Wytsma does a beautiful job of tracing the biblical narrative into the subject of justice, showing how the heart of God is intimately connected to justice. He looks at how justice can be lived out through the various parts of the Christian life, and will help many see how God's heart of justice can be connected to everyday life.

TYLER BRAUN, AUTHOR OF *WHY
HOLINESS MATTERS: WE'VE LOST OUR
WAY—BUT WE CAN FIND IT AGAIN*

We all want "justice", but what does that really look like? For people? For the planet? *Pursuing Justice* helps us think through and work toward biblical justice for all of God's creation. Read it, live it, enjoy it.

TOM ROWLEY, EXECUTIVE
DIRECTOR, A ROCHA USA

PURSUING

THE CALL TO LIVE & DIE FOR BIGGER THINGS

JUSTICE

KEN WYTSMA

WITH D. R. JACOBSEN

THOMAS NELSON
Since 1798

NASHVILLE   DALLAS   MEXICO CITY   RIO DE JANEIRO

Published in Nashville, Tennessee, by Thomas Nelson. Thomas Nelson is a trademark of Thomas Nelson, Inc.

Published in association with the literary agency of D. C. Jacobson & Associates LLC, an Author Management Company, www.dcjacobson.com.

Thomas Nelson, Inc., titles may be purchased in bulk for educational, business, fund-raising, or sales promotional use. For information, please e-mail SpecialMarkets@ ThomasNelson.com.

Lyrics: "Secret of the Easy Yoke," David Bazan © 1998. Bug Music. All rights reserved. Used by permission.

Unless otherwise indicated, Scripture quotations are from the Holy Bible, New International Version®, NIV®. Copyright © 1973, 1978, 1984, 2011 by Biblica, Inc.™ Used by permission of Zondervan. All rights reserved worldwide. www.zondervan.com

Scripture quotations marked ESV are taken from THE ENGLISH STANDARD VERSION. © 2001 by Crossway Bibles, a division of Good News Publishers.

Scripture quotations marked KJV are taken from the King James Version (public domain).

Scripture quotations marked MSG are taken from *The Message* by Eugene H. Peterson. © 1993, 1994, 1995, 1996, 2000. Used by permission of NavPress Publishing Group. All rights reserved.

Scripture quotations marked NASB are taken from the NEW AMERICAN STANDARD BIBLE®. © The Lockman Foundation 1960, 1962, 1963, 1968, 1971, 1972, 1973, 1975, 1977, 1995. Used by permission.

Scripture quotations marked NKJV are from THE NEW KING JAMES VERSION. © 1982 by Thomas Nelson, Inc. Used by permission. All rights reserved.

Scripture quotations marked NLT are taken from the *Holy Bible*, New Living Translation. © 1996, 2004, 2007. Used by permission of Tyndale House Publishers, Inc., Carol Stream, Illinois 60188. All rights reserved.

978-0-7852-3830-0 (IE)

Library of Congress Control Number: 2012953829

978-0-8499-6466-4 (HC)

Printed in the United States of America

12 13 14 15 16 QG 6 5 4 3 2 1

CONTENTS

CONTENTS

THE INTERLUDES

To Tamara

". . . but the just shall live by [her] faith."
Habakkuk 2:4 KJV

For the beauty of your trust and the sincerity of your love.

Justice, *and only* justice, you shall pursue.

DEUTERONOMY 16:20 NASB

INTRODUCTION

'm a first-generation American. My dad, Johannes Wytsma, was born in Holland during World War II. It took most of my life, but he eventually shared the stories of that era with me. He told me how my grandfather, to avoid Nazi capture, had to dress up as a woman throughout 1944 and ride a bike more than twenty miles to get food for his family and pregnant wife. He told of how they survived by eating tulip bulbs and potato skins discarded by German soldiers.

After the war, my dad's family immigrated to the United States. My grandfather was determined to make a better life for his wife and their three children than they had known in Holland. In 1953, they stepped onto American soil, speaking no English and with only a twenty-dollar bill to their names. My dad was eight.

My father never forgot where he came from. In 1979, my parents sponsored a Cambodian refugee family to live with us. The family of five was fleeing the genocide in their country under the Khmer Rouge regime, which eventually claimed the lives of a fifth of the country's population.

They showed up with shaved heads—a common practice in refugee camps to guard against lice—and only spoke Khmer. Fauy Long, the father, spent the first day they arrived writing a letter to my father using a Cambodian-to-English lexicon. He wrote of the genocide, the refugee camp in Thailand, the horrors of the Killing Fields, and, in the heartbreaking clarity of his translated words, "people eating people."

That year our family was featured in *People Helping People*, a documentary about individuals like my parents who made sacrifices for the benefit of others. I remember racing my BMX bike around our cul-de-sac for the film crews with a vague sense of pride in my parents. Even at age seven, I understood they were doing something different from most adults I knew. Something better.

I'm convinced that's why my sister, Laura, is such a passionate advocate for refugees seeking asylum in the United States. She is an award-winning lawyer who has been recognized on numerous occasions for her ongoing pro bono work with refugees fleeing persecution. Like my dad, she never forgot where her family came from—or where others come from either.

LATECOMER

As for me, until I was twenty-two, I treated life as if it existed for my amusement and pleasure. In the words of Henry David Thoreau, my goal was to "suck the marrow out of life"[1]—as long as that didn't require too much effort.

That all changed when my destructive lifestyle began to cause serious health problems. When I finally saw a doctor, he looked me in the eye and told me I wouldn't live past my twenties if I continued damaging my body at such a significant rate. That shook me up—what good is hedonism if I can't be around to enjoy it?

I began reading for the first time in my life, searching for answers about the meaning of life and wrestling with my own mortality. I was determined to figure out if God existed or if I was going to continue down a different path. I soon became convinced that the Bible was true. I quit partying with my fraternity, joined a Christian group on campus, and spent hours and hours reading the Bible and every Christian book I could find.

That summer—between my fourth and fifth years at Clemson University—I traveled across the country to a Christian summer camp in Big Bear, California, doing my best to throw myself at this newfound faith.

When I returned to campus at the end of that summer to finish my engineering degree, the word spread quickly: *"Wytsma went and got religion."* But the truth was, I didn't feel as though *I'd* "got" anything—I felt, instead, that *Someone* had gotten hold of me. And it didn't take long for God to deconstruct my former fraternity self and rebuild me—a man given a second chance at life who was being called to give his life away.

PURE RELIGION

About the time I began going to church and reading the Bible, I came across a verse in the book of James that puzzled me. "Religion that God our Father accepts as pure and faultless is this: to look after orphans and widows in their distress" (1:27).

Religion? That was pure and faultless? What was so important about orphans and widows that they made the top of God's priority list?

I mulled over this passage for months. I knew God was calling me to give my life away, but I wasn't sure exactly how. One Sunday I decided to put the idea to the test—I'd simply start looking after orphans and widows, as James had written. It would be an engineering experiment.

But where would I find them? The best plan I could come up with was to drive fifteen miles through the South Carolina countryside to a nursing home that seemed as if it was in the middle of nowhere.

For that whole spring semester, I drove back and forth to the nursing home on Sundays, and usually once or twice during the week. I'd envisioned a grand experience: the chance to live out my new faith and to sit under the wise tutelage of the quintessential wise grandfather type who would regale me with war stories and thank me profusely for my generous sacrifice.

Reality was far different. There was the senile woman who told me the same story every week. There was the man who had lost his mind and made guttural noises and often wet himself. When my closest friend at the home, an older gentleman I'd sometimes buy cigarettes for, began inappropriately grabbing the Clemson University girls who worked there, I challenged him on his behavior. He cursed me, and we never spoke again.

My grand plan became a series of tedious afternoons spent serving people who gave me absolutely nothing in return.

One particular Sunday evening, my frustrations turned to prayer. I was driving back along the country road, windows down and the humid air pouring into the car. What was I supposed to be learning about pure and faultless religion through all this? What could I get from people who had nothing to give, but required so much energy and effort to love?

Like most insights, the answer was the question. Looking after orphans and widows—those who require everything and seem to give nothing in return—is the very picture of God's love for us.

It wasn't about God needing anything from me—His delight came in the giving, not the receiving. God's love for me sacrificed, forgave, and endured all things, not because I was a good return on His investment, but because God's love is pure. And that meant it wasn't about what I could get so much as what I had already been given.

Pure religion, then, is a reflection of God's love.

When we act justly—when we give our lives away—we have the best chance of glimpsing what grace truly is and experiencing, along the way, what Jesus calls "complete joy" (see John 15:11). On that late April evening, I understood that we are never closer to God than when we are pursuing justice by serving others. No secondary agenda. Just the purity of sacrificial love.

SEEDS OF HOPE

Imagine Jesus, sitting on a rock, with His disciples gathered in a loose ring. He's looking around, searching for a way to *somehow* get through to them. He stands, walks to the edge of a nearby field, and plucks a head of wheat. He rolls it between his rough palms and blows away the chaff. Holding a single kernel up to the light, He looks at His friends.

"Unless a seed falls to the ground and dies," He says, "it remains only a single seed. But if it dies . . ." He tosses the seed into the field and locks eyes with the disciples one by one before driving home the point. "If it dies, it produces many seeds."[2]

When we die to ourselves—when we give our lives away—God takes our lives and uses them to bring new life and restore creation and goodness.

If it is impossible to change the world, God wouldn't have told us to try. We know what is required of us. To act justly. To love mercy. And to walk humbly with God. We're called, in the words of Wendell Berry, to practice resurrection.[3]

Giving our lives away as Jesus calls us to do requires an understanding of justice—of God's grand and redemptive purpose for His creation. Jesus isn't calling us to only give our *words* away, though our words certainly matter. Jesus, who is called the Word in John's gospel, came to do more than preach and teach . . . He came to give His life away on behalf of others, for the glory of God.

Giving our lives away requires us to understand biblical justice. Justice is a word that has often been hollowed out, muddied, and even shunned, but one we must necessarily redeem to its full significance if we are to embrace a God of justice and His call to be agents of justice.

Justice is rooted in the character of God, established in the creation of God, mandated by the commands of God, present in the kingdom of God, motivated by the love of God, affirmed in the teaching of Jesus, reflected in the example of Jesus, and carried on today by all who are moved and led by the Spirit.

In a broken world full of inequity and injustice—from human trafficking to racism to gender violence, and from gossip to consumerism to petty anger—can we really treat our lives as God's? Can we redeem and energize the concept of justice and embrace the fullness of God's plan for creation? Can we expect to find true life and happiness in obeying Him as we seek to give our lives away for others?

I think we can. I think we must—and that's what this book is about.

KEN WYTSMA
BEND, OREGON

ONE

REDEEMING JUSTICE

What Justice Is and Why It Matters

Never doubt that a small group of thoughtful, committed people can change the world. Indeed, it is the only thing that ever has.[1]

MARGARET MEAD

Justice, sir, is the great interest of [people] on earth. It is the ligament which holds civilized beings and civilized nations together.[2]

DANIEL WEBSTER

God calls everyone to pursue justice—but how?

My friend is a police officer because he believes in upholding our country's justice system. I understand that conviction, and I wouldn't want to live without the rule of law.

World Relief, an international relief and development organization for which I have enormous respect, works on behalf of some of the most vulnerable people in the world. I am proud to partner with them.

Many of my spiritual mentors have demonstrated to me, year after year, a commitment to pursuing discipleship and righteousness. Their goal is to become more like Jesus in the way they think, believe, and act.

Another friend is a teacher in an English as a Second Language (ESL) program. She believes, as do I, that education is a way to provide equity of social access to people in a community who might otherwise be at a disadvantage throughout their lives.

The church I pastor, Antioch, organizes outreach and missions into the categories of food, shelter, and love. This lets us connect our people with others in the community who are already working in these areas.

I've been blessed to interact with colleagues who teach and write about justice, history, and ethics. They've helped me understand what the past can teach us about how we ought to live in the present, and how that can shape the future.

Several pastors I know work in countries that have been torn apart by generations of war, hunger, and political instability. They give their lives to help bring justice to suffering families and communities, and to help bring the perpetrators to justice.

I'm incredibly grateful to be surrounded by such a diversity of people pursuing justice. Their example challenges and inspires me. They, like so many others I meet in my congregation and at schools and conferences around the country, are daily giving their lives away on behalf of others.

However, this array of justice stories also presents a question, one you have perhaps asked yourself: *If I want to pursue justice with my life, how and where should I start?*

It's natural to want direction or a clear call. For most of us, however, that never happens. We aren't told explicitly to move to a certain city or take a certain job or study a certain thing . . . yet the hunger remains to "change the world."

That's exactly why it's vital to consider the widest, most biblical definition of justice we can. Each of these applications of justice is good, but none is complete. Justice is something far broader than a single life can hope to capture, no matter how well it is lived. Justice can be messy on its borders and unclear in the exact ways it ought to be understood or pursued or applied—and that's a good thing!

It means that God, who is perfectly just, and who desires justice for all of His creation, can ask us to use our unique talents and passions and experiences to pursue justice. *Wherever* we find ourselves, we can make a difference—and that difference starts with understanding more about what *justice* really is.

A WIDER VIEW

Back when I was studying philosophy in graduate school, we learned to distinguish the difference between simple concepts with a single or easy definition, and complex concepts that required multilayered definitions. Often, for these more complicated concepts, a cluster of definitions was needed to fully capture their meanings.

There are many singular examples of justice, some of which we looked at to begin this chapter—but the wider concept of justice requires a cluster definition to fully capture its meaning. In a cluster definition, the parts of a whole are *necessary*, but no single part is *sufficient*. This is familiar to us—if you drove a car to work today, you drove a cluster concept. Many parts of a car are *necessary*—axles, a steering wheel, the brakes—but no single part is *sufficient* to define the whole car. You don't drive your engine to work, and neither could you drive your car to work without the engine. Similarly, no individual application of justice in the real world is, by itself, sufficient for understanding all of justice, even though each sphere of concern is important.

The biblical concept of justice has a lot of shared space with synonyms such as *love, mercy, charity,* the *law, righteousness,* and more. Justice is a sum of many parts, with many similar overlapping concepts, as the following illustration makes clear.

One of our most important tasks in this book will be to hold up justice and examine its many elements together. Like art students instructed to study a still-life composition at the center of the room, we will strive to see justice from many angles and appreciate its unique qualities. We need to consider its meanings, its theology, and its history. In our effort to understand justice, we must take as wide a view as possible.

This is one reason for the interludes I've included between many of the chapters in this book. I've learned from diverse voices, and I wanted to bring imagery, poetry, short meditations, and even interviews to help illuminate a brighter understanding of justice.

THE MOSAIC OF JUSTICE

When I was in Turkey recently, I toured the Hagia Sofia, a former church in Istanbul that was first dedicated as a Christian worship site more than fifteen hundred years ago. It was converted to a mosque in 1453, when Sultan Mehmed II sacked Istanbul (then called Constantinople), and reconverted by the Turkish government into a nonreligious museum in 1935.

Inside the museum is one of the most iconic and compelling works of religious art in the world: the *Deësis* mosaic, which dates from the mid-thirteenth century. In it, the figure of Jesus looks wisely and sympathetically at the viewer, making a sign of blessing with His right hand. He is clothed in a blue robe draped over a golden shirt, and a halo frames His head.[3]

To create this mosaic, which is a picture formed from the careful arrangement of small pieces of colored glass, stone, or tile, an artist must have painstakingly added color and form, bit by gleaming bit, until the shape of Jesus began to emerge. Centuries later, visitors continue to take delight in the mosaic, every piece of stone working together in a stunning whole.

Here's a thought experiment. Suppose, when I was in Turkey, I had flipped open a pocketknife and, when no one was looking, pried away a single fragment of the mosaic. Then, upon arriving home, I set the piece of blue stone on the kitchen table and proclaimed to my family, "*This* is one of the most beautiful works of art in the world!" No matter how lovely that single shard was, in no way would it capture the glory of the whole.

Justice is like a mosaic. It's not *only* about single pieces—it's *also* about all the pieces working together in a stunning whole. All too often we believe that our desire to pursue justice can only be lived out or understood in a single shard. Criminal justice. International development. Creation care. Education. Anti-trafficking. Works of mercy and love.

All of these shards are vital parts of God's mosaic of justice.

SHARDS INSTEAD OF THE WHOLE

Many of us want to pursue justice. Even if we don't understand justice as a whole, even if we are thrown for a loop by the words *social justice*, we want specific injustices to be rectified. So we pursue a single cause, which is wonderful . . . unless we allow that to be the sum total of our engagement and understanding. I may volunteer to help homeless veterans, and you may send money to build a well in Africa, in lieu of birthday presents. But if we let those good, necessary things become *sufficient* for understanding justice, we're neglecting far too much.

When we think a single shard of the mosaic of justice describes the whole, it's as if we're cataloging one particular butterfly and assuming we've understood every other species that swoops and sways through the sky.

In Francis Schaeffer's words, we "have seen things in bits and pieces instead of totals."[4]

One of my fellow pastors once stated that it was fine for me to preach about justice, as long as I started giving equal time to other areas of the Christian life, such as marriage and spiritual growth. I realized I'd failed to communicate to my congregation the reality that justice is universal. We can study justice by itself, but we must also incorporate it when we study nearly every other subject, from marriage to spiritual growth.

In that sense studying justice is like studying grammar. We can learn how the structure and elements of a particular language work together, but we also need grammar to study nearly every other subject, from history to sociology to law. Grammar is laced throughout these subjects, and we cannot understand them apart from it.

We're familiar with how a concept can be thoroughgoing and foundational. Think of truth. We wouldn't suggest that truth was an optional add-on, a subject that should only be studied and preached about occasionally. Rather, we understand truth to be so crucial that it is a universal—it is upon the foundation of truth that we build our ideas about other subjects. Truth is not simply one valuable subject among many; it is, in a sense, the one subject that is part of all others.

I've come to see justice in similar terms. Through studying, reading the Scriptures, traveling, dialoguing with brothers and sisters around the world, learning how to serve with my life, and always trying to ask good questions, I've become convinced that justice is every bit as universal as truth.

Put simply, truth corresponds to what is; justice to what ought to be.

We understand truth is a universal, a paradigm, a lens through which we can look to see what is real. Justice, likewise, is a lens through which we can look to determine what ought to be in our relationships both with God and with others.

Truth and justice as lenses for perceiving reality.

Justice has many facets, but we can't lose sight of the fact that justice itself is never peripheral. Rather, it is integral to the way we think, pray, act, hope, believe, work, spend, live, and love.

This isn't really a book about how to *do* more justice. Pressuring people to act is, ironically, a good way to ensure that people burn out, and that *less* justice gets done. It can also potentially even create injustice.

Rather, this book is about recovering the full-orbed biblical concept of justice and inviting it back into our lives. When we understand that justice is rooted in the character of God and flows from the heart of God, we can begin to see that it permeates all of life.

The heart of this book is an encounter with the heart of God, and God's heart beats with justice.

AN ONGOING DEFINITION

Justice is the single best word, both inside and outside the Bible, for capturing God's purposes for the world and humanity's calling in the world. *Justice* is, in fact, the broadest, most consistent word the Bible uses to speak about *what ought to be*, and it has been used throughout the centuries by Christians and non-Christians alike to describe vital areas of human and divine concern.

To "do justice" means to render to each what each is due. Justice involves harmony, flourishing, and fairness, and it is based on the image of God in every person—the *Imago Dei*—that grants all people inalienable dignity and infinite worth.

Justice describes both our rights—what we are owed—and our responsibilities that we owe others and God.

Justice is broad enough to speak about truth, love, forgiveness, and grace, and it is woven consistently throughout Scripture.[5] It conveys, through the prophetic images of Scripture, a picture of what God's kingdom will look like, and what it can begin to look like now.

During a radio address in 1933,[6] Dietrich Bonhoeffer, the German theologian and pastor killed by the Nazis, offered three possible stances for Christians to address systemic or state-sponsored injustice: speak truth to and criticize the state; give aid to victims of the state; and directly engage the unjust system . . . "not just to bandage the victims under the wheel, but to put a spoke in the wheel itself."[7]

In this I see a spectrum of justice, moving from dialogue to works of compassion and mercy to actively attacking unjust structures. All are part of justice, and all can and should be done. Abolitionists in the 1800s wrote newspaper editorials, organized the underground railroad, cared for injured slaves, and boycotted the products of the slave economy—all while working to pass laws banning slavery. They didn't pit one aspect of justice against the others, but pursued justice along the whole spectrum as the building of God's shalom demanded.

A biblical understanding of how expansive justice is will carry us into a strong, broad, and deep appreciation of the fullness of God's heart for His creation.

A SCEPTER OF JUSTICE

Throughout history, a scepter has been a near-universal symbol of a ruler's sovereign authority—of his or her expansive responsibility and power. A scepter defines the kingdom, linking the ruler as a person to the kingdom as a whole. What happens to the kingdom happens to the ruler, and vice versa. When a pharaoh carried the scepter of Egypt, not only did he possess absolute authority over Egypt, but Egypt became his primary concern.

The psalmist said of God: "Your throne, O God, will last forever and ever; a scepter of justice will be the scepter of your kingdom" (Psalm 45:6). God's primary concern, His sphere of influence, is a kingdom defined by justice.

If we know the kingdom, we know the king.

To know God, we need to know His will for His kingdom, and to understand His will for His kingdom, we need to understand justice.

There are more than 2,100 verses in the Bible that mention poverty. Rock singer and humanitarian Bono called attention to this in his address to the National Prayer Breakfast in 2006, stating, "It's not an accident. That's a lot of air time, 2,100 mentions."[8] By contrast, praying and prayer are mentioned less than a quarter of that.

Justice isn't a nice addition to God's otherwise perfect character. If we ignore justice, like ignoring love or truth, we create a *caricature* rather than the divine *character* we meet in Scripture and in our lives. Justice is a hallmark of God, a distinctive and pure feature of His character that defines Him and His will for the world.

Justice—a right and equitable relationship with God and with people—is truly a word worth redeeming.

HUNGRY FOR JUSTICE

That's part of what led me, along with a group of colleagues, to launch The Justice Conference. We wanted a way to gather people around a crucial conversation, to get twenty-first-century Christians talking about the word *justice* itself, carefully but with open hearts and minds.

"All virtue," wrote Aristotle, "is summed up in dealing justly."[9] We need to begin pursuing justice by escaping fragmented causes and the latest social fads. We need, instead, to consider the big idea of justice, a theology of justice, and how it relates to God.

The most helpful conversation to begin with focuses less on specific actions and more on a deeper understanding of God's character. In Psalm 146:6–9, God's power as Creator is linked to His design for justice to be enacted in His creation, demonstrating that justice is an aspect of His character as foundational as love and truth.

> He is the Maker of heaven and earth,
>   the sea, and everything in them—
>   he remains faithful forever.
> He upholds the cause of the oppressed
>   and gives food to the hungry.
> The Lord sets prisoners free,
>   the Lord gives sight to the blind,
> the Lord lifts up those who are bowed down,
>   the Lord loves the righteous.
> The Lord watches over the foreigner
>   and sustains the fatherless and the widow,
>   but he frustrates the ways of the wicked.

People are hungry for justice. They want justice for those they know who are suffering injustice. They want it for themselves and for their communities. They want to practice justice, experience justice, and know God through the universal quality of justice.

These things are what God wants too.

AN INVITATION

My race, gender, class, and education have shaped me to recognize some facets of justice and injustice more readily—and to be blind to issues that are clear to my brothers and sisters who are different from me.

Recently I tried to capture some of my understanding of justice in a poetic exploration called "Justice Is."

> Justice is rooted in the character of God
> and flows from the heart of God.
>
> Justice is woven into the fabric of God's creation,
> part of the Image of God in every person.
>
> Justice is commanded in God's Scriptures
> and integral to the promise of the gospel.
>
> Justice is incarnated in the life of Jesus,
> inseparable from His words and deeds.
>
> Justice is highlighted in Jesus' concern for the poor
> and demonstrated in His death and resurrection.
>
> Justice is the early church sharing what they had,
> meeting the needs of others near and far.
>
> Justice is the saints building hospitals and caring for orphans
> instead of pursuing worldly wealth and self-interest.
>
> Justice is the abolitionists laboring to end transatlantic slavery,
> recognizing the God-given dignity and worth in each person.

Justice is the legacy of those who fought for civil rights,
who began to dismantle systems of violence and exploitation.

Justice is the worth and equality of people in every land,
for we are all God's creation and God's children.

Justice is God's grand design for His creation,
a hope for every man, woman, and child to flourish in God's
kingdom.

This book is my story. It is the story of learning what "Justice Is" and what that means for me every day. In it I share some of the voices God has used thus far to bless, teach, rebuke, and shape me. It is a story that has yet to be finished, but I trust God will continue to draw me closer to Himself and to what He cares about. My desire is to speak with a humble voice, knowing that my story is incomplete. Yet I also believe that my story is part of a useful conversation in our world.

What does it mean to have a robust, biblical understanding of justice? What does it look like to give your life away? What bigger things might God be calling us to live and even die for?

This book is not an in-depth study on any *particular* application of justice to a single issue. That is not because particular applications of justice don't matter—they do. But this book is an invitation to explore God's heart for justice and why justice matters to God . . . and why it should matter to us as well.

It is my prayer and hope that this book will be part of your own journey toward justice, and that as you continue to read and study and live and question, you will sense God leading you in the way you should go. Deeper into relationship with God. Deeper into justice. Deeper into love. Deeper into giving your life away on behalf of others for the glory of God.

I can't know what that will look like for you because it looks different in every life. But I do know that it can begin with conversation. Conversations require voices, so I pray that as you grow nearer to God's heart, you will discover the particular voices in your life that God wants to use to shape you.

God is inviting you to join Him in a dynamic relationship—to come to know Him, through justice, in a new and life-changing way.

> "Justice, *and only* justice, you shall pursue,
> that you may live and possess the land which
> the LORD your God is giving you."
> DEUTERONOMY 16:20 NASB

TWO

DYNAMIC ART

Justice as a Way of Knowing God

What you *do* in the present—by painting, preaching, singing, sewing, praying, teaching, building hospitals, digging wells, campaigning for justice, writing poems, caring for the needy, loving your neighbor as yourself—*will last into God's future.* . . . They are part of what we may call *building for God's kingdom.*[1]

N. T. WRIGHT

Not that [Bonhoeffer] believed that everybody must act as he did, but from where he was standing, he could see no possibility of retreat into any sinless, righteous, pious refuge. The sin of respectable people reveals itself in flight from responsibility. He saw that sin falling upon him and he took his stand.[2]

EBERHARD BETHGE

BLINDERS

Imagine a faithful Christian woman living in Stuttgart, Germany. She believes in Jesus, goes to church each week, and reads her Bible every day after breakfast. At night, before turning out the lamp, she prays for the leader of her country, who is keeping Germany safe and strong. When her neighbors are low on food, she shares what little she has with a cheerful heart, and though her clothes are threadbare, she trusts that God will continue to provide for her, just as He provides for the lilies of the field. The year is 1944, and Hitler's Final Solution to eliminate the Jews is already well under way.

Imagine a faithful Christian man living in Charleston, South Carolina, in 1944. He has just turned eighteen, and at last he can follow in his older brother's footsteps and enlist in the United States Army. Even though his brother is fighting across the Pacific from island to island, he wants to be sent to the European theater. He's sick of the newsreels showing Hitler's panzer divisions rolling through formerly peaceful towns, and he feels a gut-level disgust for the way tyranny and totalitarianism are crushing the continent under their iron boots. He kisses his mother good-bye and serenely rides the whites-only bus to the local recruiting station.

How could they both—the German woman and the American soldier—be so blind to the injustices surrounding them? From our perspective, their ignorance would be laughable if it didn't have such painful, real-world consequences. How is it possible to be a faithful Christian while turning a blind eye to the Holocaust or to Jim Crow laws? Same war, same religion . . . and same basic failure to see the tatters of goodness and justice being ripped apart each day right in front of them.

When was the last time we considered—seriously considered—our own moral blindness?

PRAYING WITH TEARS

Dietrich Bonhoeffer, who was hanged on Hitler's order just twenty-three days prior to Allied victory in 1938, reportedly said,

"Only he who cries for the Jews is permitted to sing Gregorian chant."[3]

Prior to the Second World War, Bonhoeffer visited and taught at Union Theological Seminary in New York. While there, he was disturbed by the racial issues facing African Americans and intrigued by the response of many American theologians arguing on behalf of racial justice and against racial inequality.

In 1939, Bonhoeffer returned to Germany on the last scheduled steamer before the start of the war, convinced he must endure the war's terrors if he hoped to aid his countrymen in its aftermath. He continued his outspoken advocacy for the Jews throughout the war. Knowing that Bonhoeffer could have escaped the persecution of the war, and prolonged his life, gives a deeper layer of pathos to his assertion, for surely he "cried for the Jews" with his very life.

Gregorian chant is a form of worship music from the Middle Ages, and Bonhoeffer was juxtaposing the religious image of monks engaged in sung worship with the vivid picture of someone lamenting the horrors of oppression. He was testing his devotion to God, measuring it against a felt compassion for the suffering.

If we don't cry, we shouldn't sing. The connection between lament and justice is an oft-neglected relationship. Engagement in justice and our worship and knowledge of God are inextricable.

DIAGNOSING BLINDNESS

I'm haunted by this question: *What am I blind to?* What are the things of which I and my generation are unaware? Where am I a part of a majority group, and by default, likely ignorant of issues on the margins? It's far too easy to go with the flow.

Christians in Germany got it wrong about Hitler. Christians in the United States got it wrong about Jim Crow laws. I get it wrong and you get it wrong. When we read the Old Testament Prophets and sense the sharpness of God's righteous anger, we wonder how the Israelites, their leaders, priests, and teachers could have been so ignorant of the mind and heart of God concerning the justice issues of their day. Likewise, we can bet future generations will look back at us and wonder how *we* could have been so blind to God's design for His world.

We don't *want* to be hypocrites, certainly. We don't want to be critical of other generations and peoples while remaining blind to issues of our day. But it's a fact: it's much easier to see someone else's acts of injustice when they're written on a piece of paper and disconnected from our current context. Isn't it harder to see our own shortcomings amid the difficulty of dealing with stress, fatigue, health concerns, parenting, dreams for the future, the economy, and growing old?

I wonder, however, if God sees us the same way He saw the Israelites. Are we, like them, too comfortable, too disconnected, too insensitive, and too selfish? Are we singing songs of praise to a God who's red faced with righteous indignation at our blindness to the plight of others? And if we've missed God's desire for us to pursue justice, how can we claim to know Him?

KNOWING GOD

At a gut level, many of us want to know God. We want to know who He is, what His plan is, and what He wants of us. We weary ourselves with countless activities in pursuit of Him: Sunday school, worship services, Bible studies, prayer meetings, evangelism, personal purity . . . and the list goes on.

I remember reading J. I. Packer's classic *Knowing God* back in college. This amazing work taught me much of what I know about God, but as good as it is, Packer would never want me to substitute his book for a life lived in relationship with God. Just as we would never claim to know someone personally after reading his or her biography, we must not mistakenly assume we know God because we learn about Him in church or from books. To truly know someone, we need to spend time with that person, participating in his or her world.

God is among the vulnerable, seeking their good. When we join Him in this, we begin to know Him better because we are in relationship with Him and His children. As Bonhoeffer pointed out, there's a connection between justice and our ability to know God.

The distinction between *static* and *dynamic* art is a helpful way to see the difference between knowing about someone and knowledge that comes from being in relationship. A painting is static. It can tell us many things about the painter, but we can never claim to completely know the painter in a personal way simply from viewing the art. However, when we participate with an artist in the creation of the art, we come much closer to a personal relationship. For example, imagine a choir, an orchestra, and a conductor—this type of art changes, develops, and grows in response to relationship. As individuals contribute to dynamic art, the art takes on collaborative life. Beethoven's famous Fifth Symphony had really only begun when he finished inking the score, for then it was ready to be brought to life. Even now, more than two hundred years later, we are still enraptured by Beethoven's musical magic as his artistic vision is brought into being by those who participate in it.

STATIC ART   DYNAMIC ART

The musician who carefully follows the score and pays close attention to the direction of the conductor will be in closer communication with the original artist. Participation with the artist and knowledge of the artist are somehow connected—and this is true of God as well.

God's creation involves both static art and dynamic art. Part of His static art is reflected in the skies and in nature. We are familiar with verses that speak of how we know God through such art (emphasis added):

> The heavens *proclaim* his righteousness,
>   and all peoples see his glory. (Psalm 97:6)

> The heavens declare the glory of God;
>   the skies proclaim the work of his hands.
> Day after day they pour forth speech;
>   night after night they *display knowledge*. (Psalm 19:1–2)

The heavens—the sun, the moon, and the stars—literally communicate something about God. They *display* knowledge. The heavenly bodies are visible, tangible evidence of who God is. We know God through His created order that exists in the skies and shows in the sunrise, sunset, and colors of the rainbow.

However, God's static art only tells us *part* of who God is. We tend to understand the role Scripture reading plays in learning about and knowing God, and many of us understand the connection between prayer and solitude in knowing God, or the connection between purity and an understanding of God's holiness. Fewer Christians, however, make the connection between our ethical action toward others—our justice or lack of it—and our knowledge of God.[4]

If we gain knowledge of God through His static creation, how much more do we gain through God's dynamic creation of His people and the symphony of justice He desires to play in and through them?

Just as Psalm 19 shows how we know God through creation, Psalm 9:16 shows how we know God through justice: "The LORD is known by his acts of justice; the wicked are ensnared by the work of their hands."

We know people through their actions, whether just or unjust. As philosopher Paul Moser has written, "[the apostle] John regards a filial attitude of loving obedience toward God as necessary and sufficient for properly knowing God."[5] Static art helps us know by seeing; dynamic art helps us know by seeing and participating.

When God asks us to know Him in this dynamic sense, He is, in effect, saying, *Know Me by knowing how I bring justice and shalom together in a beautiful, just society. Understand your unique, individual, and active part in restoring what I intended.*

I was nineteen when I stumbled upon a way to connect

dynamically with my dad. I was driving home with him from college, and somehow we started talking about politics. I hadn't known before then, but Dad had majored in political science.

My father is an introvert. He's quiet, wise, pensive, and incredibly deep. He probably found it hard to connect with much of what I'd been into during college, but when we started talking about current affairs and politics, it was natural and fun. I quickly learned we could talk for hours about anything connected to world affairs, politics, or the historical development of political theory.

Once we spent hours talking about the Cold War, and it was one of the most fascinating historical lessons I'd ever learned. I loved the times we connected like that. Dad would open up, and I'd learn more than I ever thought possible. It was fun and fascinating at the same time.

The best part, however, was discovering a new, shared language; talking politics was a way to feel close to and know my dad.

DYNAMIC ART AND SHALOM

God's dynamic art is the part of creation that includes people, God's purposes, and the future—in other words, things not yet fully realized. Dynamic art is the part that involves us in collaboration and relationship. The grand plan, the great orchestration God wants to achieve through his dynamic art, is peace, unity, goodness, and relationship—all to His glory. The Hebrew Scriptures call this *shalom*.

God's dynamic plan is predicated on *shalom*—the intended state of peace and wholeness that all of God's creation is meant to experience. This isn't *peace* as we Americans conceive of it, like snoozing in a hammock; rather, it is an active presence of what is right, true, nourishing, joyful, and the like. *Shalom* is the plumb line, and when we see injustice in the world, we see that things are not as they ought to be. Put another way, injustice and sin tear the fabric of *shalom*—and shalom is the all-encompassing desire of God for peace and goodness throughout His creation.

The astonishing reality is that we are also part of God's plan for mending the fabric of *shalom*. God's intended peace isn't a neutral absence of conflict; rather, "[it] expresses completeness, wholeness, harmony, fulfillment . . . [and] unimpaired relationships with others."[6] Dr. John Stackhouse, a theology professor at Regent College, described *shalom* in an interview, saying:

> Shalom is this wonderful Hebrew word that literally means "peace" but it means "flourishing"—I think it's the closest English word we have for it, and it means each individual element flourishes—each person, but also each tree, or each animal. It also means each of those relationships flourish. It also means that every group, every system, a family or a business or a school or a nation, flourishes. . . . So it's this literally global idea where everything . . . lives up to its potential. . . . God created the world, and God wants it all back. God doesn't just want human souls to come up and live in a kind of heaven with Him. He is looking forward to a new sky and a new planet, a new heaven and a new earth, with a new humanity, a renewed humanity, to work out with Him the best flourishing of this wonderful world that He's made.[7]

To *work out* with Him. That's dynamic, and it requires us to give our lives away. *The Message* Bible, a paraphrased version, captures that divine/human collaboration in John 14:

"Believe me: I am in my Father and my Father is in me. If you can't believe that, believe what you see—these works. The person who trusts me will not only do what I'm doing but even greater things, because *I, on my way to the Father, am giving you the same work to do that I've been doing. You can count on it.* From now on, whatever you request along the lines of who I am and what I am doing, I'll do it. That's how the Father will be seen for who he is in the Son. I mean it. Whatever you request in this way, I'll do." (vv. 11–14 MSG; emphasis added)

Jesus Himself announced the work He was going to do when He began His public ministry: "to proclaim good news to the poor . . . to proclaim freedom for the prisoners," and "to set the oppressed free" (Luke 4:18). Then He lived out those words, giving His life away, day after day.

Justice, goodness, unity, and *grace* are all words that describe the harmony God desires. They are His musical notes, melody, rests, and crescendos—the music He has written for His creation. We are meant to participate in concert, dynamically, with God's plan.

Jesus is giving us the same work to do that He did. We can count on it.

Sin rends the fabric of *shalom*. It trades our just actions for injustice, love for hate, unity for self, righteousness for unrighteousness, healing for violence. Sin repeatedly stretches, tears, and eventually unravels God's creation. When we seek our own selfish ends, we rebel against God's righteousness and upset the work of *shalom*.

C. S. Lewis wove this thinking together while discussing sin. "We poison the wine as He decants it into us; murder a melody He would play with us as the instrument. . . . Hence all sin, whatever else it is, is sacrilege."[8]

Sin is dissonance where there should be harmony. It vandalizes God's dynamic art. That is why justice is a universal—because it is the act of righting the wrongs that sin creates. Without justice there can be no *shalom*. *Shalom* flourishes in the presence of justice.

Biblical *shalom* requires the active pursuit of what ought to be. Knowing God means spending time with Him, in His world, doing what He is already doing. God's ongoing work in His creation, His dynamic art, is to right that which is wrong. He wants to undo the effects of sin and to bring about *shalom*—isn't that why He sent Jesus?

As Cornelius Plantinga has written, "To be a responsible person is to find one's role in the building of shalom, the re-webbing of God, humanity, and all creation in justice, harmony, fulfillment, and delight."[9]

Perhaps it's possible to be neutral and not be guilty of any sin as long as we aren't fighting against God's plan. Can't we just disengage?

Ask the conductor if a member of the orchestra who refuses to play his instrument is "neutral." This is the subtle reality of idolatry. If we aren't actively following God, we are following another conductor.

Jesus used this logic in His teaching: "No one can serve *two masters*. Either you will hate the one and love the other, or you will be devoted to the one and despise the other. You cannot serve both God and money" (Matthew 6:24; emphasis added). So if God tells us that His heart is for the fatherless, for the widow, for the marginalized, for the poor and the downtrodden, we cannot turn away from these in pursuit of something else while still claiming to be serving God, can we?

Justice is a fundamental part of God's character and desires. We can't just claim to know *about* it; we must seek to *experience* it. To claim to know God without doing justice would be like claiming to play for the New York Yankees just because you own a Yankees jersey. Our trouble is that we are guilty of trying to separate what is eternally connected. We want to hold God in one hand and justice in the other, yet knowing God requires both hands to join.

FEELING JUSTICE

As a new Christian, I read in a theology book that one of God's attributes is His justice. However, that didn't provide me with any *relational* knowledge. Knowing God intimately and understanding more of His character and heart came through experiences I had later, like when I was taken undercover one night in Cambodia, where I witnessed newly trafficked teenage girls—sex slaves—from Vietnam who were to be auctioned off in Phnom Penh.

I understood God's pain and outrage in that moment because I felt it as well. God saw those girls, and His fundamental character was crying out against their violation.

God's love for those misused girls isn't a line in a textbook. It is a reality that defines Him. And we grow closer to and understand Him better as that concern comes to define us.

JUSTICE AND THEOLOGY

Let's take a closer look at what it means to know God through the dynamic process of pursuing justice. Recall that Psalm 9:16 says, "The LORD is known by his acts of justice." Knowing what God cares about, such as acts of justice, is a way for us to know Him.

In Jeremiah we encounter a powerful story in which God

condemned the injustice of Judah's king. Jeremiah was called to declare against King Shallum: "Woe to him who builds his palace by unrighteousness, his upper rooms by injustice, making his own people work for nothing, not paying them for their labor."

Then God angrily contrasted Shallum with his father, the good king Josiah, saying, "He did what was right and just, so all went well with him. *He defended the cause of the poor and needy, and so all went well. Is that not what it means to know me?*" (22:13, 15–16; emphasis added).

God was talking about justice. He is greatly concerned with how we treat each other, our use of material wealth, and the extent to which we care for the marginalized. In fact, through the prophet Jeremiah, God said that living justly is what it means to know Him. All too often, however, we fixate on the static study of God (theology) at the expense of participating with what God is doing in the world.

Yet theology *is* vital—as Richard Baxter wrote, "Nothing can be rightly known, if God be not known; nor is any study well managed, nor to any great purpose, if God is not studied."[10] Even the static knowledge of theology has something to teach us about justice, however, and can therefore become dynamic. The word *theology* comes from the Latin *theologia*, which is made from the Greek words θεος (God) and λογος (study). Theology is the study of who God is and how God relates to everything else. If justice is a way of knowing God more deeply, then justice, it seems, is a theological necessity.

I'm not saying justice is the only way to know God. But it does mean that if we want to know God fully or grow closer to Him, pursuing justice is a biblical and necessary way. Doesn't it follow that if you want a relationship with God, you will care about what

He cares about? You will work where He is working? You will care for the poor and defend the weak, since justice is at the very heart of God and part of the peace or *shalom* He desires?

In more common ways, when my daughters join me in what I'm passionate about, they begin to know me in new ways. For instance, my oldest daughter, Mary Joy, has made a choice to read challenging books because she knows how important reading is to me. My daughter Sara has begun watching and learning about football because she sees it as something I love. While both daughters are different, they share the same desire to join me in my passions as a way of knowing me and feeling closely connected.

Similarly, when we participate through justice in God's plan for goodness and unity, we can know God in new ways. Our lives can be in concert with God. As Henry David Thoreau wrote, "Justice is sweet and musical; but injustice is harsh and discordant."[11]

JUSTICE MATTERS TO GOD

Justice, kindness, and equity are central to God. He delights in them.

> "Let not the wise boast of their wisdom
>   or the strong boast of their strength
>   or the rich boast of their riches,
> but let the one who boasts boast about this:
>   *that they have the understanding to know me,*
>   *that I am the* Lord, *who exercises kindness,*
>   *justice and righteousness on earth,*
>   for in these I delight,"
>   declares the Lord. (Jeremiah 9:23–24; emphasis added)

Why aren't these things central for us? Why don't *we* delight in them?

Justice is always a felt need for the poor, for the oppressed. However, for people who have enough—or too much—it is more difficult to *feel* the need for justice. If the cry for justice, for *shalom*, isn't burning in our guts, it's easy to put it on the back burner.

Yet there are more than two thousand verses in the Bible directly related to justice. How many of those did you learn in Sunday school? How many of the worship songs you sing are based on them? Compare this to eleven hundred references to prayer and almost seven hundred mentions of the word love. There are nearly three times as many references to money—in which much injustice finds its root—as there are to love!

Perhaps it's hard to hear what Scripture is trying to tell us because we think we already know what it's saying.

Grab a highlighter and follow the thread of justice throughout Scripture—from creation to sin; from liberation to law; through the kings and the prophets. Note its sharp focus through the ministry of Jesus bringing reconciliation, redemption, and equality before God; trace it through the letters of Paul, James, John, and Peter, who command us to love, to bring praise to God by our good works, and to treat our fellow humans lovingly and justly in response to God's love for us.

Justice sharpens the point of prophetic poetry and convicts the believer that those who follow Christ, who call themselves Christians, necessarily must care for the poor, the weak, and the oppressed. It is hypocrisy to lift certain themes out of Scripture but neglect this one.

We never worship justice. We worship God. The question is, can we worship God without justice?

Isaiah 58 answers that we can't.[12] One of the most startlingly straightforward chapters in all of Scripture, it opens with God describing His people who *claimed* to want to know Him:

"Day after day they seek me out; they seem eager to know my ways, as if they were a nation that does what is right and has not forsaken the commands of its God. They ask me for just decisions and seem eager for God to come near them.

"'Why have we fasted,' they say, 'and you have not seen it? Why have we humbled ourselves, and you have not noticed?'"

God's response spotlighted the contradiction in their lives and indicted them.

"Yet on the day of your fasting, you do as you please and exploit all your workers. Your fasting ends in quarreling and strife, and in striking each other with wicked fists. You cannot fast as you do today, and expect your voice to be heard on high.

"Is this the kind of fast I have chosen, only a day for a man to humble himself? Is it only for bowing one's head like a reed and for lying on sackcloth and ashes? Is that what you call a fast, a day acceptable to the Lord?"

God then contrasted the Israelites' failed devotion with His true desire for them:

"Is not this the kind of fasting I have chosen: to loose the chains of injustice and untie the cords of the yoke, to set the oppressed free and break every yoke? Is it not to share your food with the hungry and to provide the poor wanderer with shelter—when you see the naked, to clothe him, and not to turn away from your own flesh and blood?

"Then your light will break forth like the dawn, and your healing will quickly appear; then your righteousness will go before you, and the glory of the LORD will be your rear guard. Then you will call, and the LORD will answer; you will cry for help, and he will say: Here am I." (vv. 2–9)

Empty devotion is a disappointment to God. Justice is a delight.

Religion, routine, and ritual carry with them the appearance of wanting to know God, as does external piety. They demonstrate an apparent eagerness for God to come near. Yet, as God said in Isaiah 58, this is not what He wants. God wants His people to approach Him by living just lives.

If we expect our voices to be heard and our fasting to be recognized, God declares that these efforts must be united with justice, charity, hospitality, and mercy. If we do these things, God will answer our cries. We will look for Him and He will say, "Here I am."

CONVERSATION

Knowing God isn't just about studying Him from a distance. To know God's heart and His plan, to be in relationship with Him, we need to be with God, pursuing His desires in the world; that is, *pursuing* justice.

But what does that really mean? What does it *look* like to pursue justice? And while we're asking that question, what about these: What does Jesus say about justice, and how does that fit with our ambitions in life? What if justice is just the latest church fad that inevitably leads to failure or religious guilt? What if we don't know any victims of injustice or don't have much to give? What if we don't have the time? And, what if *we're* the ones in need of justice?

We're going to wrestle with these and other questions throughout this book. Even the briefest overview of the Bible lets us see that justice is one of God's central concerns.

Let's join the conversation.

> Evildoers do not understand what is right,
> but those who seek the LORD understand it fully.
>
> PROVERBS 28:5

INTERLUDE

THE GARDEN

By Jeff Johnson

> One of the most important resources that a garden makes
> available for use is the gardener's own body. A garden gives the
> body the dignity of working in its own support. It is a way of
> rejoining the human race.[13]
>
> WENDELL BERRY

What do snap peas, bell peppers, and kale have to do
with God's work of justice in the world? Perhaps more
than you think.

In the Western world, we often have no idea where the food
we consume comes from. We have lost touch with part of what it
means to be human. For countless generations, folks have fostered
a relationship with the soil based on mutual health and benefit:
we cultivate and care for the soil, and that same soil nourishes our
bodies with food.

Yet today we have relegated our relationship with food to a
plastic-wrapped, microwavable affair of convenience.

Food is an essential and profound element of what it means to
be human. Our families, cultures, and stories center around the
dinner table.

Think of Jesus and the tax collector. Why was sharing a meal with this shady member of society so scandalous compared to having a conversation with him on the street? Because sharing a meal with someone is an intimate experience. When we eat together, we don't just share food—we share ourselves and create memories.

Are you satisfied with the memories you've been creating around the table, or have those moments been replaced by a five-minute trip to the drive-thru?

Dear friends, discover for yourselves the joy of being a gardener. Sink your hands deep into the soil and plant your snap peas, bell peppers, and kale. Discover the slow joy of growing new stories. Celebrate a just harvest that is meant to be shared.

In doing so, you may cultivate more than vegetables. Your love affair with the land may begin to change the world.

THREE

ADVENT

The Gospel and Justice

To believe in future rewards is to believe that the long arm of
the Lord bends toward justice, to believe that one day the proud
will be overthrown and the humble raised up and the hungry
filled with good things. . . . Like a bell tolling from another
world, Jesus' promise of rewards proclaims that no matter how
things appear, there is no future in evil, only in good.[1]

PHILIP YANCEY

Preaching a gospel absent of justice is preaching no gospel at all.[2]

DR. JOHN M. PERKINS

The Society for the Propagation of the Gospel in Foreign
Parts was formed in 1701 by the Church of England under
the rule and authority of King William III. The Society's goal
was to preach the gospel in the Americas and the West Indies. Its
governing board, according to author Adam Hochschild, "included
the Regius Professors of Divinity at Oxford and Cambridge and the
head of the church, the Archbishop of Canterbury."[3] To help fund

this costly enterprise, the Society owned the Codrington sugar cane plantation in Barbados.

The plantation fields were worked by African slaves.

Each slave brought to the Society's plantation was branded across the chest with the word *SOCIETY*.[4] When the branding failed to sufficiently reduce escapes, "the chief deterrent was the lash, plus, at times, an iron collar."[5] The slaves were subjected to miserable living and working conditions, and many died within several years.

The clerics on the society's board noticed the plantation's high death rate, but made no move to change how it operated. "I have long wondered & lamented," wrote the Archbishop of Canterbury to a fellow bishop in 1760, "that the Negroes in our plantations decrease, & new Supplies become necessary continually. Surely this proceeds from some Defect, both of Humanity, & even of good policy."

His conclusion?

"But we must take things as they are at present."[6]

This story draws as sharp a contrast as any I've ever heard between our ability to focus on preaching and proclaiming the gospel and yet completely failing to see its clear relevance to justice and the material needs of our fellow humans. We always have the ability, it seems, to cross oceans to make converts, yet—as Jesus discussed with the Pharisees in Matthew 23—neglect the weightier matters of the law, like justice and mercy and faithfulness.

BALANCING THE SPIRITUAL AND MATERIAL

Is it possible to talk about the gospel without talking about justice?

We sometimes see the gospel and justice as separate, like two sides of a teeter-totter. We think talking about the requirements of justice or the material aspects of life, raising that side of the teeter-totter, will diminish the gospel and our focus on the spiritual aspects of life. The assumption is that if one is highlighted, the other is diminished. This kind of either/or thinking, or dualism, is actually a heresy historically referred to as Gnosticism.

This is not how the Hebrews understood God, however. To them, the spiritual and material sides of life were united and integrated. When we think about the gospel this way, our picture changes. Rather than being in competition, as with the teeter-totter analogy, the spiritual and material aspects of life can be pictured as the two sides of a train track—meant to be inextricably connected in one purpose.

SPIRITUAL
(HEAVEN)

MATERIAL
(EARTH)

JUSTICE IS COMING

We are familiar with the idea that the Old Testament prophets spoke to the coming of Jesus. We often assume the whole reason Jesus came to earth was to bring individual salvation. Yet the very prophets who spoke about the coming Messiah also wrote about Him bringing hoped-for justice. Understood this way, justice isn't *added* to salvation; rather, salvation necessarily includes community and justice.

Far from minimizing justice, then, the birth and ministry of Jesus affirm justice as integral to the good news. Seven hundred years before Jesus was born, Isaiah prophesied that justice would be one of His primary concerns: "Here is my servant, whom I uphold, my chosen one in whom I delight; I will put my Spirit on him, and he will bring justice to the nations. . . . He will not falter or be discouraged till he establishes justice on earth" (Isaiah 42:1, 4).

Notice the theme in the verses below:

> Zion will be delivered *with justice*,
>> her penitent ones with righteousness. (1:27)

> The Lord is exalted, for he dwells on high;
>> he will fill Zion *with his justice* and righteousness. (33:5)

> Listen to me, my people;
>> hear me, my nation:
> Instruction will go out from me;
>> *my justice* will become a light to the nations.
> *My righteousness* draws near speedily,
>> *my salvation* is on the way,
>> and *my arm* will bring justice to the nations.
> The islands will look to me
>> and wait in hope for my arm. (51:4–5; emphases added)

God's plan of salvation and restoration, both temporally and finally, are organically connected to the restoration and institution of justice. Justice cannot be divorced from God's heart and purposes—it permeates them. In fact, a central truth of the gospel is this: God's grace enacts and restores justice.

JUSTICE HAS ARRIVED

Fast-forward to the night Jesus was born, and we see further development of the Messiah's theme of justice.

When the angels announced the coming of the Messiah, they proclaimed good news of *shalom*: peace on earth. Because this baby had been born, there would be peace on earth and goodwill toward people.

Later, as recounted in Luke 4, Jesus began His public ministry by unrolling the scroll of Isaiah and choosing to read prophesies specifically connecting the Messiah with justice.

"The Spirit of the Lord is on me,
because he has anointed me
to proclaim good news to the poor.

He has sent me to proclaim freedom for the prisoners
and recovery of sight for the blind,
to set the oppressed free,
to proclaim the year of the Lord's favor." (vv. 18–19)

He then stopped reading, rolled up the scroll, gave it back to the attendant, and sat down. With the eyes of everyone focused on Him, Jesus said, "These prophecies about the Messiah are being fulfilled today in your hearing."

Later, John the Baptist developed doubts about Jesus and essentially asked, "Are You really the Messiah, or did I get this wrong?" Jesus sent word back to John that the blind were receiving sight and that people were being healed. He declared His works of justice in fulfillment of the prophesies in Isaiah as evidence that He was the Messiah.

INTIMATELY CONNECTED

In John 15, Jesus said that He is the vine and His followers are the branches. Clearly, as we partake in the good news, as we become followers of Christ through salvation, we are knit *into* Him.

Later, in John 17:18, as Jesus prayed to His Father, He said that He was now sending His followers into the world, just as His Father had sent Him. He went on to say that His branches would bear fruit. So can we be reconciled to God without understanding God and beginning to do what He desires? Can we be connected to Jesus without bearing fruit? Can we have the Holy Spirit in us without producing a sharable harvest of love, joy, peace, patience, kindness, goodness, faithfulness, gentleness, and self-control?

No. Jesus calls His followers to be flourishing branches. His desire is that we become a living part of Him, extending His kingdom into the world. We must join with God to become stewards of His creation, involved in establishing justice, because that's what God is already doing.

The gospel is more organic than we sometimes make it. The promise of salvation is frequently laced with imagery of justice, righteousness, and goodness. We cannot extract one piece of God's plan for salvation and think we have the complete picture or the whole good news.

There are at least three main components of salvation: *justification* (being forgiven of sin and made right with God), *sanctification* (the process of becoming more like Christ), and *glorification* (the end, being made like Christ in heaven). Sometimes, however, we focus purely on that first element—justification—and think it's the entirety of salvation or the Christian gospel.

Justification *is* connected to the decision to follow Christ. It is the *moment* of turning, the visible transaction or conversion. It's like being drafted by a professional football team. There is a specific moment in time when a player is drafted and joins the team, but that's not where the story ends.

In fact, that's where the real story begins. Next comes the strengthening and conditioning process. According to Ephesians 2:10, "We are God's workmanship, created in Christ Jesus to do good works, which God prepared in advance for us to do" (NIV). That's sanctification, and it happens over a lifetime. It is the *process* of spiritual growth. It informs and gives energy to our sacrificial love for others, whereby we become more like Christ. That process ultimately leads to glorification, when we are transformed into our resurrected bodies to dwell with God forever—and to the moment when we long to hear, "Well done, good and faithful servant."[7]

When we focus exclusively on the preaching of justification, we're reducing the grand narrative of the good news down to a moment of decision and spiritual transaction. As such, anything to do with earthly or material concerns becomes secondary or superfluous.

The good news, however, requires the preaching of the whole narrative of redemption. Our picture of the gospel cannot hang together as a whole if we remove the material from the spiritual aspects any more than a piece of cloth can hang together if we remove the horizontal threads from the vertical ones.

So what does that have to do with *justice*?

In *justification*, when we are justified, God's justice is satisfied and Christ's righteousness becomes our own. Though we are unjust people, we can have fellowship with a just God. Then, as we are *sanctified*, day by day, we grow into the ability to do what a justified person would do. And just people do just things. We are growing into a degree of Christlikeness—becoming more like the Messiah, who was fully just and who came to enact and restore justice.

Ultimately, God's work will be finished, and we will be fully transformed into people who can stand in the presence of a just and holy God; that is, we will be *glorified*. Justice will then be restored and complete.

Ironically, many of us have never made the connection that these common theological terms—*just*, *justified*, and *justification*—are actually justice language at the heart of the good news. *Justice is a thread running throughout the gospel.*

Jesus came with the good news that He was going to accomplish spiritual redemption, which has everything to do with justice. He also saw this redemption extending into the material world and being represented by a kingdom community in which justice would flourish and the marginalized would be welcomed. As He taught the disciples to pray, "Your kingdom come, your will be done, *on earth as it is in heaven*" (Matthew 6:10; emphasis added).

The story of salvation isn't either spiritual or material—heavenly or earthly—rather, it is *both*. Therefore, we can't separate justice from the gospel any more than we can separate thunder from lightning.

GOOD NEWS

In his autobiography, *Surprised by Joy*, C. S. Lewis related that one of his problems with Christianity was the unknowability of God. If God is who He says He is, how is it possible for a human to know

Him? Lewis used the example of the character Hamlet, the epony-
mous hero of Shakespeare's play. How could Hamlet, the fictional
prince, ever know Shakespeare, his creator? It is seemingly impossible for the two worlds to meet.[8]

But Lewis realized that there *was* a way for Hamlet to meet
his creator—Shakespeare would need to write himself into his own
play. If Shakespeare was a character in the play *Hamlet*, then the
character Hamlet could meet him and begin to understand him.

That is what happened at the first Christmas. God wrote
Himself into His own story through the person of His Son, whom
John's gospel calls "the Word," and this was cause for great joy:
"And there were in the same country shepherds abiding in the
field, keeping watch over their flock by night. And, lo, the angel of
the Lord came upon them, and the glory of the Lord shone round
about them: and they were sore afraid. And the angel said unto
them, Fear not: for, behold, I bring you good tidings of great joy,
which shall be to all people" (Luke 2:8–10 KJV).

The "good tidings of great joy" that the angel announced was
this: the Messiah—God in the flesh—was coming to earth. Of
this event, the prophet Isaiah wrote, "The people walking in darkness have seen a great light" (9:2).[9] The advent of God's promised
Messiah meant that the established order was upended. The ninth
chapter of Isaiah, which prophesied the coming Messiah, tells the
story that no human would dare create:

- In the absolute weakness of a baby, God would shatter the
  yoke that burdened His people and remove the rod of their
  oppressors (v. 4).
- On the shoulders of a peasant, God would place a new
  government—one that would bring lasting peace (vv. 6–7).
- From out of a downtrodden nation oppressed by a powerful

empire, God would establish a new kingdom and uphold it with justice and righteousness beyond the end of time (v. 7).

Thousands of years ago, God sent His Son to advance the cause of God's kingdom. The Scriptures sing in chorus of that kingdom, weaving peace, justice, and righteousness into a never-ending song of great joy to all people. That good news pulled the shepherds to their feet, just as it pulls our hearts toward a God we feared was unknowable but whom we discovered was walking and talking right beside us.

If the message the angels heralded so long ago is still true—*good tidings of great joy*—then that message of joy leads us into justice. Jesus entered the world to herald something new, shown in the tidings given first to poor shepherds in the fields, to foreigners, to outcasts—that He had come to give His life away, even to the least of these.

So, too, can we.

CONSPIRACY

Christmas was the advent of something huge . . . so huge we want to wrap our wallets around it.

In 2011, Americans spent more than $450 billion dollars[10] on holiday shopping—more than the annual GDP of either Sweden or Saudi Arabia.[11] The World Bank estimates that to provide everyone in the world with clean water for drinking and sanitation would cost up to $21 billion dollars each year.[12] This ever-expanding chasm between the developed and developing world is not the good news of Christmas or the gospel.

In 2006, my good friend Rick McKinley, a pastor at Imago Dei

Community in Portland, Oregon, along with several other pastors, decided to do something about the consumeristic way we celebrate Christmas. They committed to flipping the distortion of Christmas upside down. That year, the Advent Conspiracy—an international movement encouraging people to worship fully, spend less, give more, and love all—was born.

In 2010 and 2011, Imago Dei, partnering with other local churches in Portland, used the principles of the Advent Conspiracy to raise nearly one hundred thousand dollars. Church representatives approached officials from the City of Portland with a simple question: If the churches gave a Christmas gift to the city to benefit the "least of these," what would you do with it?

The city asked that the gift help serve the child victims of sex trafficking in Portland. Portland Police, along with the federal officers of the Innocence Lost Task Force, work with the Sexual Assault Resource Center (SARC) and Janus Youth Services to help bring care, healing, and access for those in need of services. In 2010, SARC and Janus had major gaps in their funding, gaps the churches were able to help plug.

Instead of giving a new gadget or gizmo for Christmas that year, many Christians in Portland kept gift-giving simple; and with money that would have typically been spent on greater extravagance, they began to work toward bringing justice to some who needed it the most.

Rick reports this side effect of giving their lives away at Christmastime: his congregation understands and worships Jesus differently all year long. Since that first year, Advent Conspiracy has grown to include a network of thousands of churches worldwide.

Can Christmas still be good news? What if understanding the full gospel—justification, sanctification, glorification—can transform Christmas? What if we can escape the clutches of consumerism and begin to live in new, prophetic ways that we've yet to imagine?

Either Christmas is what the angels said it was—good news of great joy for all people—or it isn't. When Jesus was born, when He was placed in a feeding trough for animals, He already carried a new kingdom on His tiny shoulders, a kingdom of peace, of righteousness, and of justice.

God wrote Himself into our story to change our narrative. We characters can know the Author who created us, and we can join our lives with His story as it arcs toward a perfect and eternal resolution.

The gospel brings with it good news of great joy that will be for all people. And justice is embedded in that good news. There is potential in it, and God asks those who follow Him to work to uncover and activate that potential justice.

Justice is a thorny issue and can be a stumbling block for some people. However, God promised and delivered a Messiah defined by justice, a Messiah who is calling His followers to be defined by justice as well.

If God speaks unblushingly about justice, His Messiah, and the good news of salvation, shouldn't we?

> Zion will be delivered with justice,
>   her penitent ones with righteousness.
> ISAIAH 1:27

FOUR

HUMAN RIGHTS AND HAPPINESS

Recovering the Moral Value of Happiness

All that we call human history—money, poverty, ambition, war, prostitution, classes, empires, slavery—[is] the long terrible story of [people] trying to find something other than God which will make [them] happy.[1]

C. S. Lewis

For it is not earthly riches which make us or our sons happy; for they must either be lost by us in our lifetime, or be possessed when we are dead, by whom we know not, or perhaps by whom we would not. But it is God who makes us happy, who is the true riches of minds.[2]

St. Augustine

O ver time, pursuing justice can begin to feel like a chore, an obligation we can't get out from under. But I'm about to let you in on a secret: *pursuing justice can make you happy.* In fact, I'd go even farther and say that pursuing justice *is* pursuing happiness. There's a godly happiness or joy designed for those who love to the point of sacrifice—a happiness that occurs only when our conflicting desires are finally unified.

My daughters love to eat candy, but if I let them eat all the candy they want, they'll get sick. Their desires are in conflict: the desire to eat unlimited candy conflicts with their desire to avoid a stomachache. Adults aren't much different. We want to buy new things all the time, while also being financially secure. We want to spend all of our time pursuing hobbies and pleasure, but we also want to accomplish something meaningful with our lives.

There is a better way—a way to find contentment and peace as we unify our conflicting desires.

We humans experience myriad desires: selfish desires to pursue our own pleasure as well as holy desires to know God, to be virtuous, to love others, to pursue joy. God's design for the unity of our desires is found in justice, which means being in right relationship with God and with others. Dissolving that intended unity or separating our desires from our actions creates an anemic faith and tempers the excitement and passion that are properly appointed for obedience . . . and our true happiness.

WHY ARE WE DOING THIS AGAIN?

So far we've talked about two big reasons to do justice:

1. It's *ethical*—justice is the right thing to do.
2. It's *religious*—God has called and commanded us to join Him in doing justice.

There's a third reason, however, and it's a far more experiential reason to do justice:

3. It's *personal*—doing justice fulfills our deepest longings and leads to peace and joy.

Ethical and religious motivations carry the most urgency and gravity, but they can burn us out over time and deform us into passionless, duty-bound people. Being trapped by duty on a treadmill of shoulds and oughts isn't how we were designed to live. As singer-songwriter David Bazan put it in "Secret of the Easy Yoke,"

> But if all that's left is duty
> I'm falling on my sword
> At least then I would not serve
> An unseen, distant lord[3]

Rather, God in His grace provides us the *personal motivation* to obey, and that is the joy that comes from doing good and obeying Him.

If justice is a fundamental part of God's good news, and if it truly is better to give than to receive, why do we have such a hard time jumping in and giving our lives away? Why do we cling to a thin individualism rather than embrace a robust love for our neighbor? I believe it's because we've robbed justice of one of its prime motivators: godly happiness.

There are two ways we can seek happiness—either at the expense of others or in growing the goodness of others. The first builds me up at your expense, generating mutual insecurity and/or retaliation, while the second builds us both up together. The second is the kingdom happiness Jesus calls "complete" joy that lacks nothing, the kind that naturally produces right actions and genuine love (John 15:11).

The reality is that our happiness, God's glory, and loving our neighbors are all bound together. When we realize this, pursuing justice, however difficult it may be, begins to capture our attention and effort in a holistic way.

Examining the nature and history of happiness is important because it will allow us to see the difference between selfish happiness—which gets in the way of loving others and doing justice—and the deeper happiness that God intends for us. Think of it this way: God wants you to be just, and the more just your life is, the happier you'll be *and* the happier others will be. That sounds like something worth thinking about.

RULES, RULES, RULES

When I was younger, I believed all rules were bad. Teachers had rules that bored and sedated me. Mom and Dad had rules that stifled and chafed me. Culture had rules, like dressing up for certain occasions or eating with "proper" manners, that kept me from living life the way I wanted. To my thinking, rules killed my joy.

God's rules didn't seem any different. Rules were rules, whether they were issued by my high school English teacher or by some bearded old man in the sky. Ignoring God's rules may have given me a bit of extra guilt, but I ignored them all the same. It was easy to do this because rules clearly didn't lead to my happiness. As I mentioned in the introduction, my goal was to suck the marrow out of life, and that pursuit didn't allow me much time for rule following.

Then, when I was twenty-three, I read Saint Augustine's *Confessions*. On the surface, Augustine, a theologian and bishop who lived in North Africa during the fourth and fifth centuries CE, didn't have a lot in common with me, yet I found reading him as relevant to what I was going through as anything I'd ever read. One sentence in particular was a wakeup call.

In Book 1, Augustine wrote, "For you have made us for yourself, and our heart is restless till it finds its rest in you."[4]

I'd spent my whole life up to that point running from rules and authority and trying to run *toward* happiness. So why was I unhappy and unfulfilled? Why was I still restless if I was running after all the stuff and pleasure that was supposed to fulfill me?

I sensed in Augustine a hint of something new. Somehow my pursuit of the good life—a life filled with meaning, purpose, a sense of wholeness, and satisfaction—was connected to my pursuit of God.

Instead of running *from* God to attain happiness, I realized happiness was found in running *toward* God. It began to make sense that God created us to find our ultimate satisfaction in our relationship with and obedience to him. As Saint Thomas Aquinas echoed hundreds of years later, "God alone constitutes [humans'] happiness."[5]

WHY OBEDIENCE?

Rules shouldn't exist for their own sake—at least not proper, well-intentioned rules. Instead, laws and sanctions and rules and mandates "must be used in accordance with their true nature, which is to be, not ends in themselves, but servants of people in their search for God."[6]

Bend, Oregon, where I live, has a lot of roundabouts, or traffic circles. Every entrance to a roundabout has a yield sign. These signs have become a symbol to me of the nature of rules and obedience as a means to an end.

A yield sign doesn't exist to tyrannize me by making me obey it, nor is it there to vacuum the joy from my life or prevent me from experiencing the fullness of life—it's there to safeguard and promote my life by keeping me from getting sideswiped as I navigate the intersection. My life as a citizen of Bend would absolutely *not* be better if the roundabouts had no rules. So we can say that some rules aren't life negating, but are instead life *affirming* and purposeful. Obedience leads to happiness rather than competing against it. God's rules are the same way. His commands don't exist to tyrannize us or keep us from wholeness. Rather, they're meant to guide us toward wholeness and goodness.

The Bible passage that first cracked this idea open for me was John 15:9–11. Jesus was talking to His friends on the night He would be betrayed and arrested. In the midst of saying He was like a vine and they were like the branches growing from Him, Jesus said, "As the Father has loved me, so have I loved you. Now remain in my love. If you obey my commands, you will remain in my love, just as I have obeyed my Father's commands and remain in his love" (vv. 9–10).

We're used to hearing commands in Scripture, such as the need to love and the injunction to obey. What shocked me when I first read this passage and still surprises me today is what Jesus said following the command to obey: "I have told you this so that my joy may be in you and that your joy may be complete" (v. 11).

I wrestled with that last verse for a long time. I even thought, *How can something like this be in the* Bible—"*that my joy may be in you and that your joy may be complete," lacking nothing?*

The answer is that joy is a natural end and motivation for our obedience. In fact, says the *Theological Dictionary of the New Testament*, "throughout John's Gospel, fulfillment and joy are related to the person of Jesus."[7] And one of the noteworthy features of early church fathers was that they believed that "joy is a reward for excess good works,"[8] or more simply, virtuous actions.

If joy is so closely tied to pursuing Jesus and justice, have we missed something important in our pursuit of godliness?

Contrary to a tyrannical attempt at restricting our freedom, Jesus seems to be beckoning us to something far better. It is as if He is saying, *I want you to have a relationship with Me, which means you need to obey. And I have told you all this so that you would know and have My joy in your life. That's My motivation and heart for wanting you to obey. I'm giving you rules so that you can be with Me and the Father and therefore be the happiest, most joy-filled people possible.* That was a world apart from the preacher I heard growing up who made me want to get as far away from God as possible if I wanted a chance to be happy.

As a teen, my formula went like this: ignore God so you don't have to obey so you can be happy. Jesus says the opposite: follow God by obeying so that you can experience the fullness of joy. Whoever thought *joy* could be a motivation for *obedience*?

I used to be caught up in what philosophers call the *hedonistic paradox*, or what I like to call the "hedonistic myth": when you pursue pleasure for its own sake, you tend not to find it. What I've learned since is that my pursuit of God and my pursuit of true happiness, rightly understood, *are one and the same.* As Thomas Aquinas wrote, "God alone constitutes [our] happiness."[9]

A HISTORY OF HAPPINESS

These days, happiness often means simply a license to pursue *self-gratification.* "What do happiness and justice have to do with each other?" we ask, because on the surface they seem antithetical.

When we use the word *happiness*, we usually mean one of two things: either *do whatever I want with myself*, which seems to have little to do with justice, or *the pursuit of pleasure*, which seems to be neutral with regard to justice.

But this demeans the true meaning of happiness. It wasn't always defined this way.

Aristotle defined happiness as the chief end of humans. In other words, everything else that we do or value is a means to happiness. Happiness drives ethics and character development because they are a way of fulfilling who we are designed to be: the right kind of virtuous people. As we develop character and become ethical, we begin to fulfill our potential and achieve a state of happiness.

Aristotle codified much of his thinking in a book called *Eudemian Ethics*. The central idea is the flourishing of human life and happiness and that virtuous pursuits are a necessary step toward that end. But in his other seminal book on ethics, titled *Nicomachean Ethics*, he wrote, "Both the many and the cultivated call [the good] happiness, and they suppose that living well and doing well are the same as being happy."[10]

Eudaimonia was a Greek word for happiness, and its parts actually mean "good" (*eu*) and "spirit" [*daimon*]. Can you imagine, *happy ethics* or *the ethics of happiness*? Aristotle sought to define what virtues led to the greatest flourishing and happiness of a person. These virtues, in turn, also produce good societies.

For Aristotle and many of the ancients, happiness was a state of being. They used *happiness* much as we would use the word *joy*. Aristotle's unabashed use of happiness as a driving force for doing good or being ethical was readily agreed to and picked up by many Christian scholars all the way through the Enlightenment. Augustine also saw happiness, rightly defined, as the chief end of man, as did Thomas Aquinas and later Pascal. These theologians didn't see a tension between happiness and living for God—indeed, they saw a unity.

Thomas Jefferson penned the phrase "the pursuit of happiness" in the Declaration of Independence. He was borrowing from the English philosopher John Locke, who had developed theories on just governance and argued that all people had the right to life, liberty, and property. For Locke, *life* meant the right to live—to flourish without being killed or physically harmed by another person. *Liberty* meant the freedom to move about, to not have somebody artificially limit or put boundaries on me, unlawfully imprison me, and so forth. Pretty straightforward, right?

The most intriguing part of Locke's phrase is the word *property*. By this Locke meant the right to have and to hold a place that would allow a person to fully develop his or her human potential. In an agrarian culture, property was the thing that allowed you to flourish. Land allowed you to be self-sufficient, pursue a good and stable life, and experience goodness and satisfaction.

We can even see the tie between property and human flourishing in the Old Testament: God promised the Israelites land—a land flowing with milk and honey. Land became a symbol for what was needed to be able to develop, grow, and flourish.

Thomas Jefferson wasn't altering the substance of the phrase when he switched *property* to *happiness* in the Declaration of Independence. He was basically saying the same thing: that true happiness—in the tradition of philosophers since ancient Greece, not as merely a feeling of pleasure—was a human right and goal. The pursuit of happiness means the right to pursue the full development of human potential. (This is a philosophical analysis of Jefferson's thinking in line with classical concepts, not a defense of him personally, as there were obviously inconsistencies and hypocrisies in his life.)

It wasn't until much more recently, in our highly consumerist culture, that the word *happiness* was degraded to mean merely pleasure and license without regard to ethics, morality, or the human cost of that pleasure. This is why modern-day Christians have a hard time considering happiness in a positive light, never mind as something connected to righteousness and justice. How can self-serving pleasure be tied up with others-focused justice and righteousness?

Between these two extremes, however, lies the kind of godly happiness or satisfaction—moral happiness—that is a fitting and essential part of our relationship with God and the pursuit of justice.

Jesus gave us a picture of godly happiness in His Sermon on the Mount in what we call the Beatitudes. He said:

> "Blessed are the poor in spirit,
>
>> for theirs is the kingdom of heaven.
>
> Blessed are those who mourn,
>
>> for they will be comforted.
>
> Blessed are the meek,
>
>> for they will inherit the earth.
>
> Blessed are those who hunger and thirst for righteousness,
>
>> for they will be filled.
>
> Blessed are the merciful,
>
>> for they will be shown mercy.
>
> Blessed are the pure in heart,
>
>> for they will see God.
>
> Blessed are the peacemakers,
>
>> for they will be called children of God.
>
> Blessed are those who are persecuted because of righteousness,
>
>> for theirs is the kingdom of heaven." (Matthew 5:3–10)

The word *Beatitudes* is taken from the Latin word *beati*—meaning "power," "blessed," or "happy"—that appeared for fifteen hundred years in the Roman Catholic version of the Latin Bible. *Beati* is a translation of the Greek word *makarios* that was in the original version of Matthew, a word that also meant "happy," "blessed," or even "to be envied."

It seems strange at first that Jesus' words would be translated using the Greek word for *happy*, but put in context, it doesn't seem so paradoxical. Those who are meek, merciful, peacemaking, and persecuted may not have pleasure in the moment, but they are going to find true happiness and blessing from God the Father, as well as from the human relationships they develop as they give their lives away.

We need to recover this sense of the word *happiness*. We have to learn that happiness is a vital part of the conversation about obedience, duty, and right living. Yes, there is a corrupted happiness that hampers justice. When I choose myself and my desires at the expense of community or my relationship with God, my momentary happiness is ultimately destructive. It is sin. Yet there is also a happiness that spurs justice onward, a happiness that brings community together and helps establish intimate relationship with God.

When we give our lives away, we discover that two of our primary desires—to make a difference and to be happy—are united. Happiness is the current that helps carry us along, and happiness, as strange as it may seem, provides a natural and godly motivation for doing good.

ENGINEERED FOR HAPPINESS

Without a doubt, our desire for happiness was engineered by God. When God created the world and everything in it, He pronounced it good. The Lord is our Shepherd, and He wants to lead us to green grass and clear streams. Jesus told His friends that He came so that they might live full lives and experience complete joy. When the prodigal son returned home, his father threw him a party.

As we think about what God-designed happiness truly means, however, we must take continued care not to confuse it with the ultimate goal of our happiness. We may easily consent to the fact that watching football does not afford the same kind of happiness as loving a spouse, but *neither* kind of happiness is the same as what awaits those God loves.

I've been studying C. S. Lewis for nearly twenty years, and in my experience he is one of the wisest thinkers on the subject of happiness. In *The Problem of Pain*, Lewis wrote:

> The *settled happiness* and security which we all desire, God with-holds from us by the very nature of the world: but *joy, pleasure, and merriment*, He has scattered broadcast. We are never safe, but we have plenty of fun, and some ecstasy. It is not hard to see why. The security we crave would teach us to rest our hearts in this world and oppose an obstacle to our return to God: a few moments of happy love, a landscape, a symphony, a merry meeting with our friends, a bathe or a football match, have no such tendency. Our Father refreshes us on the journey with some pleasant inns, but will not encourage us to mistake them for home.[11]

While we'll never experience the deepest, most secure sense of happiness during our lives on earth, the *longing* for that happiness—as well as the tastes of it we enjoy during this life—points to God. Lewis's list of "pleasant inns" is a peek at much that is good about being human. A tender kiss, an alpine lake, watching your favorite band play your favorite song, dancing with your friends, swimming in the sea, cheering for your team in the championship . . . these are God-given gifts.

Let me say that again: the joy and happiness we experience on earth is deeply, doubly good because it comes from God *and* points us forward to God's coming kingdom. Such joy and happiness are best found when we give our lives away to others in the service of justice and motivated by love, for only then is the mirage of self-pleasure exchanged for the joy of relationship.

In relating to happiness, we Christians often compound our problems. Since *happiness* seems to be so destructive to individuals and to society—although really the trouble is the unbridled pursuit of selfish pleasure—we try to eschew happiness. We reason that "happiness" must be unbiblical, or sinful, and in response we tell ourselves to stop wanting it.

DON'T STOP RECEIVING

Christians are really good at creating false dichotomies. We like to separate things that aren't meant to be separated. We invent either/or choices for the sake of simplicity. An example of this is contained in nine simple words Paul attributed to Jesus in Acts 20:35: "It is more blessed to give than to receive." This is one of my favorite verses, and one my wife and I have built into the fabric of our family. In some ways, this whole book is summed up in that verse.

What interests me here, however, isn't so much what Jesus was saying, but rather, what we think we hear. "Since it's better to give than receive," we tell ourselves, "giving must be good . . . and therefore getting must be bad."

That's a false dichotomy. It's as if we can't help but think of giving and getting as opposed to each other. If we're giving, we shouldn't be getting, and vice versa.

What's left, then, is poorly motivated giving, along with repressed desires and needs. We want things, we need things, but we believe those feelings are bad. We need to give, give, give because the Bible says so, because giving is good, but we can never receive.

In the messy, organic relationships where real humans live, we are constantly giving and receiving. We hunger to receive, we are inspired to give, and when we intentionally focus on giving, more often than not, we receive what we want and need.

In the previous section we looked at how God designed us to be happy. Listen to C. S. Lewis again: "It is Christian duty, as you know, for everyone to be as happy as he can."[12] What Lewis was saying is that if we are less happy than we could be, given our circumstances, we aren't going to score any points with God. Being less happy than we can be isn't a virtue. True happiness doesn't distract us from loving God and pursuing justice—it motivates and rewards us.

Augustine said in his *Confessions* that the spirit feeds on what gives it joy.[13] I've realized that the goal I had in college of sucking the marrow out of life isn't necessarily wrong. What matters is whether we choose to turn *toward* God or *away* from God in our pursuit of meaning and happiness.

The book of Proverbs says, "The appetite of laborers works for them; their hunger drives them on" (16:26). In that, I realize my appetite for life and joy, rightly understood, can actually help motivate my pursuit of God. Exploring the connection between God's commands and our joy should be an integral part of a robust, passionate, and obedient faith.

Happiness is not the enemy of the Christian message. It is essential to it.

"THIS AIN'T MY AMERICAN DREAM"

My friend Erin is a living example of how the best way to find happiness isn't to chase it . . . it's to give your life away to others.

She didn't have to give her life away. In fact, she had every reason *not* to. Erin is smart, articulate, and energetic, and for ten years she worked for high-end golf resorts. Erin was living the American Dream: a promising career, growing paychecks, travel, and the time and money to chase her favorite sports and hobbies. She was comfortable and safe.

What she knew about God was static. She knew some verses and platitudes, but she didn't have a relationship with God and wasn't pursuing His will. Then Erin became a Christian in her early thirties after sitting in the back row of church at Antioch for months. She was, in some sense, a reluctant convert.

Over time, however, Erin became more involved. An old friend from college on staff at Antioch offered her a full-time job mentoring college students in the Antioch intern program. The thought of doing something she cared deeply about stirred her heart, so she asked for more information.

No benefits and no pay.

Then she heard a sermon about faith—about how we don't really need faith and can't understand it until we literally have no idea what's supposed to happen next. She became convinced God was asking her something: *Are you willing to walk away from the American Dream and live My dream instead? Are you willing to live by faith?*

The next day she resigned from her job.

You may wonder why God called Erin away from her job at the golf resort. Surely God could have used her there as well. Why did finding true life require her to give away her money, her time, her security, her comfort, and her sense of self-identity?

I'm going to let Erin start to answer those questions. I'm inspired by her courage to not simply *say*, "Speak, Lord, for Your servant is listening," but to then *do* what God told her. During the biggest recession of the last seventy-five years, Erin quit her job because she wanted a better life. Here's how she tells it:

> The best thing about turning my back on my old life was having my eyes opened to what really matters to God. Now I have to rest in who God created me to be instead of striving to make a name for myself. I get to serve God and serve the marginalized every day of my life until I'm so tired that I can't stand up. When I do that, I get to know God's heart. If I love God, I give my life away to the vulnerable, and if I give my life away to the vulnerable, I grow closer to God. I know God—and that's true joy, happiness, and fulfillment.[14]

We're never more trapped than when we think *knowing* God is static and giving our lives away is merely for bonus points on our way to heaven. The paradox is that we need to *give up* the things the world says will make us happy if we want to actually *be* happy. What if we gave our lives away? What if we went to bed every night exhausted—and with a smile on our faces?

Everyone's story looks different. Jesus didn't ask every person He met to leave jobs or family or give away possessions, though He certainly asked some people to do those things. What He did ask of everyone was that they follow His example of giving sacrificial love to God and to others.

The surprising encouragement is that our longing for happiness is given to us by God in order for us to have the best shot at experiencing a happy life. Not fake-happy—plastic smiles and consumer slavery and constant distraction—but real, biblical happiness. The kind that doesn't come at others' expense, but increases with their good.

Real happiness is the natural motivation and reward for living and loving as Jesus commands us to. In the kingdom of God, my joy, God's glory, and the good of the community sing together in beautiful harmony, which is why it truly is better to give than to receive. We can't prevent godly happiness emerging from sacrificial love any more than we can prevent the scent of a rose emanating from the rose itself. Joy is an inseparable part of giving our lives away.

As stated earlier, there are three motivations for doing justice: the ethical, the religious, and the personal. To ignore the holistic and spiritual nature of these and remove the last one leads to a thin, guilt-driven Christianity that is inescapably rule-bound. True happiness, biblical joy, and godly satisfaction nourish us and keep us from burning out as we love and serve others. Recall the words of Saint Augustine: "For you have made us for yourself, and our heart is restless till it finds its rest in you."

Our desire for happiness was designed by God, for God, and to bring us to happiness through God. If our society defines happiness in a way other than God does, our goal must not be to dismiss happiness as somehow sinful or unbiblical. Rather, it must be to ask God for *His* definition of happiness. We are meant to long for God-given happiness, and we are meant to experience it as the fruit of following God into our broken world.

"The thief comes only to steal and kill and destroy;
I have come that they may have life, and have it to the full."
JOHN 10:10

THE WAY OF THE WORLD

By Cathy Warner

Inspired by Psalm 14

This is how fools live—
the powerful are corrupt
believing they are deities,
concerned only with personal gain.
Governments abandon the poor
and commit crimes with impunity.

In this mess God is searching,
looking for a leader who will learn
the ways of justice, who will act with wisdom.

But God's hands are empty, there is no one
to lift up, no one who is living right.
Everyone is self-absorbed, clawing at status,
clamoring for more.

God cries out, "Stop, you evildoers
who gobble my people as if they were bread,
chewing them up to feed your greed.
Quit this insatiable gorging
and call out to me."

Even if the powerful don't listen,
they won't have the last word.
God will foil their plans.
God shelters the sick, the hungry,
the destitute, provides comfort when people won't.

Yes, deliverance will come.
God will embrace those who suffer.
God will enrich the poor. They will feast
on gladness. And God's people will rejoice.

FIVE

LOVE AS SACRAMENT

How Justice Informs Love

He that has no charity deserves no mercy.[1]

ENGLISH PROVERB

Justice is the grammar of things. Mercy is the poetry of things.[2]

FREDERICK BUECHNER

What do we mean when we talk about love? A great deal of our understanding of love comes from media—movies, songs, television shows, and so on—and from nearly every popular representation of love we can generalize this: Love is defined culturally as *an intensity of desire and longing*. In essence, the more I want something, the more I love it.

Jesus defined love differently. He described the epitome of love as a person giving his or her life away.

"A new command I give you: Love one another. As I have loved you, so you must love one another. By this everyone will know that you are my disciples, if you love one another." (John 13:34–35)

"Greater love has no one than this: to lay down one's life for one's friends." (John 15:13)

The apostle John agreed with Jesus:

But whoever has the world's goods, and sees his brother in need and closes his heart against him, how does the love of God abide in him? Little children, let us not love with word or with tongue, but in deed and truth. (1 John 3:17–18 NASB)

For both Jesus and John, the measure of love was far different from what our culture tells us—for them it was focused on others rather than self. And for Jesus, the metric of love is sacrifice.

The irony, then, is that without our noticing, the meaning of *love* has been replaced with the definition of *lust*—measured by *intensity of desire or longing.*

When I first realized the subtle cultural change in the meaning of love—to make it more like the definition of lust—it was a paradigm shift for me. Love has been slowly hollowed out over time, and what remains of its meaning carries, in many contexts, the converse of its original significance.

Our culture's concept of love is primarily self-driven and pleasure-seeking. Jesus' formulation, rather, expects and anticipates sacrifice. That may sound threatening, or too difficult, but isn't sacrificial love—and not temporary lust—the kind of love *we* want from others? We want people to love us through the bad times as well as the good times; year after year, we want to know we *are* loved and *will be* loved, even if it doesn't fit an intense longing or desire of theirs.

If that is the kind of love we want, Jesus says, then it must be the kind of love we *give* others. Love is less about a focus on self than a deep and abiding concern and focus on the other.

I once heard someone teach a Mother's Day message on the nature of a mom's love for her children where the point was made that "motherhood is a call to suffer." This, of course, can be expressed more broadly as "parenting is a call to suffer." A parent's love for a child—one of the purest forms of love—shows in tangible, everyday ways that true love means serving the one loved.

Loving another as I love myself means sacrifice or suffering—it is a continual pouring out and giving up. Serving and suffering in obedience to God or in response to your calling, however, is no bleak thing. It is the sacrifice love willingly chooses, and it cannot imagine another choice.

Love that is identified primarily by the intensity of its longing or its desire isn't love—it's lust. And actions that demonstrate an ongoing willingness to sacrificially serve others are, by Jesus' definition, love.

We think we love when we ache with passion; for Jesus, the measure is sacrificial action.

THE ORIGIN OF SACRIFICE

When considering love, *sacrifice* is a fitting word with a fascinating etymology. We get it from the Latin word *sacrificium*, which means the performing of priestly duties or functions. *Sacrificium* is made up of two Latin roots: *sacer*, which means "sacred" or "holy," and *facio*, which means "do" or "make." These same Latin roots are what we see in the word *sacrament*—a visible, outward sign of inward grace—with both words having strong religious overtones.

The very roots of the word *sacrifice* have a religious connotation, an implication of sacred or priestly offering. There's a marked difference between a selfish orientation and a sacrificial one. Notice the contrast.

Self demands. Sacrifice releases.
Self craves security. Sacrifice befriends faith.
Self defends. Sacrifice risks.
Self needs to be vindicated. Sacrifice looks to God and trusts.
Self looks in the mirror. Sacrifice sees others.
Self rushes. Sacrifice endures.
Self takes. Sacrifice gives.
Self fights. Sacrifice overlooks.
Self breaks. Sacrifice bends.
Self strives. Sacrifice submits.
Self covets now. Sacrifice desires best.
Self uses. Sacrifice serves.
Self is childish. Sacrifice matures.
Self is petty. Sacrifice is noble.
Self spends. Sacrifice invests.
Self burns with momentary anger. Sacrifice overflows with
   enduring grace.
Sacrifice plants. Sacrifice nurtures. Sacrifice brings goodness
   into being.

Remember Jesus' message about the kernel of wheat? He said, "Unless a kernel of wheat falls to the ground and dies, it remains only a single seed. But if it dies, it produces many seeds" (John 12:24). We are called to sacrifice.

Oswald Chambers once said, "Beware of refusing to go to the

funeral of your own independence."[3] The problem is that as long as we are alive, we cannot ever completely kill our selfish desires, which means we are faced with choice after choice. We really *do* have to, as Paul put it, "die every day" (1 Corinthians 15:31). Those choices look different for each of us.

Dr. Randy Jacobs, an urgent care doctor, uses one day of his week to help bring dignity and respect to homeless men and women in town. He helped create a mobile medical van that he drives to homeless shelters and camps around his city, providing care for people who wouldn't otherwise receive it.

Randy also serves on the board of Kilns College and spearheads the effort to involve students in service to our community. He exudes sacrificial love, but when asked about it says, "Don't call it a sacrifice—I'm blessed by it too much for you to talk about the cost." Now, for me, that's a picture of biblical love!

Sacrifice isn't always about caring for the homeless or feeding the hungry, however. Sometimes it can look like taking care of family. This is one way in which my wife, Tamara, is one of my heroes. She wouldn't think of herself that way, but I don't know a greater example of wisdom, maturity, and sacrifice than the one I've seen in her over the years. In fact, you could say it's why I married her.

Back at Clemson, when I'd visit the old folks' home, I used to think that someday—when I wanted to know if a girl might be right to marry—I'd bring her with me on a visit. It's hard to wear a mask in a place like that. Either your heart is compassionate and giving and you see past the awkward parts, or you don't—and it shows on your face and in your body language. It's an easy way to see someone's character. I believed that principle so much that toward the end of college, I even took a few young women to the home on "dates." One of the elderly women to whom I was close would help me with a wink, a smile, or a nod based on her opinions.

In the end, it didn't work well—I was single for the next half decade.

Years later, when I met Tamara, one of the first things I learned about her was that she had moved to tiny Page, Arizona, near Lake Powell, after college, to live with and take care of her grandfather who was beginning to suffer from the early stages of Alzheimer's. Out of her entire extended family, she was the one who put her life on hold and took the baton. I knew what was in Tamara's heart when I heard she had essentially taken on full-time ministry to her grandpa.

True sacrifice always shines.

LOVE WORKS

Just west of where I live in central Oregon sits the Cascade mountain range. The Cascades are a rugged string of volcanic peaks that are snow-covered for most of the year. Watching them through the changing seasons is one of my favorite things about living in Bend. The Cascades invite me to keep my eyes up.

In the middle of this range are three individual but connected peaks: South, Middle, and North Sister. They also have a second set of names, believed to have been given by a Methodist mission in Salem, Oregon, in the 1840s: Faith, Hope, and Charity.

We are more familiar with the trinity of faith, hope, and *love* in Paul's famous verse at the end of 1 Corinthians 13. The 1611 King James Version, however, which the Methodists would have been using, translates 1 Corinthians 13:13 as follows: "And now abideth faith, hope, charity, these three; but the greatest of these is charity."

The Latin word *caritas*, from where we get *charity*, was the word in the Latin version of the Bible,[4] which was the primary scriptural text until the English King James Version, which had an obvious influence on the King James translators.

I like thinking of biblical love in terms of the word *charity*. Many of the verses on love carry a strong picture of the notion of charity. Take 1 John 3:17–18, for example: "But whoever has the world's goods, and sees his brother in need and closes his heart against him, how does the love of God abide in him? Little children, let us not love with word or with tongue, but in deed and truth" (NASB).

Charity implies movement, decision, and a regard for others. It suggests sacrificial love—love in action. (In fact, after I explained this sense of active love to my daughters, they named our hyperactive new puppy "Charity.")

The Catholic Church has a particularly rich tradition regarding charity. Charity, or a preferential treatment of the poor and vulnerable, shows up as a key tenet in the church's official social doctrine and as an imperative of the faith.

Scripture does not command us to "love" in some abstract, disembodied way, but rather to work out our love in the world. Charity puts action into the word *love*.

Love is a decision. It is an action and a pursuit. Love works. Or, as the title of Bob Goff's latest book puts it, *Love Does*.[5]

YOU CAN'T ROB CRAZY HORSE

For all the things I appreciate about the word *charity*, however, there is an aspect in which it is incomplete. Charity gives the sense of something we choose, often on our own terms. We *decide* to be charitable. The problem, though, is that we sometimes give our-selves permission to be loving in only our own circles. Charity can allow us to wear blinders that prevent us from seeing justice issues that are out of sight or beneath the radar.

I have learned a lot about this from my friend Daniel Fan, who advocates for indigenous people. He wrote a piece a few years back, and I've been pondering a single sentence from it ever since. It dealt with the tendency to neglect issues that affect Native Americans, while giving the entirety of our focus to global relief and develop-ment. The sentence that struck me was the conclusion: "You can't rob Crazy Horse to pay Bishop Tutu and call it 'Social Justice.'"[6]

Daniel was summarizing a point on the injustices to Native Americans (symbolized by Crazy Horse) that often get overlooked in our rush to help the less fortunate internationally (symbolized by Bishop Desmond Tutu of South Africa). In essence, ignoring the one to help the other is not a complete picture of justice.

The power in this phrase is the diagnosis of our tendency to seg-ment justice. This is a way of distancing ourselves from injustice—if we even notice it at all.

We all too often neglect what is close to home. Sometimes it is because we are looking at something more obvious far away. We sometimes fail to notice an at-risk child in our own community because it is easier to notice the child living in poverty overseas.

It isn't that we should pit local justice against international jus-tice, but in reality there is a great potential for hypocrisy when we focus exclusively on global issues.

I periodically meet with Garland Bruno, a Native American in his sixties who has taught me as much about faith as anyone else over the past few years. I asked him once, "What do you think about the sentence, 'You can't rob Crazy Horse to pay Bishop Tutu and call it social justice'?"

"Ken, have you seen the movie *The Help*?" Garland asked me. When I said I hadn't yet, he explained one of its key points.

The movie is set in the Deep South during the civil rights era, and a group of well-to-do, white, Southern women host a charity fund-raiser. Their goal is to collect money to send to the poor in Africa. At the same time, though, the leader of the women's group is advocating for all her friends to build outdoor bathrooms for their African-American "help" to use because they do not consider them clean enough to use the white women's indoor bathrooms. Then, at the fund-raiser, the lead woman turns to the African-American servants and, speaking of the money being sent to Africa, essentially says in a condescending tone, "You all, more than anyone else, should appreciate this."

After Garland finished talking about the movie and drawing out the cutting irony of the women engaging in charity overseas while being blind to the injustices all around—that they were personally creating, even—he slowed down. He usually speaks in a soft, gentle, and measured manner, but what he said next was even more subtle than usual.

"Ken, what I think your young friend is trying to tell you . . .," he paused to touch his nose with the tip of his finger, "is that sometimes we miss what is right beneath our noses."

He's right. It is easy to have blinders on and not see many of the things right in front of us. Many of the injustices in our immediate surroundings can easily go unnoticed or be invisible.

This isn't a new idea. Saint Augustine wrote, "Charity is no substitute for justice withheld."[7] Nelson Mandela echoed the same thought on the limitations of charity when he said, "Overcoming poverty is not a task of charity, it is an act of justice."[8]

When we understand the depth of justice, it has to go beyond compassion or charity delivered to distant places. Rather, it has to restructure the way we see the world, *including* that which is close to home and, therefore, sometimes harder to see.

We must remove our blinders and look for what has been invisible to us. Justice should be our concern everywhere—not just somewhere. For example, we can become fixated on sex trafficking internationally, yet miss the issues of trafficking and sexual exploitation in our own backyard.

Portland, Oregon's largest city, is known as one of the country's most progressive, socially aware communities, and many consider it one of the "greenest" cities in the world. At the same time, however, Portland contains more strip clubs, per capita, than any other city in the nation—a fact that contributes to trafficking and gender violence. As the *Washington Times* details, "The city [Portland] has more strip clubs per capita than glittery Las Vegas, and a tolerant attitude toward sex, both legal and illegal," and many legal clubs are "fronts for underage exploitation. [An organization called] Shared Hope estimates that the average age of minors used as prostitutes in the U.S. is 13."[9]

Oregon also has an ignominious history with race that I didn't learn until recently. Oregon used to be what was called an "exclusionary state," as it wrote into its constitution laws to exclude the settlement of free blacks. In fact, Oregonians didn't vote in favor of the Fifteenth Amendment—granting African Americans the right to vote—until 1959, almost ninety years after it was added to the United States Constitution.[10]

Stories that are new to me are the well-worn and often painful narratives others have lived for generations. My friend Garland, for instance, remembers being a kid and seeing signs in the windows in town that read, "No dogs or Indians allowed." But the particular story *you* are in can make it hard to see the narratives of place, history, gender, or race that others are living.

Anne Morrow Lindbergh, reflecting more than fifty years ago on the difficulties posed by living in an interconnected world, wrote, "Because we cannot deal with the many as individuals, we sometimes try to simplify the many into an abstraction called the mass. Because we cannot deal with the complexity of the present, we often over-ride it and live in a simplified dream of the future. Because we cannot solve our own problems right here at home, we talk about problems out there in the world."[11]

A person we have objectified and placed "into an abstraction called the mass" cannot be a person we are loving and treating justly. Neither can one who is invisible.

So again, charity, while valuable and active, is something we can choose on our own terms, and therefore it is incomplete. Justice, on the other hand, is something we often *wouldn't* choose, and it does not usually occur on our terms. Justice makes strong demands, or as Garland once put it, "Justice deserves a big drum." Therefore, however beneficial charity is, it is lacking if we stop short of justice in our immediate relationships and context.

NOT A NEW COMMAND

Love, as Scripture defines it, is measured by sacrifice. It serves and voluntarily suffers for the one(s) loved. Love is about doing and giving away. It is others-focused. And love is a sacrament, a *sacrifice* that can make internal realities present.

Charity is a necessary part of sacrificial love. It is a type of action that is initiated under the impulse of sacrifice and seeks to give, rather than receive. Charity alone, however, is not enough, because charity exists only at the times we give, and it hits only where we aim.

Justice, however, makes demands at all times and in all places—not just where our attention is focused. It requires us to see beyond our own walls and make changes in our lives and perceptions of the world that go beyond moments of charitable giving. Charity can be intermittent, while justice seeks continuity. Justice can inform and challenge both what we see and what we don't see in the world.

Eleanor Roosevelt, the great champion of human rights and chair for the drafting of the Universal Declaration of Human Rights in 1948, asked a provocative question: "Where, after all, do universal human rights begin?"

The answer she gave is profound: "In small places, close to home—so close and so small that they cannot be seen on any maps of the world . . . Such are the places where every man, woman and child seeks equal justice, equal opportunity, equal dignity without discrimination. Unless these rights have meaning there, they have little meaning anywhere."[12]

Thus, justice can be both a compass and a conscience to charity. It can broaden the scope of our efforts and invite us to pursue the highest aims of justice. As Daniel Fan put it, "Justice assumes the equality of humanity, theologically recognizes the image of God in all, and acts in a way that partners with those less fortunate, serving until, status-wise, you cannot tell the difference between yourself and those you partner with."[13]

> I am not writing you a new command but one we have had from
> the beginning. I ask that we love one another. And this is love:
> that we walk in obedience to his commands. As you have heard
> from the beginning, his command is that you walk in love.
>
> 2 JOHN 1:5–6

INTERLUDE
WOMEN—

This picture, taken on my cell phone from inside the United Nations Building in New York, is a stark and convicting illustration of the reality and significance of gender inequality across the globe.

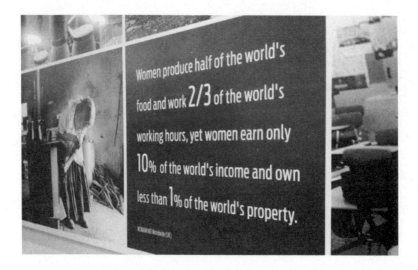

Women produce half of the world's food and work 2/3 of the world's working hours, yet women earn only 10% of the world's income and own less than 1% of the world's property.

SIX

STAINED GLASS

When Religion Gets in the Way of Justice

Of all bad men, religious bad men are the worst.[1]

C. S. LEWIS

Away with the noise of your songs!
    I will not listen to the music of your harps.
But let justice roll on like a river,
    righteousness like a never-failing stream!

AMOS 5:23–24

A 2007 study designed to identify the most common perceptions of Christianity among young adults found that 91 percent see Christians as antihomosexual, 87 percent view Christians as judgmental, and 85 percent view Christians as being hypocritical.[2]

Why do many identify Christians by what we're against, rather than by our love and care for others? In thinking about that question, consider this: In the years since the survey, AIDS has continued to ravage the world, killing men, women, and children from every race and creed. Human slavery, which even educated Christians can assume largely disappeared in the nineteenth century, has rocketed to an all-time high, with tens of millions enslaved. And each year, millions of children still die of preventable diseases like malaria. Have we missed God's direct call to us to give our lives away to the world He loves?

One way I like to draw the line is to look at how God's love for the world extends all the way to you and me being sent into it. John 3:16, a familiar verse, says, "For God so loved the world that he gave his one and only Son . . ." First John 4:9 echoes the same truth: "This is how God showed his love among us: He sent his one and only Son into the world . . ."

But then, in John 20:21, we see Jesus connecting the line to the disciples: "As the Father has sent *me*, [so] I am sending *you*" (emphasis added).

This is a lot like the transitive property from math class: if A = B = C, then A = C:

God so loved the world (A) He sent Jesus (B)

As the Father sent me (B) you are being sent into the world (C)

So in essence, we can say, "For God so loved the world that . . . you and I are being sent into the world." Through Jesus, God is sending you and me into His world to show His love and to bear witness to the restoration of justice He has provided through salvation in Christ and the advent of His kingdom.

In 1 John 3:17, John asked a profound question: "If someone has enough money to live well and sees a brother or sister in need but shows no compassion—how can God's love be in that person?"

(NLT). God's love in us should compel us to be tangibly involved in the needs of the world.

So, are we?

SINS OF THE RIGHTEOUS

Eugene Peterson, in *Tell It Slant*, wrote about sins that are peculiar to those who follow Christ—sins of the righteous. "There are some sins simply not accessible to the non-Christian, the person outside the faith," he explained. "Only men and women who become Christians are capable of and have the opportunity for some sins."[3]

Because these sins are often overlooked, Peterson coined a new word to draw attention to them: *eusebeigenic*. The second half of the word stems from the medical term *iatrogenic*, which describes a medical issue that arises because of the way a patient was treated. It means "originating from the physician" (the Greek *iatros* means "healer" or "physician," and *genos* means "origin"). *Eusebeia*, also Greek, means "godly, reverent, devout." Thus, *eusebeigenic* means an illness or sin picked up in a place of righteousness.

Peterson developed the idea, writing:

Eusebeigenic sin is difficult to detect because the sin is always embedded in words and acts that have every appearance of being righteous, godly, devout. . . . Just as iatrogenic illness is most frequently picked up in a place of healing, a hospital or clinic or physician's office, eusebeigenic sin is most often picked up in a place associated with righteousness, a church or Bible study or prayer meeting.[4]

C. S. Lewis alluded to this same idea in *The Problem of Pain*, writing, "Prostitutes are in no danger of finding their present life so satisfactory that they cannot turn to God: the proud, the avaricious, the self-righteous, are in that danger."[5]

So what's the big deal? What do sins of self-righteousness have to do with God's call to true life?

The connection becomes clear when we remember that *self-righteousness* is simply another word for *legalism*. Legalism is an inward-focused, static sense of good or rightness, and it's often defined by a *lack* of vice or sin, rather than the *active presence of good*. A legalist wouldn't purposely infect a child with malaria, but what is the legalist actively doing to ensure that child never contracts the disease?

This isn't a new problem—look at Matthew's description of the Pharisees. In Jesus' day, the Pharisees were the individuals who prided themselves on near-perfect morality. And being moral is good—but not sufficient. So it must have been quite an ironic twist, then, to hear Jesus blast external piety as evidence of the Pharisees' lack of justice.

> "Woe to you, teachers of the law and Pharisees, you hypocrites! You give a tenth of your spices—mint, dill and cumin. But you have neglected the more important matters of the law—justice, mercy and faithfulness. You should have practiced the latter, without neglecting the former. . . . You clean the outside of the cup and dish, but inside they are full of greed and self-indulgence." (Matthew 23:23, 25)

Can something so seemingly good as religion actually distract us from pursuing real faith? We tend to think the Pharisees were the legalistic bad guys, while assuming we must be the good guys, but I'm haunted by the question, do I look more like the Pharisees, or Jesus?

Bethge's description of the potential pitfall of religion is dead-on: "The sin of respectable people reveals itself in flight from responsibility."[6] I'm convinced we're only one step away from allowing comfort to replace faith, conformity to replace zeal, and consumerism to replace sacrifice.

A FRESH LOOK AT BATHSHEBA

Christians can suffer from the misconception that personal piety and individual morality simply and exclusively constitute a right relationship with God. However, the biblical picture is much different. In fact, there are more than thirty examples of "righteousness" and "justice" being used interchangeably *in the same verse*, such as:

> I walk in the way of righteousness,
> in the paths of justice. (Proverbs 8:20 ESV)

> The LORD works righteousness
> and justice for all who are oppressed. (Psalm 103:6 ESV)

So when we begin to see how *religion* can get in the way of real biblical *righteousness*—which always includes the external action of justice—it doesn't merely change the way we see the Pharisees. It can change the way we see heroes of the faith, like King David.

We often approach the story of David and Bathsheba with an isolated focus on the sin of adultery: David's problem was that he didn't take a cold shower in time, right? We even *think* we know the moral of David's story. And "moral" is the key word, because the moment David lusted after Bathsheba, he started a *moral* avalanche that eventually killed a faithful husband named Uriah, ruined David's health, and ended the life of David's young son.

In 2 Samuel 12, Nathan described a rich man who used his power and position to take advantage of a weaker, dependent neighbor.

> The LORD sent Nathan to David. When he came to him, he said, "There were two men in a certain town, one rich and the other poor. The rich man had a very large number of sheep and cattle, but the poor man had nothing except one little ewe lamb he had bought. . . . Now a traveler came to the rich man, but the rich man refrained from taking one of his own sheep or cattle to prepare a meal for the traveler who had come to him. Instead, he took the ewe lamb that belonged to the poor man and prepared it for the one who had come to him." (vv. 1–4)

Upon hearing the story, David was infuriated. "As surely as the LORD lives," he said, "the man who did this must die! He must pay for that lamb four times over, because he did such a thing and had no pity" (vv. 5–6).

Notice that David was furious because the man in Nathan's story ripped the fabric of *shalom*—he violated what *ought to be* by exercising his own power to achieve his own pleasure, no matter how it harmed his neighbor. In other words, David (and Nathan) understood that his sin was not only about failing to match a code of private morality—it was also an unjust abuse of power, the strong preying on the weak. The story and rebuke of David, although certainly including moral dimensions, is focused on justice.

UNTANGLING HYPOCRISY

It's clear from reading the New Testament that the Pharisees believed in the authority of Scripture. They loved and revered the law, and yet they were woefully wrong on many levels. So should we *stop* believing in the authority of Scripture because the Pharisees believed in it? No. In fact, most things the Pharisees believed are good and true! We need to dig deeper than that and determine *why* Jesus condemned the Pharisees and *why* Nathan condemned David so strongly.

Jesus labeled the Pharisees with a laundry list of unsavory names—hypocrites, poisonous snakes, prettied-up tombs—for one reason: they were preoccupied with the purity of their religious posture rather than the purity of their love for others. Jesus had something far better in mind than this kind of self-righteousness, so He condemned the Pharisees for their actions—or, rather, their *lack* of action: "Then Jesus said to the crowds and to his disciples: 'The teachers of the law and the Pharisees sit in Moses' seat. So you must be careful to do everything they tell you. But do not do what they do, for they do not practice what they preach'" (Matthew 23:1–3).

It's deceptively easy to *believe* a lot of good things about God but fail to live them out. Therefore, it's been said that what we *do* is actually what we *believe*. It's easier than we think to have the spiritual exteriors without the spiritual heart. We must be careful not to mistake the packaging for authentic living, or to confuse the décor of religion with genuinely loving our neighbor.

Think of James 4:17, where we are reminded of this truth: "Anyone, then, who knows the good he ought to do and doesn't do it, sins." Or Proverbs 3:27: "Do not withhold good from those to whom it is due, when it is in your power to do it" (ESV). Sometimes trying *not* to do the wrong thing is the surest way to do the wrong thing.

Eusebeigenic sin is subtle. We're often one step away from becoming the Pharisee. And the minute we care more about avoiding the bad than doing the good is the moment we're in deep trouble. Our spiritual pride blinds us to our own imperfections, causing us to become "lukewarm" from a biblical standpoint—good only to be spit out (Revelation 3:16).

True morality—genuine righteousness and justice and love—can never lead to external legalism because we cannot be fully righteous and just and loving. For that we need God's grace, every moment of every day, and grace is the stake through the heart of legalism.

OVERPLAYING MORALITY

Loveless morality has so dominated our ideas about what it means to be a Christian that it has created negative perceptions among the next generation of American adults, as we saw in the survey at the beginning of this chapter.

American Christianity is often known by what it is against. Unfortunately, when personal morality is what we focus on, then not swearing or not having sex outside of marriage or not getting drunk can become the totality of our spirituality. We define the heart of God by what ought *not* be done—while leaving undone many things that ought to *be* done.

True morality requires more than the absence of vice and sin: it requires the presence of good.

David's reaction to Nathan's parable shows us that he, as the judge of the nation, abhorred the *injustice* of the crime Nathan described. We can trace this theme of God's judgment on Sodom and Gomorrah. We tend to think of Sodom's sin purely in terms of immorality or wickedness. However, when God talked about the sin of Sodom through the prophet Ezekiel, it was injustice that was the focus: "Behold, this was the guilt of your sister Sodom: she and her daughters had pride, excess of food, and prosperous ease, but *did not aid the poor and needy*" (Ezekiel 16:49 ESV; emphasis added).

Sodom was immoral, yes. So is Bend, Oregon, where I live. So is the place where you live. But in addition to being immoral, Sodom was guilty of the sin of injustice. In her excess of food and prosperous ease, her citizens failed to aid—or even notice—the poor and needy.

Consider one final example of this theme in the book of Isaiah: "I reared children and brought them up," God said, "but they have rebelled against me. The ox knows its master, the donkey its owner's manger, but Israel does not know, my people do not understand. . . . They have forsaken the LORD; they have spurned the Holy One of Israel and turned their backs on him" (1:2–4).

How had Israel rebelled and turned their backs on God? Notice the language that describes their sin, as God clearly drew a line from Israel's idolatry to their perpetration of injustice: "Your hands are full of blood; wash and make yourselves clean. Take your evil deeds out of my sight! Stop doing wrong, learn to do right! Seek justice, encourage the oppressed. Defend the cause of the fatherless, plead the case of the widow" (vv. 15–17).

God judged the nation of Israel and sent them into exile in part because of their apathy toward the just life that God had designed for them. As Israel stopped following God, they stopped upholding justice. When Israel stopped upholding justice, they stopped following God. In this picture we see true morality and justice as related, rather than as separate realities whereby we can be moral or righteous without being just. Righteousness and justice are always woven together as threads in the same cloth when we strive to follow God.

LOST IN TRANSLATION

Over the last several years, as I've spoken across the country about biblical righteousness and justice, the most common response I hear—actually, the *overwhelming* response—demonstrates the false distinction we tend to make: "But in the Bible, *righteousness* means the same thing as *morality*, right? And justice is something different, isn't it?"

Part of the reason we commonly miss the thread of justice woven throughout the Bible, and equate true righteousness merely with private morality, has to do with how we've come to understand certain biblical terms. In Hebrew, the concept of justice is expressed by several words. The primary ones are the two relatively synonymous words *tsedek* and *mishpat*. The idea of living uprightly could not be limited to personal ethical conduct or exclusively limited to community reform. Rather, it was the outworking of a deep knowledge of God, which drives one to live uprightly and walk justly.

In English, we translate the Hebrew words *tsedek* and *mishpat* as either "righteousness" *or* as "justice," depending on the context. This is because the Hebrew sense of the words *tsedek* and *mishpat* linked the personal and communal components of "just" or "righteous" living. An example of these terms appearing together is

Psalm 36:6: "Your righteousness [*tsedaqah*] is like the mountains of God; your judgments [*mishpat*] are like the great deep" (ESV).[7]

Dr. Gerry Breshears, a theology professor for more than thirty years at Western Seminary in Portland, Oregon, explains what the Hebrew word *tsedek* means: a life in which all relationships—human to human, human to God, and human to creation—are well-ordered and harmonious. In a life full of shalom, everything is as it ought to be. The golden rule is being lived out by people in their homes, their communities, and the wider world.

Tsedek is both a personal virtue and a communal imperative. When we disconnect the two halves of the definition—caring only about personal, private morality—we do violence to God's intention for just life. As the *New International Dictionary of the Old Testament* explains: "Righteousness is not a matter of actions conforming to a given set of absolute legal standards as the Pharisees taught, but of behavior which is in keeping with the two-way relationship between God and [humanity]."[8]

In the Hebrew text, *being* righteous was inextricably linked with *doing* righteousness. Jesus made this same connection between the human heart and our actions in Matthew 12:33: "A tree is identified by its fruit. If a tree is good, its fruit will be good. If a tree is bad, its fruit will be bad" (NLT). All of this leads to a fascinating question: If *being* righteous means *doing* justice, why are we so afraid to act?

Someone may object that if our righteousness is based on our *actions*, it negates the righteousness we have through faith in Christ and His grace.

Avoiding a human-centered religion in which everything depends on our efforts is a good goal. I agree—we *can't* do it on our own! That's why a true understanding of biblical justice drives us straight into the arms of mercy and grace. But by setting the doing of justice in opposition to being righteous, we create a false dichotomy: if doing good negates God's work through the cross, then Jesus wouldn't have worked so hard again and again to command us to love one another or to look after the poor. The idea that we should resist talking about, doing, or striving after justice because it negates the work of grace is absurd. It would be like Jesus applauding legalism because it magnified His grace!

Most Christians know that not only does righteousness matter, it's necessary and obligatory too. But righteousness defined simply as personal purity isn't enough. It is the further understanding that full biblical righteousness requires an active engagement in justice that throws the circuit breaker and releases the Spirit's power in our lives and the world.

Let's dive a little deeper to prove the point that righteousness and doing justice—economic and material justice—are connected in a much greater degree biblically than perhaps we've imagined.

JUSTICE AND RIGHTEOUSNESS

The New Testament word for righteousness *and* justice is *dikaios* (or *dikaiosunae*). The word was used in the Roman world during the time Paul was writing his letters to the New Testament churches. Just after Paul wrote Romans, around 54–58 CE, there were coins circulating that are easy to date because of the image of Nero stamped on one side.

Nero was the emperor who first began stamping deities and other symbols on the backs of his coins,[9] and one of his most common designs was Lady Justice, holding scales and a cornucopia in her arms, with the phrase *dikaiosunae* around her head.[10] She was a female personification of fair dealing, and her Latin counterpart,

Lady Aequitas, was "the personified idea of equity, especially in commercial transactions."[11]

For Roman emperors like Nero, currency was a primary type of propaganda. Money touched the hands of nearly everyone in the empire, so imperial coins were effective advertising. Such coins as this one were minted in Alexandria and used to obtain a Roman citizen's grain ration. In other words, no coin meant no dinner.

For Nero, obsessed with popularity, these particular coins with *dikaiosunae* stamped on them reinforced his image as a benevolent and just ruler, especially in the eyes of the lower classes[12] who, he hoped, appreciated his impartiality and economic fairness.

Picture of Roman Tetradrachm circa AD 54–68

Returning to Paul, who often used the word we see translated as "righteousness"—*dikaiosunae*—in his letters, it seems clear he used *dikaiosunae* in a similar way. Just as Emperor Nero didn't stamp his tribute coins with a word exclusively meaning "private morality," neither did Paul use *dikaiosunae* to mean exclusively that. The word *dikaiosunae* certainly speaks to righteousness, but less in the personal, internal way where it is a synonym for purity. Instead, the word spoke about human equality and justice. About our basic need to *eat*.

When Paul talked about *dikaios* (the same Greek word often translated "righteousness" in the our New Testaments), he wasn't trying to get his readers to make a checklist of things to avoid. Instead, his intent was to help them recall that the Bread of Life broke His body for them—to give them strength and courage to give their lives away to their neighbors and even strangers, just as He had. So, unlike our modern American identification of "righteous" with morality or personal purity, the sense of the word *dikaiosune* in Paul's time had a *necessary* added meaning of justice and social fairness.

In fact, the actual definition of *righteousness* in the English incorporates justice. "The state of being just," is what you'll see in many dictionaries. Therefore, contrary to what we often think, righteousness in English, as in Hebrew and Greek, incorporates a right relationship with God *and* with others—what we call justice. When we drive a wedge between righteousness and justice, we separate two things Scripture sees as continuous, overlapping, and even synonymous. We demote justice to a peripheral type of "spiritual extra credit," rather than elevating it to something necessary for living a righteous life as a Christian. Truly, biblical justice and righteousness are two sides of the same coin—as is literally shown on the Roman coin on the previous page.

DEEPER RIGHTEOUSNESS

What if living "morally" and being "righteous" means something more than avoiding bad words, saying grace before dinner, and wearing a clean shirt to church? What if it means being just?

In light of Matthew 5:10—"Blessed are those who are persecuted for righteousness' sake, for theirs is the kingdom of heaven" (NKJV)— ask yourself when the last time was that you saw someone being *truly* persecuted *merely* for being a nice moral person. Nicholas Wolterstorff addressed this at Antioch recently, saying,

> Take for example the beatitude in Matthew: blessed are those who are persecuted for the sake of *dikaiosune*. All the translations that you can buy say "persecuted for the sake of righteousness." And my argument there is, put your head to it: persecuted for the sake of "being upright." Do you know of any upright people who are persecuted? I don't. . . . My sense of upright people is that they're either ignored or admired. Oh, I mean they may be a little bit annoying, . . . but you don't persecute them.[13]

Peruvian theologian Gustavo Gutiérrez asserted the same idea: "To opt for the oppressed is to opt against the oppressor. In our times and on our continent to be in solidarity with the 'poor,' understood in this way, means to run personal risks—even to put one's life in danger."[14]

It's interesting to think about this deeper understanding of what it means to be righteous. If we see righteousness and justice more as synonyms and less as opposites, it flips our whole mental picture of who Jesus was encouraging when He said, "Blessed are those who are persecuted for righteousness' [*dikaiosune*] sake, for theirs is the kingdom of heaven."

It is often those who are actively engaged in working for the restoration of shalom—in opposition to powerful economic and political systems—who face the most serious persecution. When we push against entrenched structures of evil and exploitation, the response our righteous deeds provoke is often severe. The person rescuing girls from brothels in Asia who gets death threats from organized crime needs to hear Jesus' affirmation and encouragement more than someone teased for being a Christian.

As with many issues, this is a matter of degrees. We don't want to create a false dichotomy. At the same time, however, we need to examine what Jesus was really saying in the Beatitudes, and to whom His message was primarily, though not exclusively, directed.

The structures of evil are often entrenched. It doesn't take long studying the history of the British abolitionists, or Corrie ten Boom,[15] or the violence against just newspaper editors in the Jim Crow South, to learn that standing for the weak and vulnerable leads quickly to very real persecution—push against injustice and it *will* push back. So how can we choose to stand up when we know we're going to get knocked down—or even killed? That's the whole point of Jesus' promise of blessing. Blessed (literally, having a full or deep happiness) are those who are persecuted for doing right, for they will inherit (literally, be blessed with) the kingdom of God. *You may sacrifice your comforts, and you may lose the life you thought you wanted by standing up for what is right*, says Jesus, *but you'll get the fullness of life God intends for you in return.*

It was for the sake of righteous justice that Jesus both foretold persecution and promised blessing. He never separated *being* righteous from *doing* justice, and neither should we.

CATEGORIES

The refrain of this book is, *Give your life away and you'll get true life back—it's time to live and die for bigger things.* Do you believe that? Really believe that?

I do, but I confess I don't live it out perfectly. It's hard to figure out finances when my daughters need braces at the same time immigrant families down the street have no health care. It takes, in a real and practical sense, *faith*.

Just think about what is meant by the phrase "the righteous shall live by faith." If you're pouring out your life for the sake of justice, for the sake of the helpless and weak, you *have* to live by faith. If you're leveraging your abilities and resources on behalf of others, instead of seeking your own gain and satisfaction, you *must* rely on God's guidance and provision. If you're not looking out for yourself, who is?

God is.

To empty ourselves creates vulnerability. If we can't create our own security, we have to *hope* for it, wait and pray for it. Giving our lives away necessitates faith because we have nothing left but our trust in God.

It's funny: here I am, talking about the connection between justice and righteousness, and trying to convince you of the theological necessity of justice to both know God and live rightly, but the translators of the King James Bible were way ahead of me. Most modern translations render Habakkuk 2:4, which is quoted in Romans 1, Galatians 3, and Hebrews 10, as saying that the *righteous* will live by faith or faithfulness. The King James and New King James versions, however, say this: "the *just* shall live by his faith" (emphasis added).

Modern translators often use the word *righteousness* in preference to *justice* because most Americans think of criminal justice or "getting justice" when they hear the word *justice*. Additionally, translators of the New Testament like to keep the word *justice* reserved for salvation passages, such as those found in the book of Romans, where *just*ification, being *just*ified, and being made *just* come into play. We like our categories clean and organized, but the unwanted effect often seems to be that we interpret righteousness as distinctly different from justice, when in reality the two are synonymous. This quickly leads to the assumption that righteousness is necessary, but justice is merely "good." We have to be righteous, but we don't *have* to be just.

This is exactly what I've been arguing against, and I hope the radical simplicity of the shared meaning of righteousness and justice comes across in these pages as plainly as it does in Scripture.

Justice. Righteousness. God calls us to walk as He walks, to go where He goes, to care as He cares, and to walk *morally* by *doing* justice. True morality requires justice. God's righteousness is predicated on His active pursuit of justice in His world, and He requires those who would seek and know Him to do the same.

The merely moral live by checklists and fear; the righteous—the just—live by faith.

POSSIBILITIES

Avoiding sin is morally good—but a lack of concern for justice indicates a moral deficiency.

The slide from a working faith to a hypocritical faith is subtle. And almost before we notice, the "good" can actually become the bad. The person passionate about religion can become the Pharisee, and the one concerned with following Jesus can become the sort of person who drove Jesus crazy.

All too often I'm hit with the irony that some Christians can focus on pursuing personal morality in a way that hinders their pursuit of justice—when did the two become antithetical?

How would it change your life—how would it *literally* change the choices you make each day—if you understood the synonymous nature of biblical righteousness and biblical justice? Would it make you feel as if you were being nudged out of your comfort zone—like a bird pushed from the nest by its mother?

Maybe that's part of what the prophet Isaiah meant when he

wrote that "they who wait for the LORD shall renew their strength; they shall mount up with wings like eagles" (Isaiah 40:31 ESV). We tend to read that as a comforting cliché, an inspiring thought to place in a picture frame or quote to a friend without really considering its meaning. But Isaiah was really saying something much more difficult—and ultimately better. He was drawing an analogy to the natural world. Have you ever seen a fledgling eagle trying to fly? It's not just ugly; it's ungainly as well. Flight doesn't come easy. And in Isaiah's word picture, flight comes only after we wait.

The just will live by faith, and waiting on God is what faith really means. That's *real* trust, not hypothetical trust or a doctrinal confession. When we give our lives away, we don't know what will happen next. That's precisely when we start to live by faith. Pushed from our nest—from comfort, from safety, from the empty dreams our culture tries to sell us—we have no choice but to rely on the God who promises to renew our strength.

God is inviting us toward a future filled with more joy than we can ask or imagine when we give our lives away.

> "But when you give to the needy, do not let your left hand
> know what your right hand is doing, so that your giving
> may be in secret. Then your Father, who sees what is done in
> secret, will reward you."
>
> MATTHEW 6:3–4

WHO BROKE AFRICA?

By national spoken word and rap artist Micah Bournes

Let me ask you something:

Who broke Africa?

And how do we fix her?

Political unrest,

    rebel militias,

        stomachs swollen with emptiness.

Water polluted with disease,

HIV, gender violence,

    the whole world is crying

    and we all wanna know,

Who broke Africa?

And why is it that this one particular continent

    is taking so long to update, urbanize,

    enforce human rights

    and figure out the right way to be human?

If only she could be like *us*,

you know—

Free.

Educated.

Healthy.

Prosperous.

    Consumeristic.

        Pornographic.

Gluttonous and never gratified yet we look with eyes of pity
upon her for being, "less fortunate."
But what if she's only less rich?
Might African youth have greater joy with a beat-up soccer
ball than we do with flat screens, laptops, new shoes, and
a hundred shirts we never wear hanging in a closet full of
things we thought would make us happy? But we remain
insecure, alone, depressed.
Now, look, I'm not saying we're no better off than Africa,
but maybe it's presumptuous to assume we are.
Life is hard in Africa, a struggle, but could the conflict be a
sign of hope, proving that she is full of those who refuse to
let injustice reign uncontested?
Africa is no damsel in distress, and we are not her savior.
Africa is a Mother in labor,
> ripe with pain and life,
> by the grace of God may we stand by her side as a mid-
> wife and friend,
> offering aid and encouragement but knowing
> that we must empower her to push by her own strength!
Walk by her own faith!
And as we work with our sister in humble love, maybe
> we will discover how to fix what is broken
> in *us*,
> for brokenness belongs to us all,
> but hope, only to those who come together before God.*

---

* A performance of this piece can be viewed at http://www.youtube.com/
watch?v=pP2RNfb3kDw.

SEVEN

REMEMBER WHAT YOU SAW

How Empathy Carries Justice

Africa! Africa! Your sufferings have been the theme that has arrested and engaged my heart—Your suffering no tongue can express, no language impart.[1]

WILLIAM WILBERFORCE

Can I see another's woe, and not be in sorrow too?
Can I see another's grief, and not seek for kind relief?[2]

WILLIAM BLAKE

I n the spring of 1963, civil rights protestors in Birmingham, Alabama, sought to end Jim Crow laws by participating in mass sit-ins and marches. The government's response included tear gas, arresting children still in high school, and—captured in iconic imagery that is now part of our nation's psyche—deploying dogs and water cannons against peaceful demonstrators.

Opinion among formerly disinterested members of the public,

in the South and across the nation, began to shift as newspapers and televisions showed images of men, women, and even children being attacked unjustly.

A similar change in public sentiment stemmed from the photograph of nine-year-old Kim Phuc. Her face is agonized as she runs toward a photojournalist naked and with napalm burns from an attack in South Vietnam. The picture appeared the next day on the front page of the *New York Times* and became an iconic image of antiwar sentiment against the Vietnam War.

Neutrality or ambivalence is harder to sustain in the face of such evocative images of suffering. When our empathy is engaged, our empathy can move us toward justice.

EMPATHY IN ACTION

Empathy is a part of the *Imago Dei* in us, the Image of God in which we were created and which all humans possess. Experiencing empathy is a characteristic of the God who created us and allows us to be social, relational, and caring human beings. The gift of empathy is the capacity that allows us to be in relationships that include the physical but also move into the spaces of emotion and spirit. The ability to empathize is what makes it possible for us to truly love one another. If God had not designed us to understand the felt reality of others, it would be impossible to live justly on behalf of others. Without entering into another's story, we are left to help from the outside, relying on our best intentions, which is often a recipe for doing more harm than good.[3]

In Romans, Paul talked about God's Spirit living within us, and how the Spirit understands, feels, and knows our struggles and pain even better than we do. That's a concise definition of *empathy*: to enter into and share another's feelings.

The word *empathy* has roots in the Greek word *empatheia* (passion, state of emotion), which comes from *en* (in) and *pathos* (feeling). Whenever we enter into another's feelings, something important happens: we value that person more. The converse is true: if we cannot participate in the unique feelings and life experiences of another person, we tend to devalue that individual, viewing him or her dispassionately or as an object.

When we slow down, engage, and are able to enter into the pain and suffering of other people, justice can follow. That often occurs when our empathy is kindled.

Certain images are so iconic, so emotive, that they kindle deep empathy and move us outside ourselves. Eighteenth-century abolitionists made effective use of empathy. A small, emblematic image of a kneeling and shackled slave was created in 1787, ringed by the now-famous question, "Am I not a man and a brother?" This powerful combination of image and text was stamped into pottery, jewelry, and medallions. The logo was designed to help people make the connection between goods they consumed, such as sugar, and the unjust system that produced those goods. As this logo and other empathetic propaganda from the abolitionist movement became more widespread, collectively they began to move public sentiment in favor of the abolitionists' cause.

The power of empathy was also activated by showing pictures of the inside of slave ships such as the *Brookes*, or letting people touch the chains and shackles with which slaves were bound. The effect of these media campaigns was to galvanize neutral or apathetic people into support of the antislavery movement. Empathy was what carried such people out of the sphere of their own concerns and into an engaged concern for their fellow humans.

Anti-Slavery Society Emblem and the Slave Ship *Brookes*

Best-selling historian Adam Hochschild wrote, "[The abolitionists] believed that because human beings had a capacity to care about the suffering of others, exposing the truth would move people to action." Indeed, Hochschild credited "the vivid, unforgettable description of acts of great injustice done to their fellow human beings" as the key element in the success of the antislavery movement.[4]

Empathy enables us to enter into and share another person's grief and sorrows, and ultimately stand with the sufferer in his or her need—just as God shares our grief and sorrows. Isaiah 53:4 prophesied of Jesus, "Surely he took up our pain and bore our suffering."

REMEMBER WHAT YOU SAW

HOW EMPATHY DIES

On March 22, 1933, the first German concentration camp was opened at Dachau, less than two months after Hitler came to power.[5] Initially the camp held political prisoners; it would be years before the infamous "death trains" began arriving, filled with Jews. The story of how that happened is a useful illustration of how deceit can twist the power of empathy for evil ends.[6]

The German government, over the course of more than ten years, systematically objectified and abused German Jews. The timeline of this process included:

1933 – The first boycott of Jewish shops and businesses

1934 – Removal of the Jews' ability to have health insurance

1935 – Nuremberg Laws introduced: removed citizenship from Jews and made it illegal for Jews to marry or have sexual relationships with non-Jews

1938 – *Kristallnacht*, or Night of the Broken Glass, one of the first instances of mass violence against Jews, in which thousands of Jews were arrested and sent to camps, synagogues were burned, and Jewish businesses were vandalized

1939 – Yellow Star introduced in Poland to identify Jews easily

1939 – First Jewish ghetto opened in Poland

1942 – Mass gassing begun at Auschwitz-Birkenau

Even in this abbreviated timeline, we can see the process of alienating and removing empathy from non-Jewish Germans to allow for persecution and violence.

111

Once empathy became apathy, non-Jews were less likely to either do justice or protest injustice. When the apathy lasted long enough, it became objectification, meaning that many non-Jews viewed Jews not as neighbors, friends, and colleagues, but as a single race with no differentiation or individual humanity. That enabled non-Jews to countenance abuse and injustice against Jews—if Jews were less than human, normal human ethics didn't apply to them. Finally, scapegoating allowed non-Jews to blame any and all problems on a subhuman, objectified underclass, thus justifying any treatment of them . . . or even making abusive treatment of the Jews a "moral duty" of the non-Jewish state. We can trace an unjust regression in all genocides.

We wonder how people could act against the clear dictates of conscience. Alexander Solzhenitsyn, who suffered under the totalitarian regime of the postwar Soviet Union, wrote:

> Justice is conscience, not a personal conscience but the conscience of the whole of humanity. Those who clearly recognize the voice of their own conscience usually recognize also the voice of justice. The obverse was equally true, that those sufficiently corrupted that they have ceased following the dictates of conscience are those most susceptible to the perpetration of acts of injustice.[7]

Chaim Kaplan was a Jew living in the Warsaw ghetto. His diary, written between 1939 and 1942, is on display at the United States Holocaust Memorial Museum. In it, he detailed how Joseph Goebbels, in charge of much of the Nazi propaganda, used what I think of as reverse empathy. During the war, he wanted to make it easier for non-Jews to be apathetic to, or even hate, the Jews, so he sent his team to film staged vignettes about how much better the Jews were living. He shot scenes of lovely houses filled with happy, laughing Jewish families, and scenes of Jewish couples enjoying intimate dinners at restaurants. His hope was that if the non-Jewish populace heard of bad things happening to Jews, they would ignore it—after all, hadn't the Jews been living so much better than everyone else?

Even this quick glance shows what the Nazis knew all too well: injustice flourishes in soil where empathy has been uprooted.

FEELING HISTORY

Back in 2002, I watched the HBO miniseries *Band of Brothers* produced by Tom Hanks, which chronicled the 101st Airborne Division on their journey from basic training to the European theater of operations, and eventually to Hitler's *Kehlsteinhaus*, or Eagle's Nest. At one point in the movie, the American soldiers are walking through Eindhoven, a recently liberated city in Holland. The cheering crowds are waving flags and celebrating the arrival of the Americans, because it means the Nazi occupation has ended. The entire city is in the streets, cheering and hugging, and the local women are rewarding the Americans with smiles and kisses.

Among the cheering crowds, two GIs notice a disturbance on a side street. They investigate, and discover a group of locals ringing several women. The women are seized—their dresses ripped from their shoulders—and forced to their knees on the cobblestone street. Then their hair is forcibly shaved, and some of the women are marked on their foreheads with the swastika.

The GIs wonder if they should intervene on behalf of the women. It turns out the women are being identified and seized by members of the Dutch underground resistance, and then publicly punished for their decision to sleep with Nazi soldiers during the occupation.

It was the first time I'd considered women being complicit with the Nazis, and I developed a bit of a smug attitude. *What a lousy thing for these women to do,* I thought.

A few days later I was with my dad, and since this had taken place in Holland, I asked him about it. I described the scene from the movie, then concluded with, "Seems like a lousy thing to do, Dad—did Dutch women really do that?"

He shot me a look as quick and stern as any I'd seen from him since my teenage years. Then he simply stated, "In those situations, Ken, it's amazing what a mother will do for a piece of chocolate for her child."

He continued, telling me what it was like when, toward the end of the war, all the Dutch men had been taken to Germany to serve in work camps and factories—most women would have wondered if they'd ever see their men again. It was a story he knew well. There was no food in the cities, and those residents left were forced miles into the countryside to scrounge for something to eat—a task made nearly impossible when there were no cars and most of the bikes had been melted down for the German war effort. He summarized that in times as desperate as that, even the unimaginable becomes imaginable.

Being connected to the human side of this complex story brought about empathy and gave me a great degree of compassion for these women, rather than judgment.

EMPATHY IN SCRIPTURE

Having placed the capacity for empathy in humanity as a part of His image, God calls on His people to activate it. We see it often in the Old Testament, especially when God commanded the Israelites to look after the foreigner or the alien—what we might call the *immigrant*.

This is something my friend Jenny Yang, the director of advocacy and policy for the Refugee and Immigration Program at World Relief, has helped me understand in more depth since I met her in 2007. When God asks His people to care for the foreigner or the alien, He often gives a specific reason, which can be seen in the following verses:

"Do not deprive the alien or the fatherless of justice, or take the cloak of the widow as a pledge. Remember that you were slaves in Egypt and the LORD your God redeemed you from there. That is why I command you to do this." (Deuteronomy 24:17–18)

"When an alien lives with you in your land, do not mistreat him. The alien living with you must be treated as one of your native-born. Love him as yourself, for you were aliens in Egypt. I am the LORD." (Leviticus 19:33–34)

"Do not oppress an alien; you yourselves know how it feels to be aliens, because you were aliens in Egypt." (Exodus 23:9)

God knows that *remembrance* of Israel's own past will provide a way to empathize with vulnerable people in their own land. God legislated rules for the nation of Israel to ensure that such vulnerable and dislocated people were treated fairly and had their needs met,[8] based on Israel's own empathetic understanding of what it is like to live on the margins of a society.

As we see in the above verses, the repeated theme of remembrance was vital.

Remember that you were slaves in Egypt . . .

Love him as yourself, for you were aliens in Egypt . . .

You yourselves know how it feels to be aliens . . .

A friend once told me that, in Jewish culture, not remembering to celebrate Passover is not considered a neutral omission. Rather, it is the same as actively forgetting it, and such forgetting is a form of pride. Remembering where the Israelites came from was a way of remembering that it was God who rescued them. Remembrance of God's provision properly produces humility and allows for empathy toward others in similar, vulnerable states.

The same ought to be true of us today. I am a first-generation American, but even if our history as immigrants stretches back farther, nearly all of us come from families who were, at some point, strangers in a strange land. And in a broader sense, all Christians are travelers and exiles, no matter which country claims their earthly citizenship, because we recognize that earth is not our eternal home. We, like the Israelites, are a people of exile. First Peter 2:11 reminds us, "Dear friends, I urge you, as aliens and strangers in the world, to abstain from sinful desires, which war against your soul." The themes of sojourning and pilgrimage are deeply embedded in Christian theology and spirituality.

That's one reason Jenny's work with World Relief is so vital. She travels around the country, engaging churches and other groups to study what Scripture says about empathy and solidarity for the vulnerable in our society. She reminds Christians that their own stories are often not so different from the immigrant stories they may encounter in their communities. "Immigrants are all around us," says Jenny, "whether a recently resettled refugee who left home due to persecution, an undocumented immigrant who cuts your lawn, or an immigrant family in your neighborhood who's been living in the United States for many years."[9] Jenny likes to connect people to the biblical narrative, which itself is filled with immigrants—the stories of Abraham, Rebekah, Joseph, Ruth, Daniel, and even Jesus, who fled to Egypt as a child and was later a returning refugee.

When I asked Jenny why empathy is so essential, she said:

> Immigrants often leave everything behind, and have little in terms of resources or friends in their new homes. Justice is not only about seeking to correct root causes of injustice—it's also about building just relationships with those in your community who can often be marginalized and forgotten. This can start with a simple conversation with someone who is foreign born as you get to know their story. Empathy is a necessary part of our Christian faith because in showing empathy, we recognize that the grace we receive from God is unmerited and unconditional— and therefore we should love unconditionally those around us, particularly the vulnerable.
>
> Scripture is clear about God's affinity for the vulnerable, as in Zechariah 7:10, which says, "Do not oppress the widow or the fatherless, the alien or the poor. In your hearts do not think evil of each other," and I'm hopeful that we can learn to practice this, for in the end, I believe the immigrant, the refugee, can be any of us.[10]

One of the statistics that drives home the messiness surrounding the realities of immigration is that there are currently more than five thousand children in the foster care system in the United States whose parents have been deported or are being detained.[11] Those children each had one or two parents—until the day they became virtual orphans. Regardless of what I think about the specific policies and life choices that result in those separations, my empathy now extends to imagine a child who may never be reunited with his or her parents.

Can you imagine yourself in a foster home, separated from your parents, and having no certainty of seeing them again?

I believe God wants our hearts to be affected by the same things that affect His. Several years ago, Jenny Yang, along with Matthew Soerens, wrote a book whose title captures this reality for me. It is called *Welcoming the Stranger: Justice, Compassion and Truth in the Immigration Debate* (InterVarsity Press, 2009). Empathy has a central role to play in helping us to be in concert with God's concerns: regardless of our public, political stance on a particular justice issue (of which immigration is only a single example), our personal attitude toward the people involved must be characterized by godly love and grace.

Sometimes I find myself becoming more comfortable with categories or labels than with the people behind them. That's when I need to *remember*—when I need empathy to move me past the labels and connect me again with the human story and with God's call to love and stand with the vulnerable.

THE TRUE END OF EMPATHY

There *is* a great deal of empathy in the world. Some have characterized this generation as a "social justice generation," and in many ways it is easier than ever before to empathize with the victims of injustice in the world. Globalization and increased mobility provide us with more opportunities to empathize than in previous generations. In fact, an astonishing *90 percent* of current nongovernmental organizations (NGOs) and nonprofits were created in the last decade.

We need to be cautious of a potential downside, however: empathy can be something we settle for. Empathy is not the goal; it simply carries us into actions that are just. For example, because sugar was imported to Britain from slave plantations in the nineteenth century, the abolitionists labeled tea, the national drink, a *blood-sweetened beverage* and refused to drink it.[12] God provided us with a capacity to feel kinship and compassion for others, but such empathy should lead, when awakened, to empathetic action. Empathy should carry justice, not stop short of it.

Empathy can begin to address existing power differentials and the unjust structures that facilitate systemic injustices because it places us in relationships with others who are made in the image of God and share equal dignity. When we are in an empathetic relationship with people, we cannot help but care about the role unjust structures play in their suffering.

Whatever has a use can be used either well or badly. The same can be true of empathy. If it becomes an excuse not to move beyond feeling and into action for the dignity and worth of others, it is not being used well.

Empathy, when used well, leads to unity and partnership. Merely feeling another's pain can result in paternalistic pity. When that feeling motivates us to extend a hand in friendship, rather than extending handouts, empathy is acting as a means toward the proper end of justice and shalom.

The danger is that we view empathy as the *end* of our engagement with injustice, rather than the entry point. We can believe that simply *feeling* another's pain is the extent of our call. Michael Badriaki, who worked with the global HIV/AIDS crisis and is now pursuing graduate studies in global health and education, calls attention to what he calls "the exploitation of images . . . and empty marketing slogans focused on soliciting strong emotions [from donors]."

What is needed, according to Badriaki, are human stories that build human relationships. "When telling the stories of people in certain African regions it is important to consider the people's voices . . . to arrive at a truthful, meaningful, and balanced story. . . . How can the stories of genuine people in Africa be narrated without the leading and willing voice of the African people?[13]

Empathy is not a capacity given to us merely so that we can *feel* badly about an injustice or a tragedy . . . and then stop. Empathy is a God-designed way to begin acting justly in the world. We see this in the example of God Himself. In Exodus 2, God's empathy was integral to His acting justly toward His people: "During that long period, the king of Egypt died. The Israelites groaned in their slavery and cried out, and their cry for help because of their slavery went up to God. God heard their groaning and he remembered his covenant with Abraham, with Isaac and with Jacob. So God looked on the Israelites and was concerned about them" (vv. 23–25).

We know what happened next in Israel's history: God's hand delivered them from slavery in Egypt.

JUSTICE FOR ALL

The connection between empathy and ongoing action is clear in the life of Auschwitz survivor and Nobel Prize–winning author

Elie Wiesel. Wiesel has spent his life fighting for justice, writing more than fifty books, speaking, and conducting leadership camps for students designed to break down the ethnic or national barriers that exist between them.

Wiesel has been instrumental in galvanizing the message of genocide prevention around the act of remembering. He believes that some things that happened cannot be allowed to happen again; we cannot stand by and watch. "My goal is always the same," he has said: "to invoke the past as a shield for the future."[14]

This is made explicit in a striking piece of art embedded in the stone exterior of the United States Holocaust Memorial Museum. The bold text implores,

Think about what you saw
(While smaller lines of text spell out our responsibility to remember.)
The next time you witness hatred
The next time you see injustice
The next time you hear about genocide . . .
Think about what you saw

Wiesel understands the importance of empathy as we address injustices in all their forms. There is no finish line where we can stop thinking about others, stop empathizing with others.

Wiesel himself might have been tempted to do just that at the inauguration of the United States Holocaust Memorial Museum on April 22, 1993. The museum was, in a sense, the culmination of a dream for him. He was the chair of the committee that led the building of the museum, an achievement that would help ensure that the past would be remembered for generation after generation.

During his speech, however, he didn't focus on the injustices

he'd experienced personally—despite the fact that his own intern-
ment at Auschwitz, Buna, and Buchenwald was an example of what
the museum was created for. Neither did Wiesel focus on the injustices experienced by others like him during World War II.

Instead, he did something I find heroic because it is an example
of the purity with which empathy pursues justice for *all*. Wiesel
stood and said to then president Clinton, "What have we learned?
We have learned some lessons, minor lessons, perhaps, that we are
all responsible, and indifference is a sin and a punishment. And we
have learned that when people suffer we cannot remain indifferent.
And, Mr. President, I cannot *not* tell you something. I have been in
the former Yugoslavia last fall. I cannot sleep since, for what I have
seen. As a Jew I am saying that we must do something to stop the
bloodshed in that country! People fight each other and children
die. Why? Something, anything must be done."[15]

At a moment when he could have turned inward, Wiesel's heart
went out to the people being killed in the Balkans. Justice has no
finish line.

Empathy is an engine that powers justice. It is ingrained in us
because God placed it there, and it is designed to help carry justice
forward.

Near the end of Wiesel's speech, he told guests, "This is a lesson. There are many other lessons. You will come, you will learn.
We shall learn together."[16]

I hope to be more like Elie Wiesel.

> A father to the fatherless, a defender of widows,
>   is God in his holy dwelling.
>
> PSALM 68:5

NUMB
(OR EVER DIMINISHING RETURNS)

By Alex Davis

This piece, part of the Exile Poster Project,[*] explores what a mind looks like that has been taken over by exploitation and consumption.

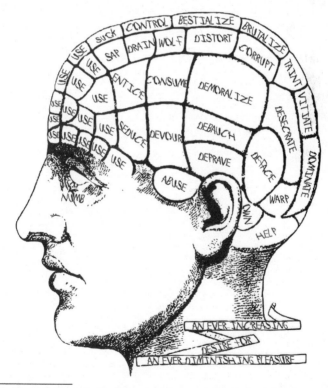

---

* The Exile Poster Project aims to confront specific injustices in Portland, Oregon, through the powerful medium of the poster. http://www.exileposterproject.com/vision.html.

EIGHT

PLAYSTATIONS AND POVERTY

Growing Up (in) a Consumer Culture

The Public is merely a multiplied "me."[1]

MARK TWAIN

So many lucky men restless in the midst of abundance.[2]

ALEXIS DE TOCQUEVILLE

O ne of the most eye-opening moments in my life happened in an unlikely place: show-and-tell at my daughter's
school. It seemed innocent enough, but the experience
there would shake Tamara and me to the core.

I had just picked up my good friend Marcel from the airport.
Marcel is a pastor in the Democratic Republic of the Congo (DRC),
one of the most violent, war-torn regions on the planet. He has
given his life to serving the poorest of the poor and the most broken of the broken. My daughter Esther was in the car, and since she
had show-and-tell coming up at school, she asked if she could bring
Marcel. He graciously agreed.

When the day arrived, my wife, Marcel, and I piled into the car
and headed to Esther's school. Once there, I noticed the overhead

lights in the classroom were off, so there was only dim light coming in through the windows. The kids sat in a line on the floor, behind a strip of tape. Marcel sat in a chair in front of them, ready to answer their questions. I leaned against a bulletin board, observing from a distance and ready to offer quick explanations to Marcel if he needed help.

The kids asked typical second-grade questions, like "Do you wear fancy clothes?" and "Do you eat green beans?" The class had recently done a study on animals from around the world, so the teacher prompted a few questions about gorillas, snakes, and zebras.

Then came the question that would change the way I see consumerism forever: "Do you have a PlayStation?"

Instant chaos. Every kid in the room was clamoring to be heard, asking Marcel if he had a Nintendo, a Game Boy, an Xbox.

Marcel looked to me for help, confusion wrinkling his forehead. He didn't know what any of those things were.

"Tell them no, Marcel," I said, "you don't have those."

Marcel smiled, looked back at the kids, and said, "No, my brothers and sisters. We don't have PlayStations."

I stood rooted in place, a sick feeling growing in my gut. Watching my friend interact with the kids, I thought about what I'd told Marcel to answer. I'd told him to say his country didn't have PlayStations.

Except what I'd told him to say wasn't true.

His country has been bleeding for centuries. Various militias and governments have come and gone, but there has been one constant: war. When civil war isn't tearing the country apart, war often spills over the border from neighboring countries. The result is an utter devastation and deprivation of the human spirit.

The DRC's wounds were opened even wider on October 26, 2000, when the PlayStation 2 was officially launched in the United States. The DRC has the misfortune of possessing some of the world's richest coltan deposits, a mineral used in the manufacture of consumer electronics. The unparalleled success of many of these products[3] led to a flurry of market speculation that drove the value of coltan up to more than *ten times* what it was worth only months before.[4]

The warlords pounced. Recognizing a golden opportunity, the leaders with military power in DRC seized as many coltan mines as they could, subsequently forcing men, women, and children into dangerous mining operations.

Marcel was doing ministry right in the middle of all of this, and his family suffered along with him. He would drive on long, deserted roads into affected areas. In his words, "The roads became the woods." Nobody else ventured there because it was so unsafe.

Marcel told me he would pray with his family before he left, and while he was gone, they would fast and pray the whole time for his safety. Every time he left he was literally putting his life at risk, yet he couldn't imagine *not* going to help these vulnerable people. Even if it cost his life.

Watching Marcel interact with my daughter and her classmates, it struck me: the suffering and tragedy he is giving his life to fight are fueled, in part, by the toys many of us are consuming.

As Marcel sat humbly and graciously in front of those second graders, there was no way he could have known.

CONSUMING THE CONGO

"We are consuming the Congo" is Micah Bournes's powerful closing line in "Life Should Be Free," a video my friends and I produced for the Enough project Film Competition, in conjunction with YouTube, and in the process won a Hollywood Film Festival award.[5] This call to action was designed to raise awareness about the electronics industry and the suffering it can cause. Here's the script:

> Look, when you use your cell phone,
> You activate the cries of a million children working through the night,
> Mining the ore that burns to tin,
> And that's exactly where this story begins:
> With a child in a cave
> In the dark, being brave,
> Surviving, hardly living,
> Serving as a slave,
> Digging minerals from the earth that always gives birth
> To a chain of events that never really ends
> 'Cause at the heart of it all
> There's an evil, strong and tall,
> With a gun in hand and a wicked plan
> To rape women and earth of all they're worth

So they can sell their greed in what we need.

It's right here.
Right now.
Today.
Hiding inside the price we pay
For the brand-new phone that says
We don't know
Or we don't care
That death and despair and war
Are what provide the means to have our well-connected lives.
It's time we stop supporting the unethical exporting of
Tungsten.
Tantalum.
And tin.
It's time for death to lose
And life to win.
So share what you know.
We are consuming the Congo.

I'm not calling for a boycott of video games and cell phones. I couldn't have written this book without my computer and smartphone. I am pointing out that we live in an interconnected world. We exist within a matrix of human relationships, economic ties, and political forces, whether we know it or not.

The philosopher Cornelius Plantinga wrote, "To be a responsible person is to find one's role in the building of shalom, the re-webbing of God, humanity, and all creation in justice, harmony, fulfillment, and delight."[6]

The way we consume directly affects the lived realities of other people, whether we want it to or not. The story we are part of is far larger than we think.

CONSPIRACY TO COMMIT CONSUMPTION

Consumerism is a relatively new phenomenon, even in America's short history. Our rabid economic machine that constantly churns out new products and services hasn't always been calibrated that way. Even as recently as the Great Depression of the 1930s, our industries weren't producing disposable, purchasable garbage in mass quantities—or importing it from overseas.

What happened?

The deliberate choice to create, market, and sustain consumerism is what happened. It was a planned development in American economics. Following World War II, marketing strategists realized that if America didn't continue to consume the amount it had during the war, our supercharged wartime economy would slow down and sputter out.

The solution was consumerism. This 1955 journal article by Victor Lebow, a marketing consultant, is a fascinating and even chilling peek behind the curtain:

> Our enormously productive economy demands that we make consumption our way of life, that we convert the buying and use of goods into rituals, that we seek our spiritual satisfactions, our ego satisfactions, in consumption. The measure of social status, of social acceptance, of prestige, is now to be found in our consumptive patterns. The very meaning and significance of our lives today expressed in consumptive terms.

The greater the pressures upon the individual to conform to safe and accepted social standards, the more does he tend to express his aspirations and his individuality in terms of what he wears, drives, eats—his home, his car, his pattern of food serving, his hobbies.

These commodities and services must be offered to the consumer with a special urgency. We require not only "forced draft" consumption, but "expensive" consumption as well. *We need things consumed, burned up, worn out, replaced, and discarded at an ever increasing pace. We need to have people eat, drink, dress, ride, live, with ever more complicated and, therefore, constantly more expensive consumption.*[7]

This was written in 1955, but it could have been written yesterday.

Wherever we are, and whatever we are doing, our lives are being broadcast. What we value and support with our time, money, and attention is part of the culture we are exporting. There is no possibility of a completely private, neutral life. All of us are exporting certain cultural values and assumptions, projecting them out into our neighborhoods, our country, and even distant parts of the world.

Every culture has a dominant export, and in every culture there are people who no longer wish to be part of exporting it. The question to ask ourselves, then, is, what is *my* life exporting?

While the idea of the "consumerism conspiracy" is frightening, I also take encouragement from it. It's good news that consumerism wasn't a natural development of Western culture or an intrinsic part of ourselves. If consumerism can be created, it can be combated. If selfishness can be taught, *selflessness* can be learned.

Although today we consume the Congo, tomorrow we can begin to restore it.

ONE CLOTH

When Tamara watched Marcel speak to Esther's class, she experienced something very different than I did, but just as negative. Outside the classroom she said, "Ken, I almost vomited."

Tamara had picked up on the spiritual undercurrent of the class, something she's sensitive to. One of the moments she remembered most was Marcel's answer to the question, "Do you wear fancy clothes to dinner?"

Marcel said, "Brothers and sisters, we only have one cloth. One cloth, set of clothes, because my countrymen, they suffer very much."

The kids' reaction nearly floored Tamara.

"That's stupid."

"Ew, gross!"

"Yuck."

The complete and utter lack of concern or empathy for the need and suffering of others was chilling. In Tamara's words, "They were all so self-focused and showed absolutely zero concern for anyone else, including their fellow students. It was nauseating."

Without guidance from their teacher, the kids were only able to ask questions that tried to connect Marcel to things they owned and consumed. Not only were they unable to imagine what his life was really like; they were unable to feel gratitude for the prosperity they enjoyed.

I spoke about this recently at Baylor University. In that talk, I traced the creation of the concept of the "teenager" to a marketing plan during the 1940s.[8] With the men off at war, and the women working in the factories, there was a "need" for a newly differentiated segment of buyers. As the postwar economy roared and the television era soared, the first generation of Americans grew up as what I call "advertising's children." That history helped me understand that the second graders in my daughter's class *can't* empathize with a man from the Congo or appreciate their own blessings—and it isn't just those second graders who are advertising's children.

It's all of us.

A THEOLOGY OF GRATITUDE

My friend Richard Twiss spoke at Antioch in 2012, and he had a poignant message for our culture about gratitude and respect. One of the most moving parts of his sermon for me was his description of the Yupik tribe: "Among the Yupik people of the western coast of Alaska," he said, "they have ideas about human and nonhuman persons and how animals give themselves to feed us. And we're to receive their life. So they have a couple of social patterns.

"One of them is that when you eat a chicken, you eat everything on the chicken. . . . You do not feed the bones to dogs; you do not throw the bones away. You either burn them, or you bury them. Or, depending on the animal, you take the bones back to where it came from, because *the primary value is gratitude and respect.* You are grateful that that animal provided the food to nourish you, so you treat this gift with respect."[9]

That is a world away from our obsession with disposable products—so far away that the deep and respectful gratitude that the Yupik tradition expresses might seem strange or awkward to some of us. But is it really so outlandish to remember that an animal died for our dinner? Is it really that odd to recall that our planet doesn't *owe* us sustenance?

Is it strange to be grateful?

The kids in my daughter's class aren't bad kids. They're living almost exactly as their context has trained them to live. These particular children for the most part have no context for understanding suffering, or real lack, so they can't understand their own prosperity—and that makes it impossible for them to be grateful.

I'm desperate to reverse the current of consumerism and ingratitude that wants to carry our kids away from God, and that's why my friend Linda Van Voorst and I began Mission Kids. Linda has one of the most generous hearts of anyone I know, and she has poured her soul into creating children's curriculum that is designed to *help parents raise compassionate and mission-minded kids.*

Linda was in my youth group while I was in grad school in Southern California, and after she graduated from Moody Bible Institute, she moved to Bend, Oregon, to help us plant Antioch. Since then, she has worked to help parents raise grateful kids who live with an awareness of who God is and what matters to Him.

Rather than keep the conversation about compassion within the walls of the church, Mission Kids equips parents to teach compassion to their kids during the week. There are activities for parents to do with kids, stories to share about other kids from less wealthy parts of the world, and other resources to help stem the tide of consumerism in our homes.[10]

If we don't stem the tide of consumerism, if we fail to teach empathy and gratitude, our kids will continue to think that suffering is "gross" rather than tragic, or stupid rather than heartbreaking.

Once I was in a meeting with a group of Christian leaders, talking about why I'd founded The Justice Conference. Struggling to sum up a host of thoughts and feelings in a single sentence, I finally said, "The goal is to try and save the American church from American culture."

My greatest frustration with consumerism is that it encourages selfishness while reinforcing the lie that happiness is found in consumption—the opposite of Jesus' call to give our lives away. And paradoxically, rejecting the consumerism of our culture is the way to find our greatest joy. What if the consumerism that plagues our churches—that plagues our hearts—could begin transforming into compassion?

I want my kids' hearts to break for the things that matter. I want *my* heart to break for the things that matter.

THIS IS NOT A CHAPTER ABOUT PLAYSTATIONS

The only reason the PlayStation 2 drove the conflict in Congo is because it was successful. Any other successful product in the electronics industry could have caused the same tragedy. Therefore, we need to be careful about what we buy and when we buy it. Is it really necessary to replace our cars every five years? Do we really need to buy the latest gaming system every time a new one is released? Is our stuff really worn-out before we replace it? And are we certain the products we're buying aren't a chapter in a tragic story in another country?

Many people who are concerned about just consumption point to fair trade as part of the answer. Merriam-Webster defines *fair trade* this way: "a movement whose goal is to help producers in developing countries to get a fair price for their products so as to reduce poverty, provide for the ethical treatment of workers and farmers, and promote environmentally sustainable practices."[11] My friend Nathan George, founder of Trade as One, said it this way: "[Fair trade is] an attempt to not just treat the poor with dignity and respect in how we would expect to be treated, but to deliberately go about finding the most marginalized."[12]

Nathan's nonprofit Trade as One is an online fair-trade marketplace that sells fair-trade food, toys, household products, and a host of other everyday items. You can even order a seasonal basket that is shipped every few months with a variety of fair-trade products, foods, and desserts. If you're looking for a way to explore fair-trade consumption and just spending, Trade as One is a great place to start. You will soon be consuming products that actually *give back* to the regions from which they came.[13]

Blaise Pascal wrote:

> It is no doubt an evil to be full of faults, but it is a still greater evil to be full of them and unwilling to recognize them, since this entails the further evil of deliberate self-delusion. We do not want others to deceive us; we do not think it right for them to want us to esteem them more than they deserve; it is therefore not right either that we should deceive them and want them to esteem us more than we deserve. Thus, when they merely reveal vices and imperfections which we actually possess, it is obvious that they do us no wrong, since they are not responsible for them, but are really doing us good, by helping us to escape from an evil, namely our ignorance of these imperfections.[14]

However we investigate our habits of consumption and our lack of gratitude, let's be willing to allow God to shepherd and disciple us into people who are compassionate and grateful, and who raise compassionate and grateful kids.

If we're part of a larger story than we realize, let's weave a narrative characterized by God's definition of enough, rather than our culture's.

> "If anyone causes one of these little ones—those
> who believe in me—to stumble, it would be better
> for them to have a large millstone hung around their
> neck and to be drowned in the depths of the sea."
>
> MATTHEW 18:6

MY JESUS AIN'T YOUR JESUS

By Daniel Fan

My Jesus ain't your Jesus.
My Jesus was born in an alley.
The hotels, they *had* empty rooms
but they told his family "No Vacancy."

When the wise men celebrated
they brought food stamps
plastic flowers
cheese.

When the authorities heard, they came too—
the INS
the cops
the social workers—
to take him away.

My Jesus, he rides on a bus through the projects
walks a mile through the sand to school
works at the 7-11 till midnight.

When you and your Jesus hang out
you're a youth group.
When me and my Jesus hang out
we're a street gang.

My Jesus didn't just send packages to the poor.
He didn't just serve in soup kitchens on Christmas Eve.
He was there every day
till they took him away . . .

thick accent
dark skin
slanted eyes
kinky hair . . .

My Jesus is black
yellow
red
and brown.

Got room in your heart for
my Jesus?[15]

NINE

COMPASSION CAN KILL

The Need for Wisdom and Accountability in Generosity

I wish to suggest that a man may be very industrious,
and yet not spend his time well.[1]

HENRY DAVID THOREAU

Never let your zeal outrun your charity.
The former is but human, the latter is divine.[2]

HOSEA BALLOU

n the closing months of the Second World War, American GIs liberated concentration camps as they pushed across Poland and Germany. The soldiers were shocked and horrified to see the emaciated men, women, and children who were being held prisoner. Motivated by compassion, many of the GIs unpacked their army rations and began feeding people.

In a final tragedy layered upon so many tragedies that had come before, the solid food shared by the American soldiers killed hundreds of people who had just escaped the Holocaust with their lives. It wasn't until the army doctors caught up with the advancing infantry that they were able to recommend nursing the starving captives back to health slowly, using liquid nutrition.[3]

It is shocking, but sometimes compassion can kill.

Compassion and giving, in a certain sense, are not absolutes—always right, always good, always helpful. Compassion and giving must be done wisely, to maximize the benefit to the recipient and to avoid making things worse. We can think of compassion as one half of effective justice; the other half is ensuring that the beneficiaries of our compassion flourish.

LONG-TERM PARTNERSHIP

One of the keys to ensuring that our compassion is wise and benefits others is to enter into long-term partnerships, rather than temporary quick fixes.

In 2009 I was working with World Relief on a book about wise giving that would bring together leading voices to speak about how to do relief and development work wisely and effectively. There was, and still is, a need to tell a more complete story about how best to leverage our time, passion, money, and skills to engage problems that are endemic in the developing world, as well as local responses to poverty—and to develop relationships that transform us in return.

On January 12, 2010, in the late afternoon, a magnitude 7.0 earthquake struck Haiti, killing an estimated 230,000 people.[4] The book was shelved, and the very things the book had been aiming for were put into practice by World Relief staff and volunteers. World Relief, having had a long-term presence in the country, was able to leverage resources and local wisdom for search and rescue, crisis response, rehabilitations, and ongoing development in the hours, days, weeks, and years that followed the disaster. It was in essence saying, *We were here before the earthquake, we are here in the midst of the pain, and we will be here for the long haul—long after the camera crews leave and the news moves on to another story.*

Were people so moved by what they saw on their television screens following the Haiti earthquake that they were inspired to rush down to Haiti and help? Absolutely. Was good accomplished? Certainly. The hard truth, however, is that harm was sometimes done by people and organizations with good intentions, but less-than-wise execution. For example, months after the earthquake, the Haitian government was given money with which to pay Haitians to shovel rubble from the roads—a dignified way for them to earn a living in the wake of the economic collapse brought on by the earthquake. In some cases, however, short-term teams were given the cleanup opportunities, preventing locals from helping to rebuild their own country. In another example, an organization I know was challenged when leaders of short-term trips made promises about building projects they were unable to fulfill, compounding the relational difficulties of those working long-term with local Haitians.

Compassion must be guided by relationship. Love must be demonstrated with respect. And the twin principles of "do no harm" and "don't do for others what they can do for themselves" must be followed.

Over the long term, partnering with people and organizations with an established and respected presence in a particular place gives us the best chance of being effective. Local leadership, local relationships, and local know-how count for more than any foreign fund-raising ever can.[5] As I've worked with World Relief over the years, I have especially appreciated their commitment to the long term and to local relationships—they never race to get in front of cameras, but rather remain in communities as long as they are called.

That's one of the lessons about living and dying for bigger things: the call to give your life away is more about the small and faithful over many years than the grand and exciting.

RELIEF AND DEVELOPMENT

When compassion motivates us to act, relief and development are two ways we engage.

Relief is like triage: it is life-saving intervention when people are hanging on by a thread and need immediate assistance. In the event of a rapid or sudden-onset disaster—such as an earthquake, tsunami, or war—development is an impossibility, at least for the moment. God anticipated the need for relief during moments of crisis. Recall Joseph helping Pharaoh store up food in advance of a famine—a decision that ended up feeding his own family after they immigrated to Egypt. Proverbs 13:23 highlights the speed with which disasters can shred a local economy, transforming the residents from poor to desperate in an instant. "A poor man's field may produce abundant food, but injustice sweeps it away."

The need for relief is real. More than three billion people— nearly half of the planet—live on less than two dollars a day. To understand what this means, consider what your life would be like if you could spend only two dollars in your local economy for all your needs: food, shelter, medicine, transportation, clothing, and so on—and that doesn't allow for scrounging fresh food from the supermarket Dumpster if you live in a wealthy country.

Close to one billion people suffer from chronic hunger. Every day, almost sixteen thousand children die from hunger-related causes and poverty—enough to fill your nearest NBA arena.[6]

These statistics are bleak, and only scratch the surface of the injustice in our world—but there are rays of hope. Recently, for the first time ever, the proportion of people living in extreme poverty fell in every region of the Global South.[7] Seven of the ten fastest-growing economies in the world are Global South nations, and seven are in Africa.[8] Relief is absolutely needed, and the best practices of relief lead to sustainable development.

Development is empowerment over time. Phrases like "Never give a handout when you can give a hand up" and "Never do for others what they can do for themselves" capture the difference between temporary triage and lasting health.

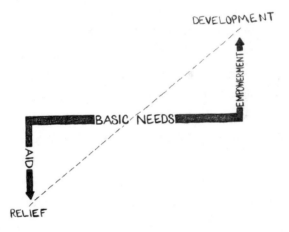

Effective relief is done with an eye toward development, and effective development is done with an eye toward resiliency so people won't need relief as often, or ever, in the future. Development that lasts is development that transforms. When relief is the only goal, we often do more harm than good, creating cycles of dependency with our paternalistic actions. Instead, relief and development aim for sustainability.

Nathan George has explained it like this: *relief* is giving a starving community free fish; *development* is teaching a community how to fish; and *sustainable development* is building an ongoing economy that can purchase those fish. Sustainable development will empower and transform that community over time.

The implication is that, to use the case of the Haiti earthquake, we ought to think seriously about the wisdom of partnering with an organization that doesn't already have "boots on the ground" in the cities and villages.[9] Rather, we should learn who was there already, is still there now, and plans to be there to partner with emerging local leaders. Such organizations, whether local, national, or international, have already built local relationships that allow them to prioritize and channel relief and make the transition to sustainable development and empowerment as soon as possible.

The end goal of development is overall resiliency, and this can only occur through relationship. As Keith Wright, international president of Food for the Hungry, has said, "I like walking with, not doing for."[10] Development isn't about flying in and delivering a cargo of superior knowledge. When development professionals "walk with" their local friends and partners, they are going somewhere together: toward the day locals can take over areas such as leadership training, crisis management, economic planning and implementation, and so on.

Some previous models of relief and development viewed certain cultures as essentially helpless and stagnant—no economic or social progress would ever be made unless a foreign expert arrived on the scene to save the day. There is another way to understand relief and development, as Keith made clear: "We're trying to reduce suffering by speeding a transition that might already be happening on its own."[11] When the transition happens and a community develops enough resiliency to build for the future and absorb or deflect shocks of all kinds—economic, political, weather related, and so forth—an intervention or relief mission that likely began with compassion can be judged a success.

"I'D RATHER BE TAUGHT . . ."

I'd like to let my friend Keith Wright tell you his story. It's one that surfaces the need for relational wisdom to partner with compassion.

Twenty years ago I went to Africa with the idea that I would "help fix" that continent's problems. What began with a well-intentioned but paternalistic instinct has become a deep love and respect for that continent—and now Asia and Latin America as well.

Over these past decades, I've learned a lot about what makes a real, measurable, transformative difference in these places:

First, I have been personally blessed and transformed by the very places I went to help; I believe God intentionally called me to Africa twenty years ago to reach me and change me, and by grace I have learned along the way how to make some contributions back.

Second, the half dozen African countries I love and have served in have enormous talent, resources, and vision that must be integral to solving their own problems and sustaining their own progress.

Last—and this is the simplest lesson—collaborative partnership is the *only* way we can make a real difference in the world, wherever we work.

A case in point is a kid who was eight years old when I first moved to Uganda—a barefoot kid with only one parent and no money for school fees. His classroom, by the way, was outside under a tree. Now he's almost thirty, and he's a good friend whose perspective I value. He's completing his MBA this year and planning to run for Parliament.

What makes me so hopeful is this: his story is being repeated over and over across the world, and especially across the Global South, which is taking control of its own development with visionary, local leaders like my friend who are spending their lives to make their countries flourish.

My other reason for hope is more personal: I'm glad I've finally figured out, after twenty years, that I'd rather be taught by him than assume I should do all the teaching myself.

RELATIONSHIP HONORS DIGNITY

Mutually beneficial relationships are vital because they are the only way to ensure we understand and honor the dignity of our brothers and sisters, whether they are our neighbors or people across the world.

Africans can fix Africa is a way of describing the need for local resources to be empowered to address local problems. Whether our compassion takes us across the street or across the world, we must leave behind our false paternalism and "fix it" mentality, and choose instead to enter into relationships with wise guides.

One of the most stark and insightful experiences I've had in relation to wise giving came in 2007 when I was in Burundi with my friends Dan and Tambry Brose, who had lived and worked near the Great Lakes for many years. We were having a conversation with their Burundian friend Emmanuel Ndikumana. He and I were both church planters and had founded colleges, so I assumed I could bring a great deal of relevant insight and value to our conversation.

After a few hours of conversation, a realization began to irritate the back of my mind. I was being arrogant. I'd approached the meeting as a chance for me to give, because I was the one with "all" the resources, and I'd assumed that Emmanuel, as a relatively impoverished Burundian, was the one who needed everything.

Determined not to be "that guy" who jetted into Africa, dispensed Western wisdom, and then left right away, I simply tried to start listening with my whole person. After hearing many stories from Emmanuel about cross-cultural engagement and missionary efforts gone bad, I asked a simple question: "What would you tell American pastors if you had the chance?"

Emmanuel didn't hesitate. He leaned forward so he could look right into my eyes. "Stop messing up my country."

He paused, then continued. "Americans always think they can come over here and give me good advice, like we don't know anything about our own country. You Americans and the way you're trying to do compassion is creating as many problems as it's solving."

As I listened to Emmanuel, the thought came into my mind: for explorers who actually want to *get* somewhere, befriending locals is more valuable than wandering blind.

Or, as stated in an old African proverb, "If you want to go fast, go alone. If you want to go far, go together."

RELATIONSHIP TAKES TIME

Forming relationships is more difficult than making charity and relief the extent of our compassion. Relationship requires us to listen and learn because the other has something to teach. Development and justice aren't only about *doing*; they're about waiting as well. When justice is nothing more than the latest fashion statement or fad, there simply isn't time or motivation to do the hard, slow work of building relationships.

And relationships always operate in two directions. We must be willing to walk our talk—if we say we care about a country, or a community, or a church, or a person, we must then give the necessary time to that relationship.

This forces us to ask some pointed questions about short-term missions. Since such trips are so brief, and seldom return the same people to the same places, are they of any use in building the sort of relationship that truly just development requires?

The shocking statistic is that short-term missions is a two-billion-dollar industry in the United States.[12] Yet many of the problems that particular communities or countries face are systemic and will take generations to solve and heal—so what can really be done in two weeks?

Does this mean that a two-week trip to Burundi or Brazil can accomplish nothing? No. What it does mean is that we would be wise to tailor our expectations and messaging to match more closely what actually happens. Whether we consciously articulate it or not, we often expect that a short-term missions trip will change us and change the place we visit in significant ways.

Change can happen; it's true. God absolutely uses short-term mission trips, and many of the career missionaries and international relief and development professionals I know were first given a "taste" of their calling on a short-term missions trip when they were in high school or college. This illustrates exactly why I believe we need to continue to fund and send folks on short-term trips, *while at the same time redefining our expectations for what they will accomplish and what they mean.*

I believe we need to call these trips by what they really are: Learning trips. Exposure trips. Relationship trips. Engagement trips.

It's important to point out that redefining expectations about short-term missions isn't "giving up" or "settling for less," as if some two-week trips really *could* transform a country forever if not for the naysayers. No, redefining how we understand short-term missions is about building cross-cultural intelligence. It's about beginning relationships that are mutually beneficial and challenging. Redefining short-term missions trips is about ridding ourselves of the illusion that we can change the world, and instead admitting that the world might need to change us.

Imagine a Burundian youth group, along with several leaders, coming to your hometown on a missions trip. You are the local pastor, and you are responsible for all the logistics of their trip: where they'll stay, who will feed them, how they'll get to and from the airport, and so on. Now ask yourself, *What do I want the Burundian youth group to do?*

If they're coming to "fix" your town, isn't that going to create more problems than solutions? How can they address the real estate bubble that depressed home prices and forced families to move into cheaper housing at the edge of town? Do they know something about narcotics crime that your chief of police doesn't know? Can they get the necessary building permits to build your church a new family center—and do they even know how to swing hammers and drive nails?

But what if they were coming to begin a relationship with you and your church? What if you spent time talking, sharing, and asking each other questions? What if they came with a list of questions to ask you, and listened carefully to your answers? What if you spent time in prayer together, reading the Bible and affirming your mutual desire to do justly, love mercy, and to walk humbly with God?

Food for the Hungry calls such relationships "C2C"— community to community. The goal is mutual transformation over a decade, rather than one-off trips. In fact, such ongoing relationships provide the sort of local structure and wisdom needed to successfully navigate any short-term trips.

Here's a truth: God has gifted Burundi with people who will help Burundi. Let's enter into relationship with them before we enter into action. As Keith said, "We can't show up in matching T-shirts and hand out glow sticks and then leave thinking we've changed Africa."[13]

WHAT WE CAN LEARN

If we educate ourselves and listen humbly, we can begin to learn what the developing world needs. But what can the developing world teach us?

A theology of suffering. The wisdom of community resources and creative thinking. An understanding of what it means to be an exile. The importance of family and extended family and networks of kin. Enthusiasm. Wise stewardship of available resources. Resiliency. Strategies for fighting materialism and consumerism. An organic connection between spiritual and material concerns. What it means to trust God daily.

In his seminal work, *Pedagogy of the Oppressed*, Paulo Freire discussed the need to engage communities in humble relationship:

"For apart from inquiry, apart from the praxis, individuals cannot be truly human. Knowledge emerges only through invention and re-invention, through the restless, impatient, continuing, hopeful inquiry human beings pursue in the world, with the world, and with each other."[14]

According to Philip Jenkins, writing for *First Things*, by 2025, more than half of the world's Christians will live in the Global South, and by 2050, "Christianity will be chiefly the religion of Africa and the African diaspora."[15] This is an amazing and wonderful possibility. The Global South is materially poorer than the Global North, but it is rising. The Global North is spiritually poorer than the Global South—and the rising church in the Global South has so much to teach those of us in the North!

Between 1990 and 2000, the combined membership of all Protestant denominations in the United States declined by 10 percent,[16] while the population increased by 11 percent. In 2008 alone, Catholic membership declined by four hundred thousand,[17] and "the United States now ranks third following China and India in the number of people who are not professing Christians; in other words, the U.S. is becoming an ever increasing 'un-reached people group.'"[18]

More missionaries are now being sent out from the Global South than from the Global North. Many of them are being sent to the United States.

We have so much to learn and so many ways to partner with our brothers and sisters around the world. Let's stop overlooking the complexities of relief and development and start learning from relationships. We often want to ride into town and fix things in short order, but real relationships take time to develop and energy to sustain. Let's listen, learn, and commit to the long term.

CALL AND RESPONSE

If we live according to the fruit of the Spirit—love, joy, peace, patience, kindness, goodness, faithfulness, gentleness, self-control—we will be living toward justice, and there can never be a law against such things. Therefore we can always seek justice through the power of God's Spirit. And as the apostle James wrote, we always should: "If anyone, then, knows the good they ought to do and doesn't do it, it is sin for them" (James 4:17).

When it comes to seeking justice, we always *can* and we always *should*.

We're hemmed in by justice, always able to practice it and always meant to practice it. And so we should be. There is no better place on earth than the road of justice because it is a road that leads us, and the fellow travelers we meet along the way, toward the center of God's will and purpose.

I know Christians who have somehow made it through six decades in church without noticing that the Bible constantly teaches about human rights and justice. We sometimes think these are new issues, new concerns, that distract from the purity of what we call "the gospel"—as if the gospel could be separated from justice without doing violence to it in the process. Yet human rights issues that feel as if they are ripped straight from the pages of our newspapers are featured in the pages of Scripture.

We read about Paul, who took up a collection for famine relief to save strangers in a distant land. We read in Esther about how genocide began, was perpetuated, and ultimately was stopped. We read in Deuteronomy about laws intended to protect the food sources on which poor people relied.

So the questions for us today are not, why *should* we take up a collection for people starving in Somalia? and, why *should* we help refugees resettle? The question is, why *shouldn't* we?

We sometimes hear a debate about whether we should focus on local or international justice, relief, and development. This is, by and large, a false dichotomy. We should be focusing on both to the extent that God calls us. Most of our energy and creativity are spent in a particular time and place, but that doesn't prevent us from keeping the wider world in our hearts and minds.

Famine, genocide, immigration, fair wages, creation care, gender violence . . . these aren't new issues. They've been in the heart of God since Adam and Eve walked, hand in hand, away from Eden. The question is, where does God have you now, and what is He asking you to do? If He is calling you somewhere else, are you willing to listen and obey?

DOING WELL, AND NOT SIMPLY DOING

In our compassion, in our response to God's call, we absolutely need accountability. It's good to do good—but beyond the impulse to do good is the need for relational wisdom and for us to evaluate our compassionate actions.

Here's a quick case study. Norway gives more of its government resources, as a percentage, to foreign aid than any other country. In the not-too-distant past, the Norwegian government decided to build a fish-packing plant in Kenya on the shores of Lake Turkana.[19] The new facility would create jobs, provide a market for local fishers, export fish, and boost the local economy. It was a compassionate idea, motivated by the best of intentions. However, there were a few problems with the plan.

First, there were no reliable roads connecting the plant with larger cities where the fish could be shipped and sold. Second, the locals were nomadic herdsmen who considered fishing to be women's work.

The result? Within a year of opening, the fish-packing plant was offline, and the local herdsmen were using it to shelter their goats from the sun—millions of dollars of aid ended up only as shade.

John 10:1–21 in the NIV bears the heading "The Good Shepherd and His Sheep." In this passage, Jesus tells a story about an effective shepherd who cares for his sheep by calling them by name, battling predatory animals, keeping them safe in their pen, and even being willing to give his life for them.

In other words, Jesus can be called the *good* shepherd because He combines compassion with wisdom to achieve the best ends for His flock. The shepherd is accountable for the state of the flock, and a flock troubled by danger or disease is not restored to flourishing by good intentions alone.

Compassion is good. Results are good. Without both good halves, we are incomplete. When God calls you into an area of justice, you are accountable for the results, to the best of your ability, and you must be willing to learn and grow and change, as Keith spoke about in his story.

In 2007, I talked with local leaders at an internally displaced persons (IDP) camp in Uganda. Several hundred people were forced to live there because of ongoing tribal conflicts.

Inside the camp stood what appeared to be a new well, yet the pump wasn't running and the ground around it was parched. One of the local leaders told me the story. A well-intentioned group had arrived at the camp unannounced. They had wanted to bring water to thirsty people, and in the course of the following week, they had dug a well and installed a brand-new pump. Then they had left.

It wasn't too long before the pump mechanism broke, rendering the well useless. The people in the camp had neither the money nor the know-how to fix the pump, and the visiting team had not provided either. Now the pump was a symbol of water that was almost close enough to drink but remained out of reach for the thirsty residents.

When doing justice or engaging in charity, good intentions do not guarantee a good outcome. We need to build and develop capacity over time. Most development organizations know and practice this, but there are still too many instances of unintended harm that begin with compassion. We need to be held accountable, like a good shepherd, for the final outcome of our love, compassion, and giving.

MUTUAL TRANSFORMATION

World Relief calls their programs "interventions." The incarnation was a compassionate intervention—God's intervention in a broken and messy world in order to bring grace and reconciliation. Our interventions need to be incarnations, following God's model.

True missions, if it's like the incarnation, take a lifetime. It requires us to be all in, to give our lives away.

Hope is rising in the Global South, as well as in the Global North. The possibilities are wide if we are willing to invest ourselves, listen, and commit to relationships that last longer than a trip during spring break.

Our world truly does require compassion. The need is great.

But compassion must be guided by wisdom and have as its end something far beyond relief. That end involves sustainable human flourishing, or shalom, and that is a goal for *everyone* involved. We are being called into partnership with brothers and sisters around the world—a partnership that both builds and is an example of God's kingdom.

> The need for more capital and better technology persists. People really do need improved access to clean water, better health care, decent education, and a living wage. But they, and we, need something far more profound. Whether we realize it or not, we all are longing for an intimate relationship with God, for a sense of dignity, for community and belonging, and for the ability to use our gifts and abilities to develop creation.[20]

Compassion alone does not guarantee effective results. Sacrificial and relational love, however, enable us to partner with others and learn from them. We are called to join the narrative of communities rather than to edit our own narrow story over the top of theirs.

The Jesus Way of loving people was steeped in humility and focused on relationship. What does the posture of Jesus look like? I believe God is calling us to unlearn some of the ways we have been doing charity and to relearn the fullness of what it means to love.

> But you must return to your God;
>   maintain love and justice,
>   and wait for your God always.
>
> HOSEA 12:6

TEN

WHY DO YOU CALL ME GOOD?

Reflecting the Goodness of God

Everybody thinks about changing humanity.
Nobody thinks about changing himself.[1]

LEO TOLSTOY

The temptation of this age is to look good without being good.[2]

BRENNAN MANNING

have a colleague in the Democratic Republic of the Congo who has spent the last decade and a half helping some of the world's most vulnerable people. He was born and raised in what is one of the most war-torn regions on the globe today—eastern Congo. His life is threatened regularly, and he faces the seemingly impossible task of trying to restore villages decimated by rape, murder, and plunder.

Some visiting executives from a large, well-known global-relief organization once toured the region. They noticed what an effective job my friend was doing, and offered him a position as the leader of their Congo operations.

He quickly turned them down.

On paper it was the kind of offer you can't refuse—higher pay, more security, great influence. A dream promotion for most Westerners. He refused for a simple reason: "God gave me the job I have. He's helped me build the relationships and the respect that I have. He has opened the door for me all these years and kept me safe on every trip out into the bush. I'm right where God has called me to be, so why would I go anywhere else? I don't just want to do good. I want to be where God wants me to be."

He serves because he loves his country, weeps for his people, and believes the only way to effect change is to trust God and the power that comes through the message of love and reconciliation in Jesus.

The way he understands goodness, it can only flow from a single source.

THE HILLS OF GALILEE

Jesus was once approached by a man who asked, "Good teacher, what must I do to inherit eternal life?"

"Why do you call me good?" Jesus answered. "No one is good—except God alone" (Mark 10:17–18).

Jesus, the most upright and good person ever to live, didn't allow people to call Him good. Instead, He pointed back to His Father.

Jesus saw Himself as subordinate to His Father. The fruit of His labor came as a direct result of the ministry His Father had given Him and the power He had through God's Spirit. Jesus used whatever was good about Himself to direct worship and glory back to God the Father—back to the source of goodness, from whom all goodness flows.

THE MOUNTAINS OF CONGO

A group of six people I know from Bend, Oregon, spent two weeks in eastern Congo to document the hardships and bring back awareness to the States. Unable to go because of the imminent birth of our fourth daughter, I received the news that a rebel group was threatening a village where our team was staying.

They took turns praying through the night. The rebels threatened the town with gunshots, but never entered the village, and moved on the next day.

But what if things had happened differently? What if somebody had lost his or her life on a short-term trip like this? What would I have said to the victim's surviving family members?

Sometimes I wonder what we're really doing. Are we trying to be good because it's an adventure? Or are we committing ourselves to justice because God is just?

I don't know what I'll say if someone I know and love is killed pursuing justice. I do know that for many of my friends, doing justice goes hand in hand with pain, suffering, and the real possibility of death.

THE HUMBLE WALK

The conversation we're having isn't about which specific acts of justice we ought to go and do. It's about how to *be* just. We know what is good and what God requires of us, taken straight from Micah 6:8—to act justly, to love mercy, and to walk humbly with God.

We can't do that. Not one of us can do what is required.

We are to *do* justly—but who among us can do justly at all times?

And so we are to *love* mercy—for our own mistakes, for the mistakes of others, for every time our hearts do not match the heart of God, we need mercy.

And what does loving mercy produce? Humility.

Quite simply, we cannot be just. We have no standing before God or our fellow humans. It is only God who can make us just, who can justify us. We can't will or act or intend or resolve or plan or move our way to being fully good people. When we try, we fail.

But when we succeed, we see, as Jesus did, God's hand in the good we did.

What we can do is center our lives on God, as justice is centered on God, all the time and of necessity. Justice both demonstrates the need for grace and is completed by grace. Paul reported to the church in Corinth what God had told him about grace: "My grace is sufficient for you, for my power is made perfect in weakness" (2 Corinthians 12:9).

We want to be good, but God *is* good. James 1:17 tells us that "every good and perfect gift is from above, coming down from the Father of the heavenly lights, who does not change like shifting shadows."

All goodness that flows into our world flows from God.

THE STREETS OF KAMPALA

I once shared a meal with Michael Badriaki at the home of mutual friends. Michael described how, in the 1990s, he'd worked at a grassroots level with churches, in collaboration with the Ugandan government's commission, to combat the epidemic of HIV/AIDS. During the first half of the decade, Uganda had one of the highest infection percentages in the world.

Traditionally, the streets and squares of the capital city of Kampala are lined with stands that sell fruit and vegetables. Michael told us, however, that during the height of the HIV/AIDS epidemic, he watched vendor after vendor convert their produce stands to sell a product with a booming market.

Coffins.

Michael paused for a long moment, reflecting on that era and on how much has changed, and then said, "We think of it now in terms of statistics, but the statistics don't have the tears."

Do I call Michael good? He doesn't want me to. He's made the story of his life the story of others, because as he says, "Human worth matters to me."

Justice for Michael is simple. He's discovered the source of goodness, and now he can't imagine doing anything other than serving God by serving others.

THE FEAR

"Be careful not to practice your righteousness in front of others to be seen by them. . . . But when you give to the needy, do not let your left hand know what your right hand is doing, so that your giving may be in secret. Then your Father, who sees what is done in secret, will reward you."

MATTHEW 6:1, 3–4

Why did Jesus say this? And why did Jesus often ask people to be silent about His miracles?

Perhaps the best acts of justice are beneath the surface.

I'm continually scared, in an age of celebrity, that I'll desire to be *seen* as just more than I'll desire to *be* just.

Once I watched a documentary about the nineteenth-century gold rush that brought people to San Francisco from all over the world. Some were still prospecting years later when the San Francisco earthquake, and the subsequent fires, destroyed much of the city.

Two brothers from Chile, who had traveled to San Francisco to seek their fortune, lost decades of work and savings. "We went out for wool," wrote one brother to family back in Chile, "and came back shorn."

Many of us go out pursuing justice, thinking we will find meaning and goodness in adopting a particular cause. We end up fatigued and burned-out. Like the Chilean brothers, we went looking for wool, but we came back shorn.

When I was writing this book, a friend of mine asked me several questions: "Why are people drawn to the concept of justice? Is it because their friends are, or because justice is the next 'it' thing to be involved in? Or is there an inherent desire in their hearts to change the world and make a difference?"

I think the answer is that we often are—and we should be—drawn to justice because of the image of God inside us.

The call to justice is a God-given whisper of what we were created for, a trace of God's true image in us that helps us believe we can be active participants in bringing about the goodness of God's kingdom.

I want to pursue justice because God is calling me, *and I want to be with God*. That is the only goal to which I want to give my life away.

THE PAGES OF LIFE

Any book is open to interpretation and misinterpretation. However, I hope some truths can't be missed:

All people matter to God.

All people deserve dignity.

All people need community, and community can be woven by justice or torn by injustice.

No matter who you are, the potential for justice and injustice surrounds you daily. And whether you are a dropout, a doctor, or a stay-at-home-parent, you can give your life away to ensure that justice prevails.

So, should we pack up and travel to the world's most dangerous places and engage purely in relief and development work? The answer, of course, is *no*. But also *yes*—and *maybe*.

The answer is based on context—your context. What gifts has God given *you*? What ways can you bring joy and peace to people? What relationships are you in?

If justice is going to happen in this world—if it's going to happen in you—it will start in the little things. Luke 16:10 says, "Whoever can be trusted with very little can also be trusted with much, and whoever is dishonest with very little will also be dishonest with much."

Start small. Value others. Focus more on your responsibilities and less on your rights.

When justice is a duty, it will weigh you down. When justice is the place where you are closest to God, giving your life away becomes your greatest delight.

We long to do good. We long to *be* good. But my friends in eastern Congo and Jesus and the prophet Micah and Michael Badriaki teach me that only God is good.

"Why do you call me good?" Jesus asks.

"No one is good—except God alone."

It is my prayer for all of us that this truth would transform the way we inhabit our lives. God does not call us to create our own goodness out of thin air, as if justice were something we could accomplish with a checklist and a bit of hard work.

Instead, God calls us to listen. The source of all goodness will surely have something to say about injustice. Then He calls us to obey. That is what it means to give our lives away. I pray each of us will have the faith to do this, on behalf of others and for the glory of God.

> Sing to the LORD!
>   Give praise to the LORD!
> He rescues the life of the needy
>   from the hands of the wicked.
>
> JEREMIAH 20:13

INTERLUDE

ONE FOR ONE

TOMS Shoes has a challenging motto: *One for One.*™ For every pair of shoes purchased, TOMS gives away a pair of shoes in a needy country. For every pair of glasses purchased, TOMS gives away a pair of glasses in a needy country.

Whatever you think about TOMS, the principle of active equality is compelling. It's a tangible representation of the golden rule. "One for one" is the mathematic equation behind "Love your neighbor as yourself."

In light of that, Tamara and I asked each other, "What if we created our own 'one for one' principle for our family?" What if we identified possessions and opportunities that symbolize blessing in our lives and made sure that, for each, we created a duplicate blessing for another? Once we began to live the principle, we learned it is a lot harder—and a lot better—than we had imagined.

The experiment began with a vacation. We've been blessed with a place to retreat in Southern California, so last year when we took our family vacation, we found a way to provide a vacation for another family we know in Palm Springs, California. Next came gardening. When we bought plants for our garden and flower beds, we purchased a gift card to the local home improvement store. We gave it to a young married couple we know who had plans to begin a vegetable garden—plans they'd been putting off for years because their need for basic necessities was more important. Then, when

167

our oldest daughter got braces, we worked with her orthodontist to sponsor a kid in our community who couldn't otherwise afford to have his or her teeth straightened.

As we've walked into the adventure of living "one for one," we've learned it isn't an exact science. A literal application of the principle would be unsustainable, both in terms of our finances and our family's time and energy. Tamara and I, along with our girls, simply talk and pray about what might be the best thing to do, and we try to follow where we feel God is guiding us.

The truth and beauty of "one for one" isn't found in a precise correspondence between everything we get and everything we give—rather, it's found in an ongoing willingness to transform our blessings into blessings for others.

In Romans 13:8, Paul wrote, "Let no debt remain outstanding, except the continuing debt to love one another, for whoever loves others has fulfilled the law." We're discovering that isn't so much an obligation as an opportunity.

Just as fruit contains seeds, every blessing from God contains an opportunity to plant the seed of another blessing. We're blessed so we can be a blessing.

Every blessing is an opportunity to be grateful. Every blessing is an opportunity to give.

ELEVEN

GOD'S LOVE LANGUAGE

The Love of Others in the Love of God

I have found the paradox that if I love until it hurts,
then there is no hurt, but only more love.[1]

MOTHER TERESA

The Bible tells us to love our neighbors, and also to love our
enemies; probably because they are generally the same people.[2]

G. K. CHESTERTON

HOW CAN THIS BE ORDINARY?

One of the most transformative moments in my life happened many years ago when I read a particular book. I'd been studying justice issues for some time, but studies and information on modern human trafficking were just beginning to be accessible. I knew sex slavery in particular had always existed, often called "white slavery," and it has been something that often hides in plain sight.

When I went to Disneyland and rode Pirates of the Caribbean

with my family, I cringed at what is meant to be a comic scene—women chased by men, tied up, and then paraded under a sign proclaiming, "Auction: Take a Wench for a Bride"—that masks a deeper, more painful history that none of us would treat as a laughing matter.[3] However, as I read this particular book about modern human trafficking, I was changed.

You can look into the statistics on your own if you have the courage. Suffice it to say they are horrifying. And each statistic hides the reality of a single woman or a single girl,[4] sometimes as young as six, who is taken from her family, imprisoned, and then raped every day—many times a day—until her body is destroyed and she is tossed into the streets. Or worse.

I finished the book without leaving my chair.

Although I had closed its cover, the story continued writing itself in my mind. Alone in the silence of my study, safe and secure, I pictured my daughters. They were safe and happy. I pictured the girls the book described, each of whom was someone else's daughter. How could we live in a world where such things happened? Where such things were increasing in frequency? Where such things were, in a twisted sense, almost normal? The very thought made me ill.

My first instinct was to do something. I knew I couldn't solve the issue from my study, but I had to do something, didn't I? If the book had shaken me up, it needed to shake up others. I wanted to buy twenty-five cases of the book and give one to everyone at my church. I wanted to blog about it. I wanted to start a nonprofit to fight sex trafficking.

Before I could *do* anything, however, I heard God asking me to wait. Not because actions weren't important, but because it was time for me to *feel* the injustice. It was time for me to understand that my heavenly Father felt every cry of pain and fear from every trafficked girl. He hated that evil, He hated the economic systems that enable modern-day slavery. He hated that His children were oppressed, violated, thrown away like trash. And He wanted me to feel that too.

Once, over lunch, a friend launched into a graphic description of a recent knee surgery. I set my sandwich down, untouched. You probably know what I said to him: "You ruined my appetite."

Before I read this book, I wanted a certain kind of life. I had specific dreams. Some of them were frivolous, like all of us have, but most of them were good ones. Dreams for ministry, church growth, and family. I had an appetite for success. But that night, when I first connected some of the most abhorrent evils in the world with my own daughters . . . well, it ruined my life because it ruined the appetites that governed my life. When the cover of that book closed, I was no longer able to stomach the things I used to desire.

I was ruined, for good.

THE PRINCIPLE OF EXTENSION

Suppose someone abducted one of my daughters and took her to a faraway place where I could not find her, and then harmed her. My person—my interest, my intention, my love—extends to my daughter, and therefore anyone who harms my child harms me. Anyone who could help my child but chooses not to also harms me. Conversely, anyone who helps my daughter helps me.

God feels the same way. This is the principle of extension: that God takes our actions personally when it affects His possessions and purposes.[5] It's as if we are acting toward Him.

God has made it abundantly clear that He loves all people with

perfect love. Therefore, harming any person means harming someone God loves. Ignoring him or her means ignoring someone God
loves. If we have the power to help someone God loves, and we
choose not to, we are refusing to help God.

> Whoever oppresses the poor shows contempt for their Maker,
>> but whoever is kind to the needy honors God. (Proverbs 14:31)

> Whoever is kind to the poor lends to the Lord,
>> and he will reward them for what they have done. (Proverbs
>> 19:17)

There is a direct reciprocity between God and those He loves.
To harm one is to harm the other; to love one is to love the other.
Someday our King will ask whether we loved the people He loves.
"Truly I tell you," He will say, "whatever you did for one of the least of
these brothers and sisters of mine, you did for me" (Matthew 25:40).

A covenant is a solemn, even sacred agreement. God has made
a covenant between Himself and His creation. God is redeeming
His creation, from plants to pandas to people. Scripture tells us
that God has a preferential option for the poor, the orphan, the
widow, the alien. That shouldn't surprise or offend us, because
we do as well. Don't we treat preferentially the one in the greatest
need? Don't we treat the broken bone before the headache, and
give food to the starving before helping the hungry? A preferential
option is not preferential love; rather, it is a natural part of the
economy of life.

Jesus preferred the skeptic and the sinner over the self-righteous.
He preferred the poor over the rich. He preferred everyone who was
living along the path that led to His Father's love.

Jesus doesn't command us to look after victims of sex

trafficking because it's a thankless task His Father doesn't want to do. He commands us because we are meant to participate with God in service that will bring us true fulfillment and liberate others. Justice is humanity collaborating with God in a covenant of love and care for all people. And God is inviting us to begin the journey toward justice where He is already, by the principle of extension: sitting in solidarity with the bruised and broken.

HURTING THE KINGDOM

The word *concern* comes from two Latin roots: *com*, meaning "with," and *cernere*, "to sift." Miners sift bits of gold from rock with vibrating conveyor belts or water-filled pans. In *Raiders of the Lost Ark*, Indiana Jones tries to sift just the right amount of sand through his fingers as he crouches before the booby-trapped pedestal where an idol rests. To feel *concern* is to do much the same thing.

When we are concerned about something, we sift our perceptions, our emotions, as we try to understand the subjective side of life. If a thing concerns us, it means it matters to us, and we care about it even if we don't know precisely what to do about it. A parent may be concerned for a child who is struggling to make new friends at school, yet have no clear path forward. When a thing does not concern us, it means it has sifted through our fingers like sand, and fallen to the floor.

How many of God's concerns no longer concern us? How many never did?

God's concern for people is infinite. There is no one outside His concern. God allows no person to slip through His fingers; He holds each of His children in the palm of His concern.

The more we know God, the more we understand what

concerns Him. The way to do more justice is not simply to *do* more justice—it is to grow closer to the heart of God. Guilt may motivate action now, but concern motivates a just life. Guilt is normal, but it can be debilitating over time.

God's kingdom and creation are coextensive with God, the King. His sphere of concern extends to the ends of the earth. God's being and character aim at a particular end—at redemption and the restoration of *shalom*. If we are not aimed at the same end, in dynamic partnership with God, we are *necessarily* working against His concerns. It is like two mountain climbers roped together as they advance toward the summit; if one climber decides to stop climbing or to descend back to the valley, that climber is necessarily working against the first climber's purpose.

We tread lightly when we know someone truly loves something. When the college student parks beside you in his cherry '65 Mustang, you take care not to ding the doors. Even though the car is not his actual person, if something happens to it, he'll take it personally. His sphere of concern covers his car.

Relationships intensify this concern. And God has made it abundantly clear that His sphere of concern extends to all people, with a Father's preferential treatment for those who need Him most. "For the LORD your God is God of gods and Lord of lords, the great God, mighty and awesome, who shows no partiality and accepts no bribes. He defends the cause of the fatherless and the widow, and loves the foreigner residing among you, giving them food and clothing" (Deuteronomy 10:17–18).

Are you harming the subjects of God's kingdom? Are you refusing to help the men and women He loves through your neglect, ignorance, or selfishness?

When you hurt the kingdom, you hurt the King.

RIGHTEOUS ANGER

Understanding God's sphere of love and concern reveals the difference between righteous and unrighteous anger. While anger is an emotion that usually rends the fabric of a group or institution—as when an angry child kicks in a sand castle—the righteous anger we see from God, the prophets, and even Jesus is a reaction to the perversion of God's plan.

Anger rips. Righteous anger mends. Anger normally protects its own interest, but righteous anger fights for the interest of others who are oppressed. It's the anger my daughter Esther felt when she asked me, "Daddy, why did some people think it was okay to steal other people?" Slavery isn't okay; she knew that, and that made her angry. Righteously angry, just as God is.

God's righteous anger should elicit the same emotion in us.

Are we advocating for God's kingdom? Are we angry about the things that anger Him? Are we *really* loving as God loves? Are we speaking His "love language"?

A SIXTH LOVE LANGUAGE

The five love languages are familiar to many of us from the *New York Times* best seller by Dr. Gary Chapman of the same name. Each love language is a way a lover expresses love to his or her beloved. They are (1) words of affirmation, (2) quality time, (3) receiving gifts, (4) acts of service, and (5) physical touch.[6] We can picture these working (and needing work!) in our own relationships. The insight that love can be expressed through varied forms is profound, and it has helped countless people understand their relationships.

When a wife feels that her husband does not express his love for her enough because he rarely says, "I love you," sometimes the truth is that he is declaring his love every time he washes her car.

What links the five love languages, despite their differences, is that they are all personal and relational. They are all direct. We speak, spend time, give and receive gifts, serve, and touch people we love, whether they are our spouses, children, parents, or friends.

What I've wondered lately is this: What if there is a sixth love language we've been missing?

One summer, several of our Antioch interns stayed at a rental home owned by one of our friends, and they were asked to take care of the lawn. None of the interns knew the owner.

When the interns left at the end of the summer, the lawn was the color of dirt.

Even though the owner made it clear that his sphere of concern extended to the lawn, the interns' concern stopped short of that. When we don't love someone else's sphere of concern, it's usually because we love the sphere of our own concern too much. Did the interns actively hate the green lawn? Did they long to harm the owner? No. But as a result of their inaction, they destroyed the lawn, and in so doing harmed the owner. Their own sphere of concern— their internship, building friendships with other interns, exploring Bend and having fun outdoors—was too small to encompass what their benefactor said *he* cared about.

The interns claimed it was nobody's fault that the lawn died. I'd say the opposite: it was the fault of everyone who lived there. Killing the lawn was abuse by omission. In other words, the interns needed a sixth love language, a love language that could be expressed to a stranger and that would motivate them to go beyond simply avoiding harm to actually doing good.

I wonder if that love language is justice.

We can unpack this by looking at Hosea 6:6, where God revealed what active love should look like. "I desire mercy, not sacrifice, and acknowledgment of God rather than burnt offerings." This was making a correlation between His desire for mercy and an acknowledgment of Himself. Mercy, evidently, is an *acknowledgment* of God.

An acknowledgment of what, exactly? Of God's existence? Of His omniscience?

No, our mercy—which is the visible and just outworking of a tender and loving heart—is an acknowledgment that *God is love.* That He cares for people. That He has asked for and commanded our love and that we hear His words, understand the import behind them, and care enough about Him to follow through.

When we have mercy and we forgive others, love them, bear with them, and lift them up, we are affirming or acknowledging what God desires.

Our love spotlights God's love. And our mercy gives testimony to God's mercy. But to take it farther, our love must enact *justice,* because our justice equates to love. God doesn't ask us to only love those who love us, or those who are easy to love. God asks us to learn a new love language, one we can speak to His entire kingdom.

IT'S NOT ABOUT ME

My three-year-old recently broke her arm. That wasn't the first time she'd hurt herself, and it likely won't be the last. When I want her to stay safe, sometimes I say to my ten-year-old, "Mary Joy, I need you to protect your little sister." Mary Joy is not the focus of my intention, or my attention, even though I am speaking directly to her and giving her a direct command. My priority is keeping Mary Joy's little sister safe—something that's best accomplished when Mary Joy, the strong, protects her little sister, the weak.

When God commands us to serve others, it's not about us.

That's part of what the Pharisees and religious rulers got so spectacularly wrong, and Jesus called them on it every chance he got, sometimes by using the words of the Prophets. The Pharisees thought God's commands existed to govern—and ultimately approve—their personal relationships with God, rather than understanding the infinitely bigger picture: that God's commands had far more to do with others.

When my children are outside my direct control, like when they're playing down the street or home with a babysitter, I erect rules and boundaries to keep them as safe as possible; I use my parental authority to issue commands to others to ensure the satisfactory treatment of those I love. God has issued similar commands to help protect His children and help them flourish. We receive those commands—to love, to serve, to be merciful—not primarily as a way to guarantee or prove our individual righteousness, but rather so we can live for the sake of others, living and dying for bigger things.

Proverbs 22:2 tells us that "rich and poor have this in common: the LORD is the Maker of them all." Psalm 146:9 reminds us that "the LORD watches over the sojourners; he upholds the widow and the fatherless, but the way of the wicked he brings to ruin" (ESV). Psalm 68:5 declares that "a father to the fatherless, a defender of widows, is God in his holy dwelling." And Jeremiah 21:12 insists that we "administer justice every morning; rescue from the hand of the oppressor the one who has been robbed, or my wrath will break out and burn like fire because of the evil you have done—burn with no one to quench it."

So every day we wake up and ask, "What is right? What is just? Where is God, and what does He care about? How do I labor to be the kind of person who makes God's world a just world? How can I work to redeem and reconcile people trapped in sin and systems and help bring about *shalom*?" We ask these questions at the office, in the car, at school, and on vacation.

Loving our own, and responding politely to those who injure us, is not the limit of what Christ called us to. He called us to a radical ministry of reconciliation. We're not asked to avoid harming others; we're commanded to do good.

The ethical demands of God's love force us into the awkward position of not just changing one or two behaviors, but of revaluating our entire framework of life. God's love, on one hand, is overwhelming and crushing; on the other, liberating and joyous.

Do we love God when we love others? Does God receive love from us, even when He is not the direct object of our time and energy? Yes. This is the truth of Matthew 25.

It's surprising, but the word *orphan* is used far less in Scripture than the word *fatherless*. In America, we think orphans have no parents. In some cultures, however, an orphan is someone who's lost *a* parent. Often the father provides the resources and social position to protect and provide for his children. When a child loses a father, the child often loses opportunities to thrive, or even to experience basic levels of comfort. In certain cultures, a fatherless child has lost the fullness of what it means to be inside another's sphere of concern. God's preferential love seeks out the fatherless. *I've got them now,* God says, *in My sphere of perfect concern, and I'm asking for your help.*

Imagine a single mom. Her eleven-year-old loves baseball. She doesn't give a flying you-know-what about baseball, but because her son loves it, she hasn't missed a game in over two seasons. Sometimes she has to work double shifts to make sure she's free, but when the umpire yells, "Play ball!" she's always sitting right behind the dugout, cheering for her boy. If a man begins to date that single mom, if he says he loves her, he must love her son. Period. The mom's sphere of concern wraps around her boy's life, and it always will. So if this man wants to tell the single mom that he loves her, without being a liar, he must be right there at the ball game, beside the mom, cheering for her son.

If we care about the kingdom, we work toward the same end as the King. If we love someone, we love what that person loves. God is absolutely clear about who and what He loves.

Who and what do you love?

Beloved, let us love one another, for love is from God,
and whoever loves has been born of God and knows God.

1 JOHN 4:7 ESV

MONSTERS

I was in my living room early one morning when my oldest daughter, Mary Joy, entered. She was terrified because of a nightmare about monsters.

Have you thought about monsters? It seems as if every scary thing is a twisted caricature of what is whole and complete. A monster is a perversion of a good creature or a good person. Similarly, evil often takes the shattered or deficient shape of what once was good.

Saint Augustine believed that evil doesn't exist independently, but parasitically, as the twisting of good. If this is true, spiritual growth involves the unbending of what is twisted, an unbending that happens only through the work of God's Spirit. Becoming like Christ means becoming what God originally intended for us to be before sin bent us.

Too often, however, we approach spiritual growth as a chase. We run and hide from monsters, real and imagined, just as Adam and Eve hid from God in the garden. Yet in this world there is nowhere we can run, nowhere we can hide, that will be free of monsters. Often they live within us. Other times the monsters aren't meant only to frighten us—they're meant to point us to the reality that our entire world needs to be remade and straightened by God's power.

Which is what we need as well.

Perhaps there was a hint of all this as I held my daughter in the

La-Z-Boy™ that morning. I rocked her in my lap, her small body curled into the shape of mine.

"Mary Joy, you are so very special, and I love you."

I whispered nothing to her about monsters and whether they were real, nothing about whether they could reach her. Rather, I whispered to her about the reality of goodness, and that she could reach it.

TWELVE

THE ANATOMY OF APATHY

How We Settle for Less than the Golden Rule

The Negro's great stumbling block in the stride toward freedom
is not the White Citizens Councilor or the Ku Klux Klanner
but the white moderate who is more devoted to order than to
justice.[1]

MARTIN LUTHER KING JR.

The sad truth is that most evil is done by people
who never make up their minds to be either good or evil.[2]

HANNAH ARENDT

In a case that is often cited as an example of the "bystander
effect," a woman in Queens, New York, was attacked repeatedly over the course of thirty minutes while dozens of people
nearby either saw or heard what was happening. No one physically
intervened, and the police were not sufficiently alerted.

This wasn't an isolated event. Every day, people witness

preventable crimes or tragedies and do nothing. A bystander may be willing to call 911, yet often allows that single action to be the extent of his or her responsibility.

There are at least two assumptions present in the bystander effect. The first is that if there are many people who *could* do something, I don't have to. The second is that if *I* am not the one committing the crime, I don't carry any guilt for the crime's occurrence.

If we do the minimum we think is required of us, we can believe we have done enough. If we avoid doing something bad, we can believe we are good people.

If the "moral arc of the *universe* bends toward justice,"[3] as Martin Luther King Jr. so eloquently expressed, then why does *our* moral arc bend toward apathy?

THE COMMAND TO LOVE

In Leviticus 19:18, we read God's command to "love your neighbor as yourself." Jesus repeated this command in Matthew 22:39.[4] This principle exists in many cultures, and is sometimes known as the *ethic of reciprocity*. We know it as the golden rule: *Do unto others as you would have them do unto you.*[5]

American culture, however, has twisted the golden rule into the silver rule: *Do not do unto others as you would not have them do unto you.* And that one extra word—*not*—makes all the difference.

The golden rule requires action—*do* unto others—while the silver rule allows for passivity and neutrality. The golden rule makes just actions necessary, while the silver rule can allow just actions to be optional. We like to talk about the golden rule, but we often *live* the silver rule. That's because, though the silver rule prohibits directly wronging or harming someone, it doesn't require us to intervene in injustice. It may keep me from stealing, but it doesn't demand that I share or give to someone in need.

A preference for the silver rule is subtle, but I can even see it in the way my girls sometimes do their chores. Recently I told one of my daughters to pick up the dirty clothes on the floor of her room. Several minutes later, when I went to check on her, I had to step over several crumpled-up shirts in the hallway outside her door. She glanced up at me as I entered.

"What?" she asked. "*What?*"

I looked down at the dirty clothes in the hallway.

"Those?" she said. "But you told me to pick up the clothes in my *room!*"

The golden rule—do unto others as you would have them do unto you—tells us to do good, no matter what. The silver rule, however, sanctions indifference. It requires obedience to the minimum being asked for. The golden rule, on the other hand, seeks to do the fullness at the heart of what is being asked for.

If my daughter is told to pick up the floor of her room, all she must do is keep a tiny fraction of a tiny rule. *Dad said to pick up the clothes on my floor, so that's all I have to do.* According to the silver rule, picking up the dirty clothes three feet away in the hallway wasn't necessary. The golden rule, of course, would have prompted her to pick up all of her dirty clothes that she saw—and probably even some of her sister's dirty clothes without being asked.

Whether we're talking about household chores or the serious injustices that mar our relationships and our world, there is a crucial difference between gold and silver: "Do good" versus "Don't do bad" or "Do the minimum good." It isn't just dirty clothes that don't get picked up because of apathy.

THE NEED TO BE IN NEED

A subtle reason for apathy is that justice rarely has much to do with our daily lives. Unless we've personally been victims of injustice, we can take for granted that life is generally fair.

If we aren't in a truly vulnerable position, the real victim of a genuine injustice, then our felt needs simply don't connect us with the suffering of others. Instead, our felt needs focus on what *we* need at any given moment to feel convenient and comfortable. Just as empathy connects us with the suffering of others, so apathy prevents us from connecting with anything beyond our immediate desires. One of the greatest obstacles to real, biblical justice is simply its apparent lack of relevance to our daily lives.

This brings to mind G. K. Chesterton's challenge to his contemporaries who doubted the validity of Christianity in Edwardian England. "The Christian ideal has not been tried and found wanting. It has been found difficult; and left untried."[6]

The *Christian* ideal is truth and justice expressed through love; apathy is dogma and indifference expressed through self-interest.

The problem with apathy toward justice is that it becomes unsustainable when we become the ones in need. When we finally experience injustice—or when we finally feel empathy with a single human being suffering injustice—detachment is no longer an option. This is highlighted by the following lines of poetry, attributed to Martin Niemöller, a German Lutheran pastor during the Nazi regime:

> First they came for the socialists,
> and I didn't speak out because I wasn't a socialist.

Then they came for the trade unionists,
and I didn't speak out because I wasn't a trade unionist.
Then they came for the Jews,
and I didn't speak out because I wasn't a Jew.
Then they came for me,
and there was no one left to speak out for me.[7]

Apathy is sustainable only as long as injustice doesn't harm us—and we don't care that it's harming others. Apathy lasts only until injustice knocks on our door, and we're forced to look into its eyes.

Apathy seems far different from injustice. When I actually *commit* an injustice, I'm sinning in a way that's gross and obvious. Such actions violate the golden rule *and* the silver rule. Harming others is overt. And if someone called such actions evil—if someone called *me* evil for doing those things—that person would be right. Apathy feels different. It isn't gross and obvious—it's refined, subtle . . . even acceptable sometimes. Yet just how different *is* apathy from injustice? Suppose we drive the speed limit and serve on the PTA—can we ignore workers' rights on coffee farms in Guatemala? Suppose we go to church every Sunday and sponsor a neighborhood kid in her Jog-A-Thon—can we ignore the plight of Native American kids one county over who are desperate to get a quality education?

Apathy only requires us to not intentionally harm others. Anyone who isn't actively evil can be exonerated by following silver rules. At the end of the day—of almost any day, regardless of what we have done or left undone—apathy tells us that it's perfectly acceptable to live with illusions of our own justice.

Sometimes we start to believe our own propaganda.

RECONCILING PRAYER

When I witnessed Cambodian girls enslaved by sex trafficking, it changed the way I understood my own prayers.

Every day, young girls, like the ones I witnessed in Phnom Penh, utter cries only God hears and shed tears only God sees. The same could be said of a young man wrongfully accused of a crime and unable to afford effective representation, or the worker being discriminated against because of her ethnicity or gender. I reflected on the cumulative magnitude of their prayers. God hears the cry of the oppressed, and at the same time, God hears my prayers.

I was shocked to realize that my prayers, that I'd always thought of as spiritual, might in fact be discordant noise in the mind of God, who is attuned to the urgent pleas of the vulnerable—my requests in one ear, their cries in the other.

In my life I have prayed for small favors from God, asking God to help me endure a cold during a busy week at work or to help me do well on something for which I didn't prepare. These requests mattered to me at the time. They even seemed urgent. Yet witnessing the evil in which the Cambodian girls were trapped forced me to ask God if my prayers were creating dissonance.

I began to critique my own prayers, striving to pray in harmony with God's heart and the needs in God's world. When I have all I truly *need*, surely prayers in concert with the heart of God will be prayers in which I offer my time, energy, and resources to participate dynamically with God. Surely they are prayers in which I can be part of the answer to the cries of those in desperate need.

My mind pictured the great irony of this by crafting a mental image of two teenage girls, one huddled in a brothel and the other curled in a comfortable bed. The girl in the brothel utters a cry for help, while the other girl prays that God will give her a new car. Both girls are expressing felt needs, but seeing the juxtaposition of those needs in my mind highlights the dissonance. This mental image—which Jessie Fleury helped me illustrate in the picture below—causes me to ask myself, "When I pray, where am I on the continuum?"

If we realize that God sees both girls, and is specially present with the suffering and vulnerable, shouldn't that begin to redirect selfish and self-directed prayers? However imperfect my prayer life is, I want to learn how to pray more and more in concert with God's knowledge of and will for His world.

This dissonance reveals the difference between the golden rule and the silver rule in our families, our communities, and the entire world. Avoiding bad allows us to keep our hands clean. Doing good often asks us to get our hands dirty—but that's how *shalom* spreads.

It's easy to defend our adherence to the silver rule. *My wife started the argument . . . I'm not equipped to help those kids who are dropping out of school . . . It's not like I caused the earthquake.* As long as we're not the ones instigating the problem, we tell ourselves there *is* no problem—those are issues for others to work out, because we have enough issues of our own.

We see this in Luke 11. Jesus had been speaking to crowds about difficult topics, and now He was sitting down to a well-deserved meal, only to have the resident religious experts find something wrong with His behavior. Jesus hadn't washed His hands, yet He was getting ready to eat, to which His host, a Pharisee, loudly drew attention. Jesus was hungry, but He was willing to go a few rhetorical rounds—and when we read what He had to say, we learn something profound about the difference between the golden and silver rules.

"Now then," began Jesus in Luke 11:39, "you Pharisees clean the outside of the cup and dish, but inside you are full of greed and wickedness." Jesus then connected the Pharisees' thoughts and motivations with their public actions, saying, "Did not the one who made the outside make the inside also?" (v. 40).

The Pharisees were fond of asking tough questions, but I imagine that when the tables were turned, they hemmed and hawed. It's easy for us to dismiss the Pharisees' complaint against Jesus—that He was breaking ritual purity laws—because we see such issues as outdated and irrelevant. How many of us would suggest that digging into a meal when you're hungry without washing your hands is a sin?

Jesus didn't stop there, however. He continued in verse 41: "But now as for what is inside you—be generous to the poor, and everything will be clean for you."

Jesus went straight to the heart in verse 42, noting the difference between the Pharisees' outward purity and what was really inside them. "Woe to you Pharisees, because you give God a tenth of your mint, rue and all other kinds of garden herbs, but you neglect justice and the love of God." Jesus drew an indelible link between the Pharisees' outward actions and the motivation in their hearts. They were living by the silver rule, and kicking the golden rule by the wayside. Then He drove His final point home: "You should have practiced the latter without leaving the former undone."

To summarize, let's look at what Jesus didn't say. He didn't say, "Worry about external purity—that's what makes you righteous." He didn't say, "Practice justice, but don't bother about external purity."

What He did say, in so many words, was, "Practice justice *and* keep the law."

Earlier I mentioned James's definition of pure religion: "Religion that God our Father accepts as pure and faultless is this: to look after orphans and widows in their distress . . ." That verse finishes with a second requirement, one that mirrors the way Jesus confronted the Pharisees: ". . . and to keep oneself from being polluted by the world" (James 1:27).

Jesus and James both made it clear that we cannot artificially separate morality and justice. We need to practice justice *and* keep the law, both in terms of personal morality and in terms of ethics— the way morality extends to society. If doing justice is a rescue boat we steer into the storm of injustice, personal morality ensures that the hull is sound and watertight.

Personal morality and ethics dovetail. Both are part of our full understanding of justice, and neither can be achieved when we allow apathy to keep us on the sidelines.

GOLDEN GUILT

The golden rule requires me to love, give, sacrifice, serve, initiate, speak up, create, listen, practice justice, and much more. The silver rule only requires me to not harm anyone.

Some days, to be honest, the silver rule seems appealing. I could wake up, eat breakfast while reading a book, and head out the door to my office. Doing what I just described wouldn't harm anyone. Since I didn't commit any obvious evil before I arrived at the office, I could consider myself a pretty good person.

Is that an easy life? A doable life? Yes, but that doesn't describe my best life. What opportunities to do good am I missing when I choose silver? What opportunities to serve and bless my family am I neglecting, for example, even as I'm eating breakfast and getting ready for work?

Yet the golden rule is difficult to practice. Every time we fail to treat others as we would like to be treated, we get farther from the ideal. The gap between what we ought to be doing and what we're *actually* doing causes us to feel guilty. Since we don't enjoy feeling guilty, we ignore the golden rule. No golden rule means no guilt. But still, we know we're supposed to be following *some* rule . . . which is why we latch on to the silver rule. We can keep it without leaving the house. We can keep it while eating lunch in our cubicle at work. We can go through entire *days* without breaking the silver rule. Since we can follow it so well, we must be doing something right. Perhaps we're righteous after all, and we have nothing to feel guilty about.

Or perhaps not.

We Christians can sometimes jump the gun in declaring ourselves righteous. If there's a chance to separate people into binary categories—good and bad, righteous and unrighteous—most of the time we think we're pretty good. In Matthew 25:31–46, Jesus tells a parable about this very thing. It makes a profound point, and it is worth reading in its entirety.

"When the Son of Man comes in his glory, and all the angels with him, he will sit on his glorious throne. All the nations will be gathered before him, and he will separate the people one from another as a shepherd separates the sheep from the goats. He will put the sheep on his right and the goats on his left.

"Then the King will say to those on his right, 'Come, you who are blessed by my Father; take your inheritance, the kingdom prepared for you since the creation of the world. For I was hungry and you gave me something to eat, I was thirsty and you gave me something to drink, I was a stranger and you invited me in, I needed clothes and you clothed me, I was sick and you looked after me, I was in prison and you came to visit me.'

"Then the righteous will answer him, 'Lord, when did we see you hungry and feed you, or thirsty and give you something to drink? When did we see you a stranger and invite you in, or needing clothes and clothe you? When did we see you sick or in prison and go to visit you?'

"The King will reply, 'Truly I tell you, whatever you did for one of the least of these brothers and sisters of mine, you did for me.'

"Then he will say to those on his left, 'Depart from me, you who are cursed, into the eternal fire prepared for the devil and his angels. For I was hungry and you gave me nothing to eat, I was thirsty and you gave me nothing to drink, I was a stranger and you did not invite me in, I needed clothes and you did not clothe me, I was sick and in prison and you did not look after me.'

"They also will answer, 'Lord, when did we see you hungry or thirsty or a stranger or needing clothes or sick or in prison, and did not help you?'

"He will reply, 'Truly I tell you, whatever you did not do for one of the least of these, you did not do for me.'

"Then they will go away to eternal punishment, but the righteous to eternal life."

We like to think we get to heaven by knowing about God or calling ourselves Christians. Who, then, according to this parable, is invited into the Father's kingdom to receive a reward? Those who acted with justice and love to the vulnerable: the hungry, the stranger, the poor, the diseased, the imprisoned. Why? Because what they did for the vulnerable was received as if it were done for God, and what was not done for the vulnerable was received by God as harm produced by apathy.

Matthew 25 demonstrates the principle of extension that we looked at in chapter 11: *God takes our actions personally when it affects His possessions and purposes. It's as if we are acting toward Him.*

Earlier in Matthew, in His seminal teaching that came to be known as the Sermon on the Mount, Jesus defined the golden rule as "so in everything, do to others what you would have them do to you, for this sums up the Law and the Prophets" (7:12). This is a shocking statement—the "Law and the Prophets" represents countless generations of religious, ethical, and prophetic teaching. Yet Jesus summed all of that up with a single rule of action: *do* to others what you would have them *do* to you.

What do you want out of life? The same thing everyone wants:

health, freedom, good relationships, happiness, a chance to work and meet your needs. And what do you want when you are somehow deprived of these things? You want someone to help you restore them. You want someone to enter into relationship with you for the purpose of restoring justice to your life. When you're starving, when you're impoverished, when you're sick or in prison, who will help you: someone following the silver rule or someone following the golden rule?

Matthew 25 highlights a wonderful truth for us: following the golden rule counts as loving others *and* loving God. The connection is direct. "Truly I tell you," the King will say, "whatever you did for one of the least of these brothers and sisters of mine, you did for me." God never asks us to choose between *doing* justice and *loving* Him. In fact, He asks the exact opposite—He asks us to do both at once.

In Jesus' parable of the sheep and the goats, the ones considered righteous go to eternal life. The righteous are the ones who are given the Father's inheritance, "the kingdom prepared for you since the creation of the world" (v. 34). The righteous are the ones who give their lives away in acts of service and justice to the vulnerable on earth. They are the ones who follow the golden rule, no matter where it takes them.

I find it interesting that the unrighteous in this parable, those who are separated from God and "go away to eternal punishment" (v. 46), followed the silver rule. They may have even followed it perfectly. "Lord, when did we see you hungry or thirsty or a stranger or needing clothes or sick or in prison, and did not help you?" they ask (v. 44). They didn't personally *harm* the hungry, the stranger, the poor, the diseased, or the imprisoned.

Many societies in the world—including ours—are increasingly

governed by what the nineteenth-century economist and philosopher John Stuart Mill termed the "harm principle,"[8] which goes something like this: in a free society, a citizen can act with freedom, provided that citizen's actions do not harm other citizens. A clear example of this is America's stance on cigarette smoking. When cigarettes were considered harmless, or when it was thought they only harmed the smoker, antismoking laws were virtually nonexistent. When a series of authoritative studies were released proving that second-hand smoke harmed others, the attitude changed in less than a generation. Today, smoking is illegal in many public places—in some states it is illegal in *all* public spaces—because we know it harms others.

Yet justice and righteousness require more than not harming another, as Matthew 25 makes clear. Justice and righteousness require us to stand for and with the vulnerable. Jesus is asking us to do more than avoid harming others. He's saying that the only way to know His Father is to give our lives away to others and to do good to others—and by extension, to do good to our Father.

REVERSING THE QUESTION

Martin Luther King Jr. was assassinated on April 4, 1968. The day before he was gunned down, he spoke at a church in Memphis, Tennessee. In what is now known as the "I've Been to the Mountaintop" speech, King discussed Jesus' parable of the good Samaritan. He listed traditional reasons to "determine why the priest and the Levite didn't stop": they were late for a religious meeting, perhaps, or maybe purity laws prevented them from touching the wounded and bleeding man on the side of the road.

King then took a turn for the personal. "But I'm going to tell you what my imagination tells me. It's possible that [the men who didn't stop to help the victim] were afraid. You see, the Jericho Road is a dangerous road."

Fear can stop justice in its tracks. *What if the same people who attacked the man are waiting to attack* me? *What if the injured man is only faking in order to lure me to him so I can become his victim?*

I think of the words inscribed at the United States Holocaust Memorial Museum: "Thou shalt not be a victim. Thou shalt not be a perpetrator. Above all, thou shalt not be a bystander." I wonder how many times fear or apathy has created bystanders?

King concluded this section of his speech with an insightful and powerful analysis of the self-interest and fear that often keep us from acting on behalf of others. "And so the first question that the priest asked, the first question that the Levite asked was, 'If I stop to help this man, what will happen to me?' But then the Good Samaritan came by, and he reversed the question: 'If I do not stop to help this man, what will happen to *him*?'"[9]

We can always find a way to rationalize unlove.

We may not *choose* apathy, but when we choose *anything* other than love and empathetic justice, we get apathy by default.

> If anyone has material possessions and sees a
> brother or sister in need but has no pity on them,
> how can the love of God be in that person?
>
> 1 JOHN 3:17

RACE IN AMERICA

A conversation with Lisa Sharon Harper, founding member and board member of Evangelicals4Justice, as well as author of *Left, Right & Christ: Evangelical Faith in Politics* and *Evangelical Does Not Equal Republican or Democrat.* She is currently director of mobilizing for Sojourners.

Lisa, in what ways is racism still an issue in our country?

It's common to assume that ending racism in America or the church really only involves ending individual prejudice. But racism, by definition, is the use of one's power to actively or passively keep another group down. Our most common picture of racism is the guys in the pointy hats who live in a black-and-white world. But the problem of race in America has shape-shifted since then. Now it's not only about people's individual prejudices—though that is still an issue—but it's also about unjust systems and structures that have been put in place over time.

Sometimes the crafters of these policies, laws, and structures intentionally created systems to make life easier for some over others. Other times inequity was an unintentional result. What's important, though, is that these structures are still in place. They have not yet been dismantled. So we might be living our lives not knowing that we have benefited from stuff put in place a long time ago that just never got taken off the books or dismantled. And at the same time, the person of color who sits next to us in the pew might be struggling to navigate the obstacles, hurt, and pain that are the products of those same systems.

Until we dismantle policies, laws, and structures that intentionally or unintentionally result in inequitable access, race will still be a problem in America.

And I'm not talking about equality of *outcome*. No one is saying that every person in America should or will have the same salary, or that everyone wants and deserves a two-car garage and a home in the suburbs. Some want to farm, and some want to live in the city. We want to work at different things. But I am saying that our policies, laws, and structures must call for equity of *access* to the dream for everyone. We are all, after all, created in the image of God.

How does following Jesus change how we love our neighbor?

If we say we are followers of Jesus, we must say that we are trying to love our neighbor. But that begs the question, which neighbor? Is it my neighbor next door or the one who lives on the other side of the tracks? Is it only my neighbor who is middle everything— middle-class, middle America, middle-aged—or is it my neighbor who is poor as well? And it has to be a both/and! We are *all* created in God's image. So when we say we follow Jesus, and we say we are trying to love our neighbor, we have to look at how our hands and feet and votes are affecting our neighbors.

Jesus talks about this in the parable of the good Samaritan. He talks about costly love, love without limits. Sometimes we're content to hold the living water Jesus promised in our own personal cup. But that living water is supposed to be a geyser, gushing out into *all* of life, with the intent to love not only the people who are like us, but people who are unlike us, and even our enemies. I think we can measure the volume of our love by how far our love reaches from our own spheres of concern.

What encourages you when you think about race in America?
I am genuinely encouraged by many of the young people I meet in our country. They are the most diverse generation in American history and, as a result, they're having more interactions with people different than themselves. They have an openness and they care about poverty and immigration and the victims of sex trafficking and creation care. They care about all injustice, and that gives me hope. They know they are part of *systems* that are unjust, and they understand that those systems need to be confronted. They genuinely want to be among "the just ones," even if it comes at a cost.

If you could say one thing to American Christians, what would it be?
We need to return to teaching Scripture. We have a scripturally anemic church. Think about this: John, in Scripture, says that Jesus *is* the Word! And here we, as a church, have basically tossed out serious study of God's Word. We have fill-in-the-blank study guides, and we quote verses out of context. You know it's bad when people are so starved for Scripture that they feel like fill-in-the-blanks are helpful. Scripture is supposed to be a *feast*! We have fed folks appetizers so often that they've started to think that's the whole meal. It's not.

In the evangelical church especially, one of our markers is that Scripture is supposed to be our highest authority, yet so many of us don't know how to read it well. We need really good biblical teaching. We need God to give us a new, more holistic hermeneutic. We need eyes to see in Scripture what we've missed before, especially God's value and design for *all* people. We've lost our way, and too often our highest authority has become self-interest or money or political ideology. I wonder sometimes if those things can rule the people in the pews more than Scripture does.

What portion of Scripture is foundational to the way you understand justice?

For me, it all begins with the creation story in Genesis 1. When humans are created in the image of God, it's such a high point in the story that the text breaks into song! Being created in the image of God affects *everything*. The homeless guy pushing the shopping cart and the CEO on Wall Street are both made in the image of God, so at the most fundamental level of their existence, they are equal, and therefore deserve equal protection and opportunity under the law—and equal love.

At the end of the day, I think that if Jesus can defeat *death*, He can certainly defeat *dysfunction*! He's been to the very bottom, and we can be hopeful that He can defeat what we're dealing with.*

---

* For more on this theme, see Lisa Sharon Harper's *Left, Right & Christ: Evangelical Faith in Politics and Evangelical Does Not Equal Republican or Democrat* (New York: The New Press, 2008).

JUSTICE IN SOCIETY
Why Justice Is Always Social

I think the first duty of society is justice.[1]

ALEXANDER HAMILTON

Justice in the life and conduct of the State is possible only as
first it resides in the hearts and souls of the citizens.[2]

PLATO

I n what evangelical historian Timothy L. Smith referred to as
"the great reversal,"[3] a phrase later echoed by theologian John
Stott, the twentieth century saw liberal Christians claim love
and justice as primary concerns and conservative Christians claim
evangelism and missions.

While Christianity has been known historically for unifying
"heavenly" and "earthly" concerns, the polarization of the liberal/
conservative split in the last hundred years has resulted in a swath
of evangelicals overemphasizing "spiritual" matters at the expense
of the charity and justice that have been hallmarks of the church.
Some in the conservative church have focused so intently on the

heavenly kingdom that redeeming earthly culture and structures has fallen by the wayside.[4]

We'll see in this chapter that much of the current division surrounding justice is due to what is called the "social gospel." Many today view the function of justice in society through the lens of a late-nineteenth and early-twentieth-century movement called the social gospel, even though the two subjects are not synonymous. Consequently, the Christian call to do justice in society can generate more heat and disagreement than it should.

When we identify certain political views with the social gospel or the phrase "social justice," we tend to allow arguments over *means* to keep us from the biblical *end* of a just society. We confuse the politics and policies of justice with the *need* for justice. This is like confusing specific exercise plans (means) with the need to get in shape (ends). The former is a way of implementing the latter, but not synonymous with it.

In the following sections, I'll trace the history of the social gospel and the origin of the phrase "social justice." Then I'll suggest a way forward using careful definitions, a balanced approach to history and theology, and an open ear to the calling of Scripture. It is my hope that we can find areas of common cause that cross the political spectrum and unite us around following the example of Jesus.

TOO RISKY?

The first time I heard the phrase "social gospel," it was said with a bit of a sneer—with the kind of tone some Christians reserve for concepts that reek of heresy or compromise. As time went on, I was taught that the social gospel was something sinister, a grand conspiracy that used

Christian language to defend a project devoid of Christ. This fear of the social gospel only grew as I continued learning and serving in conservative churches, extending itself to nearly anything associated with "the world" or even with justice itself. Doctrine and evangelism were safe, but altruism—or selflessly loving people in society, to put it another way—seemed too risky.

I once suggested that our church give Christmas trees to single moms and widows and offer to hang their Christmas lights for them, but the senior pastor shot down the idea. Since I didn't also have a strategy to get the single moms and widows into church and "save" them, my plan was just social gospel.

This chapter is about justice in society—often referred to as *social justice* since justice is fundamentally and intrinsically relational and built into the fabric of society. I'm going to begin with a concise overview of the history of the social gospel because it's linguistically similar to the phrase "social justice." Though the social gospel and social justice are not the same thing, they share a common focus on social action.

Additionally, I believe the fear and mistrust I encountered and continue to encounter regarding justice have a great deal to do with a misunderstanding of what the social gospel was and is—a conflation of what is clearly good and what is, rightly, controversial.

A BRIEF SKETCH OF THE SOCIAL GOSPEL MOVEMENT

The social conditions of the late 1800s gave rise to the social gospel movement. America was in a state of rapid social transition as industrialization led to rapid urbanization. Living conditions in the cities were often squalid, and working conditions were worse.

Factory workers, including vast numbers of women and children, worked up to fifteen hours a day, six days a week. That can seem like just another statistic until I think of my daughter: she's scarcely tall enough to ride the roller coasters at Disneyland, yet in the 1800s and early 1900s she could have been employed in a dangerous factory all day long. In 1900, 1.75 million children between the ages of ten and fifteen were employed full-time in buildings with poor sanitation and little safety, commonly given the most dangerous jobs.[5]

It was in this cultural soil that the social gospel took root. Social gospel proponents, who were Christian ministers and activists, lobbied for safety legislation for factories and child workers, public health regulations, stricter tenement housing codes, and labor unions, motivated by the conviction that the Christian church couldn't speak about salvation and love without engaging the social issues plaguing the country. Henry Emerson Fosdick, pastor of New York's Riverside Church, said that "any church that pretends to care for the souls of people but is not interested in the slums that damn them, the city government that corrupts them, and the economic order that cripples them . . . [promotes] a dry, passive do nothing religion in need of new blood."[6]

The social gospel was driven by the Progressive movement and Christian postmillennialism. Progressives believed the positive forces of industrialization could be matched by positive social programs in an effort to help society evolve into a new and just reality, far different from the social evils produced by pure, unfettered industrialization, urbanization, and capitalism. Postmillennialism, a theological assumption that the kingdom of God would emerge on earth before the return of Christ, fueled the belief that it was the responsibility of the church to usher in that kingdom of God by fighting vice, corruption, employee abuses, and so on.

Social gospel reformers helped workers and immigrants improve their lives by offering services such as daycare, education, and health care to the poorest of the poor living in neighborhood slums. A minister named Charles Sheldon wrote a novel in 1896 called *In His Steps*, which remains a classic. Sheldon's framing question, "What would Jesus do?" expressed the heart of the movement—something evangelical teens would rediscover in bracelet and T-shirt form in the 1990s.

Given that the social and working conditions in America's cities were so horrific, it was unsurprising that so many churches and individual Christians agreed that the gospel, if it was truly good news, ought to be making an immediate difference in both the hearts *and* the daily lives of people who heard it.

The spread of the social gospel is epitomized in the life of Walter Rauschenbusch, a pastor who emerged as the most notable voice of the movement. Rauschenbusch was shaken by the gritty social conditions he saw during his time as a pastor in Hell's Kitchen, Manhattan, and in 1892 he responded by helping to form the Brotherhood of the Kingdom, a group committed to advancing the idea that "the Spirit of God is moving men in our generation toward a better understanding of the idea of the Kingdom of God on earth."[7] He was immensely frustrated by what he perceived to be an overemphasis on the otherworldly nature of salvation in the revival teaching of the time. Rauschenbusch believed that Christianity was, at its heart, revolutionary, and its purpose was to redeem society and the entire person, not just the "soul." This was surely a vital goal for a man who had seen so much human tragedy.

Rauschenbusch did more than advocate for justice, however—he was profoundly influenced by both German higher criticism and the liberal theology that arose from it. Higher criticism, among other techniques, downplayed or denied the historical veracity of many scriptural accounts. So as the social gospel spread, it began to be identified with a skeptical view of the Bible and an emphasis on purely societal changes, rather than on people being transformed externally *and* internally.

This wasn't something the conservative sector of Christianity could generally support. Ninety essays were written between 1910 and 1915 by conservative leaders, outlining orthodox doctrine and attacking liberal theology, higher criticism, socialism, and many similar institutions. These publications, called *The Fundamentals*—from which the word *fundamentalist* derives— intended to affirm traditional Protestant belief. At the same time, however, they widened the gap between conservative and liberal Christianity and increased conservative suspicion of the social gospel.

To Rauschenbusch, engagement in social struggle and the fight for justice was necessary for every individual. "This is the greatest moral task conceivable," he wrote. "Every Christian motive is calling us to do it. If it is left undone, millions of lives will be condemned to a deepening moral degradation and to spiritual starvation." He fiercely argued against what he saw as the irony of his detractors, who criticized him for losing God, saying, "Does it look probable that we will lose our contact with God if we plunge too deeply into this work? Does it stand to reason that we shall go astray from Jesus Christ if we engage in the unequal conflict with organized wrong? What kind of spirituality is that which is likely to get hurt by being put to work for justice and our fellow men?"[8]

The detractors of Rauschenbusch, however, believed that in his obsessive quest to work for justice and his fellow humans, he'd forgotten about God and detached Jesus from the historical veracity of the Bible, making Jesus into nothing more than a social agitator and advocate.

The term "social gospel" has become an established symbol of the theological split between liberalism and fundamentalism. As the split between liberal and fundamentalist understandings of the gospel has widened over the last century, slow shifts in society and theology have led to the general identification of social agendas with liberal concern, while doctrine and biblical accuracy are commonly considered part of the fundamentalist project.

Today, however, there is a growing desire among Christians of all sorts to discern and differentiate the *social awareness* of the historical social gospel movement from the specific theology that undergirded much of the movement. There is a desire to mend the artificial divide—the false dichotomy—between material and spiritual and return to a robust gospel message that includes the proclamation of Jesus and the embodying, person-transforming, society-changing love of Jesus.

Woe to us if, when confronted with the countless injustices in our world, we think we must choose either right belief or right action. Orthodoxy and orthopraxy (right belief and right practice) go hand in hand for the followers of Jesus, just as they did for Jesus Himself when He ministered on earth. Reasoned and mature reflection is essential. Paul, in 1 Thessalonians 5:21, wrote, "Test everything. Hold on to the good." This is exactly what is needed when we approach the social gospel and its influence on what we call social justice. Many in the church have spent decades arguing *against* the social gospel from a theological perspective without arguing *for* justice and love. Arguing theology isn't the same thing as doing justice or living a just life, commands about which the Bible is quite clear.

Rick McKinley, pastor of Imago Dei Community in Portland

and a professor at Multnomah Seminary, expresses the Christian mission and calling this way: "Taking the whole gospel, to the whole person, to the whole world."[9]

DEFINING SOCIAL JUSTICE

Even if we understand some of the history of the social gospel movement, how does that relate to social justice? We may hear that phrase being bandied about by politicians, pastors, and pundits, but what really *is* social justice? Should Christians be engaged in it? Does biblical justice include social justice, or is social justice really another way of saying the social gospel?

The phrase *social justice* was first coined by the Jesuit Luigi Taparelli D'Azeglio in the 1840s during the struggle for Italian national unity.[10] Taparelli was influenced by the works of Saint Thomas Aquinas and sought to use Aquinas's natural law theory to mediate the extremes of capitalist and socialist economic thought of his day. It seemed to Taparelli that neither extreme represented what was best, or what was most biblical, for society. At that time, social justice did not embody any particular philosophy or view of the world but rather represented a middle path between the socialists and the laissez-faire capitalists who were struggling for control of the Italian economy.

When the movement migrated to the United States, various theologians and philosophers added specific ideas to it, such as a living wage for workers, and an alternative to both the communists, who were gaining power in the 1930s, and capitalists who sought profit without regard for the working class. Later in the twentieth century, philosopher John Rawls used a Platonic perspective to define what might constitute a just society in a modern context, including the conviction that historic inequalities such as racism should be actively addressed until the inequalities are resolved.

A way of looking at social justice, therefore, is seeing it simply as justice in society, where "social justice" is a piece of the total area in which justice operates.

Thomas Patrick Burke, president of Wynnewood Institute, has argued that Taparelli would define social justice as "justice between man and man."[11] Or as Ryan Messmore, an essayist for the Christian journal of thought *First Things*, explained:

> Today, political activists often use the phrase "Social Justice" to justify government redistribution of wealth. In the mid-1800s, however, Taparelli prefaced "justice" with "social" to emphasize

the social nature of human beings and, flowing from this, the importance of various social spheres outside civic government. For Taparelli, these two factors were essential in formulating a just approach to helping those in need.[12]

When we use the phrase *social justice*, therefore, it is important to note that we are not committing to the particular goals of any single political party, economic theory, or theological stance. More accurately, we are seeking to understand how the Bible's clear call to be in right relationship with both God and our fellow humans is best accomplished in our society.

Perhaps the definition can be even simpler. "Social justice" describes the elements of a just society. If that sounds obvious, like a tautology or a truism, perhaps that is because we so over-defined social justice in the twentieth century.

As my friend Mike Yankoski, author of *Zealous Love* and *Under the Overpass*, pointed out to me in an e-mail, the fact that *love* took on new connotations among the free-love generation of the '70s doesn't mean we stop using the word *love* if we don't agree with those connotations. Similarly, the fact that people may use the word *god* to refer to something other than the God of the Bible doesn't stop Christians from using the word. *Justice* is a rich, biblical word, and we all live in societies, so talking about social justice isn't just a good idea—it's necessary.

THE POLITICS OF JUSTICE

The Greek word for *city* is *polis*. The word *politics* derives from Aristotle's work *Ta Politika* and means "the science of government."

Politics is one of the fascinating subsets of science wherein, unlike math and chemistry, there can be wide disagreement about truth. The structure of a country's banking laws doesn't lend itself to the same precision as mixing sodium metal (Na) with chlorine gas (Cl) to produce table salt. It isn't just that the ends are open to debate— they are, and there is no single and fixed answer that humans around the world agree should be the *telos*, or end goal, of society. It's that the means are open to debate as well. With both means and ends in flux, it's no wonder that politics generates so much contentious debate.

Social justice necessarily involves politics because it takes place in a *polis*—in organized groups of people attempting to live together. Even when Christians agree on the *end* of biblical justice that protects the vulnerable and allows for *shalom*, there is still the question of *how* that end is best achieved. We've traced the history of the social gospel movement enough to see how contemporary Christians can sometimes mistakenly identify specific instances of "doing justice" with specific liberal positions in theology or politics. We might trace a representative conservative Christian argument against social justice like this:

1. Social justice is an extension of liberal political philosophy. It is an abuse of government power, creates entitlement, is tainted with socialist ideology, and removes responsibility from the poor, replacing hard work with charity from government programs.
2. Rather, Jesus emphasized personal love and responsibility as means of building a just society.
3. Therefore, social justice is certainly not good, is possibly very bad, and is far different from what Christ commanded.

For other Christians, however, social justice is not about particular political programs in contemporary America. Rather, social justice denotes particular *concerns* about which the Bible is very clear, such as caring for orphans and widows, fighting racism, helping sick and diseased children, promoting economic and educational initiatives, dealing with refugees, and so on, all in the social sphere of our societies. Their argument for social justice can be expressed like this:

1. Jesus commanded His followers to love indiscriminately—neighbors, enemies, friends, self, God, and so on.
2. Social justice means acting on Jesus' command in whatever society we live, as well as around the world.
3. Therefore, social justice is near to the heart of God and a joyful obligation for His children.

There is clear and compelling common ground in the debate over what social justice means and what it does. That common ground is, of course, the Christian injunction to love in word and deed.

We sometimes think that the gospel can remain entirely apolitical, but as Lisa Sharon Harper once said to me, "Have we introduced the gospel to our politics?" Social justice, because it involves and influences what happens in the *polis*, necessarily involves politics. It isn't so much *if* politics and the gospel might interact . . . it's the *how* of politics that often generates the most heat and friction.

As I've given more and more of my time and energy to pursuing justice, I've had a chance to meet people from all walks of life who are unified around the biblical mandate to work and pray for justice in society. These folks take the idea of justice in society—caring for orphans and widows, fighting ongoing racism, helping children suffering from AIDS, promoting economic and educational initiatives in developing countries, addressing hunger, ending the horror of human trafficking and modern slavery—as a given. They can, and do, argue about the specific politics of how best to accomplish these goals, but the goals themselves are never in doubt.

If we don't like a particular policy, let's not impugn social justice as a category; instead, let's offer a better policy that will honor God and enact justice in the societies we share. Let's not argue against helping orphans; instead, let's find a better way of helping orphans.

For the sake of those living with injustice, we must be precise: social justice as a goal—working to ensure that a society is as just and free of evil as possible—is a part of the biblical universal of justice, and is therefore necessary. Working for justice in society does not mean a commitment to any particular political party, economic theory, or legislation. No matter how we argue that justice is best enacted in a society, we cannot let that debate prevent us from heeding God's clarion call to give our lives away for the sake of others.

Social justice is already happening in this country, just as it has happened over and over in the past. The abolition of slavery. Women's suffrage. Child labor laws. Controls on pollution and toxic substances. Free public education. Civil rights legislation. A vanishingly small number of people, and no faithful follower of Christ, will argue that such instances of justice are a negative in our society.

When we concern ourselves merely with "spiritual" or "heavenly" concerns, we drive a wedge between organically connected elements of life. This dualistic way of thinking—it doesn't really matter what happens to our "flesh" if we're bound for heaven anyway—is foreign to the Hebrew way of thinking and the full-orbed testimony of Scripture, and veers dangerously close to the heresy of Gnosticism, in which all earthly concerns are bad by definition. The next step in that line of thinking is often an obsession with personal purity and morality that has no regard for the difficulties or sufferings of others.

The Bible heralds visions of both heaven and earth—why don't we? Our job is to think about heaven and earth, soul and body, individual and society, as Scripture does: as an amalgam of God's holistic concern.

Politics is an easy way to talk about causes that require nothing more from me than checking a box on a ballot sheet. The gospel, however, cannot be reduced in such a way. God is relentlessly relational, and He expects His children to be as well. If we follow Jesus, then we will be led, regardless of our political views, into social situations that are uncomfortable, difficult, or costly. And why will we be led into such situations? Because we are salt and light. Because the world will know we are Christians by our love. Because when we love others, we're loving God. Because we are to let no debt remain outstanding, except our continuing debt to love one another.

JUSTICE MATTERS IN SOCIETY

Injustice often manifests in society. How a society addresses the concerns and needs of its weakest members is a large part of biblical justice.

Much of the prophetic language of the Old Testament chastises the nation as a whole and its leaders in particular for the systematic

FOURTEEN

REDISCOVERING WORSHIP

The Role of Justice in the Pursuit of God

[People] are not flattered by being shown that there has been a difference of purpose between the Almighty and them.[1]

ABRAHAM LINCOLN

[Worship] is a fully integrated life.[2]

LUKE HENDRIX

One of the key insights of the Protestant reformers was that worship didn't happen only in church—it happened during the week as well, when believers worked as bakers and builders to the glory of God. And one of the enduring legacies of the Catholic and Orthodox churches is the care and craft focused on worship in church, from ritual to liturgy to the very architecture of the church itself.

Unfortunately, today many American Christians are caught *between* these rich traditions, not benefitting from nor being transformed by either. We can often equate worship narrowly with Sunday morning music. At times we've lost the scriptural depth

221

that speaks to how we approach and worship God through our everyday actions.

We don't readily see the significance of justice in our pursuit of God. Isaiah 58 is a case study in how God defines worship—and it might just change the way we understand both worship and justice.

The unique power of Isaiah 58 doesn't flow from God's use of sharp prophetic language. There are certainly many passages in the Old Testament, and the New Testament as well, where strong language is used. Rather, the power comes from *what God is speaking sharply about.*

Isaiah 58 stands as one of the few passages in Scripture that directly challenges and confounds some of the very actions we deem most righteous and good: prayer, fasting, and seeking God.

RETURNED FROM EXILE

The whole of Isaiah spans the Assyrian and Babylonian exile. This particular chapter was written to the community of Jerusalem after they had returned home. The people were in the middle of an economic depression, trying to resettle themselves and rebuild their community. Families were broken, relationships were fractured, and trade wasn't booming. The Israelites were refugees returning to their homes, unsure about their future and their ability to even survive.

We begin with God speaking to Isaiah:[3]

> "Shout it aloud, do not hold back.
>   Raise your voice like a trumpet.
> Declare to my people their rebellion
>   and to the house of Jacob their sins.

For day after day they seek me out;
they seem eager to know my ways,
as if they were a nation that does what is right
and has not forsaken the commands of its God.
They ask me for just decisions
and seem eager for God to come near them."

God was setting the stage. He wanted His people to know that, despite their seeming eagerness to come near, there were serious sin issues. Yet in the verses that immediately follow, Israel spoke back to God, defending themselves against the charge of sin. In fact, Israel had a complaint about God's seeming lack of attention regarding their fasting.

"'Why have we fasted,' they say,
'and you have not seen it?
Why have we humbled ourselves,
and you have not noticed?'"

The Israelites were humbly praying and fasting, seeking God and trying to reestablish their relationship with Him. But God wasn't responding, and He was about to tell them why:

"Yet on the day of your fasting, you do as you please
and exploit all your workers.
Your fasting ends in quarreling and strife,
and in striking each other with wicked fists."

The Israelites were being inundated with the difficult issues that came from having lived in exile, but they were not working to resolve them or loving one another. Instead, they neglected each other as they prayed and fasted and asked God to deliver them. In his commentary on Isaiah 34–66, John D. W. Watts said, "God's choice for worship is acts which would remedy these conditions."[4]

Israel was approaching worship as a way to get what they wanted: God's attention and blessing. That relationship was short-circuited, however, when Israel failed to reflect God's character either to its own society or to the surrounding culture.

Ralph Waldo Emerson wrote, "That which dominates our imagination and our thoughts will determine our lives, and our character. Therefore, it behooves us to be careful what we worship, for what we are worshipping we are becoming."[5] When we focus our worship on what we want, we'll become nothing more than consumers.

Israel, similarly, was going through the motions of worship—fasting, praying, and so on—without any foundation or motivation beyond their desires. They were seeking God daily in order to be blessed by God, yet God was asking them to worship in order to be a blessing to *others*. Don't miss the crucial end of this verse, in which God gave what sounds like an absolute prohibition:

> "You cannot fast as you do today
> and expect your voice to be heard on high."

That's a serious statement. God seemed to be saying that He would not listen to their prayers! This chapter suggests that sometimes there's a reason God doesn't answer our prayers. It's not that God is being indifferent or unreachable—sometimes He doesn't answer our prayers because of *us*.

It is almost as if God was hitting His chosen people while they were down in Isaiah 58, perhaps because the only way to get them to look up was for them to reach rock bottom. I call this concept *strategic anarchy*—think Jonah in the belly of the whale or Jesus overturning tables in the temple.

Israel's behavior was so distasteful to God that He railed against their broken sense of worship:

> "Is this the kind of fast I have chosen,
>   only a day for a man to humble himself?
> Is it only for bowing one's head like a reed
>   and for lying on sackcloth and ashes?
> Is that what you call a fast,
>   a day acceptable to the LORD?"

Couldn't we easily substitute our familiar, post–New Testament worship practices, like fasting, singing, worship nights, and Christian concerts, into that verse?

"When fasting, accompanied by grief over sin and repentance from sin, leads to new resolve and compensating action," wrote Watts, "it can be both useful and therapeutic. When it becomes an end in itself, it is sterile and counterproductive."[6]

Do we fast to manipulate God or to humble ourselves? When we pray on our knees, are we bending them to His will?

HEALTHY WORSHIP

It's crucial that we understand the kind of worship God desires. He told Israel in the next several verses of Isaiah 58 what sort of worship pleases Him:

"Is not this the kind of fasting I have chosen:
to loose the chains of injustice
    and untie the cords of the yoke,
to set the oppressed free
    and break every yoke?
Is it not to share your food with the hungry
    and to provide the poor wanderer with shelter—
when you see the naked, to clothe him,
    and not to turn away from your own flesh and blood?"

God seems to be saying that the purest form of worship, the worship He finds most pleasing, is *justice*. If so, does that change the way we think about the word *worship*? Have we artificially narrowed it?

Recently I was asked to speak at an anti–human trafficking conference. The main question the conference was intended to address was, "How is the church going to abolish slavery?" As I was listening to other speakers and pondering that question, I concluded that if the church is going to help abolish slavery, it isn't going to do it during the two-hour Sunday morning services we attend.

It occurred to me that there is a distinction between the church *gathered* and the church *scattered*. For two hours on Sunday morning, we are all gathered in one place for what we call "worship." For the rest of the week, we are scattered apart, busy living our lives.

For many of us, our intentional focus on God and His purposes happens during church. But Isaiah 58 seems to be suggesting that God is more concerned about how we spend our scattered time than our gathered time. It is when we are scattered that we will fight injustice . . . or contribute to it. The real impact of the church will be felt, for better or worse, where it connects to the messiness of the remaining 166 hours in the week.

What if Sunday morning was the prelude to what the church does during the week? What if musical worship was the warm-up to the melody of our justice throughout the week?

A RELATIONAL NECESSITY

God's concern about how we spend our scattered time means we can't enter fully into relationship with Him unless we are living justly. We can't please God without pleasing worship. In chapter 2, I described justice as a theological necessity. Perhaps justice is a relational necessity as well.

In chapter 11 I talked about how justice is God's kingdom, a part of His sphere of influence. I illustrated it by saying that if my daughter was kidnapped, anyone who harmed my daughter would be harming me, and anyone who helped my daughter would be helping me. If you are harming my daughter, or if you are choosing not to help my daughter, you and I cannot have a healthy relationship. Quite the opposite.

The next few verses of Isaiah 58 speak directly about God's desire to restore the relationship broken by injustice:

> "Then your light will break forth like the dawn,
>   and your healing will quickly appear;
> then your righteousness will go before you,
>   and the glory of the Lord will be your rear guard.
> Then you will call, and the Lord will answer;
>   you will cry for help, and he will say: Here am I."

The end of this section is particularly powerful: "He will say: Here am I." That's as relational as it gets. God's desire is so strong for us to love our neighbors and promote *shalom* that injustice is an insurmountable barrier to healthy relationship with Him.

"*Then*—that is, when actions on such social issues demonstrate true worship as Yahweh wants it—*you may call and Yahweh will answer.* There is a proper order to be followed. First, do what is known to be God's will and what one is able to do. Then pray to God with assurance of being heard and answered."[7]

LIGHT RISING IN THE DARKNESS

Does your life inspire worship? As Isaiah 58 neared its conclusion, God continued to promise His people blessings that were contingent on the people's actions.

> "If you do away with the yoke of oppression,
>   with the pointing finger and malicious talk,
> and if you spend yourselves in behalf of the hungry
>   and satisfy the needs of the oppressed,
> then your light will rise in the darkness,
>   and your night will become like the noonday."

God wanted the nation of Israel to "spend themselves," to give their lives away for the hungry and the oppressed. They were to be "a peculiar people,"[8] who were like a light shining in darkness because of their fairness, their equity, and their goodness in all spheres of life.

Matthew 5:16 states, "In the same way, let your light shine

before others, so that they may see your good works and give glory to your Father who is in heaven" (esv). First Peter 2:12 echoes this, saying, "Live such good lives among the pagans that, though they accuse you of doing wrong, they may see your good deeds and glorify God on the day he visits us."

The logic is this: if we act justly in our neighborhoods and across the world, not only will other people be blessed, but they will see our good works and glorify God—another example of the bounty inherent in God's economy.

Your worship is your leadership. It is your influence. It is your mission. Your worship is how people will perceive you and it is ultimately where people will follow you.

If pursuing justice is a necessary component of worship, does that change the way we should think about worship pastors? As I have pondered what Isaiah 58 has to say about worship, I've begun to wonder if we're asking the right questions when we hire worship pastors.

Anyone hiring a worship pastor expects that he or she can play a musical instrument, sing, and blend various styles of music together in a way that will please the congregation. Those are valid concerns, but are those ultimately *worship* concerns?

One of my favorite things about Justin Lavik, the worship pastor at Antioch, is that he's a leader in thinking about and pursuing local justice in our city. He is as dedicated to leading in the realm of justice as he is to excelling as a musician.

With the way Isaiah 58 defines worship, there is a sense in which everyone is a worship leader. If every Christian in the world were living with exactly the same amount of faith as you are, would God applaud? When your neighbor is looking for something better out of life, are you providing a true alternative?

JOY

The final result of pursuing God through holistic worship is joy, and the promises in Isaiah 58 continued to be lavished on God's people if only they obey God's commands.

> "The LORD will guide you always;
>> he will satisfy your needs in a sun-scorched land
>> and will strengthen your frame.
> You will be like a well-watered garden,
>> like a spring whose waters never fail.
> Your people will rebuild the ancient ruins
>> and will raise up the age-old foundations;
> you will be called Repairer of Broken Walls,
>> Restorer of Streets with Dwellings."

Working in parallel structure, God reiterated the point. If Israel would take away the yoke and treat people fairly, stop accusing and blaming others, stop speaking wickedness, and begin to pour themselves out on behalf of the hungry and oppressed, *then* God would guide them, strengthen them, and bless them as they continued the task of rebuilding their society after exile.

The final condition in God's promise—the final way in which worship and the proper activities of worship are defined—was a reminder to Israel to keep the Sabbath holy. If His people would honor Him on the Sabbath, and stop seeking their own pleasure or desires, He would bless them above all others on the earth.

In other words, they'd experience joy! The conclusion to Isaiah 58 is inspiring and heartening.

"If you keep your feet from breaking the Sabbath
and from doing as you please on my holy day,
if you call the Sabbath a delight
and the LORD's holy day honorable,
and if you honor it by not going your own way
and not doing as you please or speaking idle words,
then you will find your joy in the LORD,
and I will cause you to ride on the heights of the land
and to feast on the inheritance of your father Jacob."
The mouth of the LORD has spoken.

We find our greatest joy and fulfillment by worshipping God in right relationship, as we pursue His purposes in our broken world. This highlights the paradoxical nature of joy discussed earlier—that when we seek our own joy, we fail to find it, but when we give our lives away on behalf of others, we find joy.

Or, as God said in Isaiah, our light will rise in the darkness.

"The mouth of the LORD has spoken."

HOW SWEET THE SOUND

In many ways, Isaiah 58 boils down to this: to "spend ourselves," to give our lives away, is true worship.

Like Israel, we are a people of exile, in desperate need of restoration. Our world is in ruins around us, but God promises that in true worship "ancient ruins" will be rebuilt and that we will "raise up" the foundations of many generations (v. 12).

Perhaps today it is time to take the simple step of asking God what He would have us *do*, even as we sing in worship.

Jesus says in Luke 19:40 that if we are silent about God's glory, the very stones will cry out in praise. God doesn't ask merely to hear *our* songs in worship—He asks us to hear *His* song that is meant to be sung among every tribe and nation, among poor and rich, among healthy and sick.

John Newton, the slave trader turned abolitionist pastor who wrote "Amazing Grace," understood that to sing God's song is to do God's work, and to do God's work is to sing God's song. The worship God accepts is a song of healing and justice, and we are called to sing it with our lips only after we have lived it with our lives.

In the words of the beloved hymn "Lead On, O King Eternal," penned by Ernest W. Shurtleff in 1888,

> Lead on, O King eternal,
> Till sin's fierce war shall cease,
> And holiness shall whisper
> The sweet amen of peace.
> For not with swords' loud clashing,
> Nor roll of stirring drums;
> With deeds of love and mercy
> The heavenly kingdom comes.[9]

> The sacrifices of God are a broken spirit;
> a broken and contrite heart,
> O God, you will not despise.

PSALM 51:17

THREE-YEAR-OLD JUSTICE

By Tamara Wytsma

My daughter at the age of three
may know more of justice than you or me.
"Mommy, everyone makes mistakes,"
my little reminder to have more grace.
She's learning that it's good to share,
and when you split, be sure it's fair.
Be a good helper with a happy heart,
pick up your stuff and do your part,
when there's a problem, you work it out,
and never whine and never pout.
Always be kind, better to give than receive,
be responsible, don't take more than you need.
Just basic stuff—after all she is three—
pink tutus and giggles and simplicity.
But what if these virtues my three-year-old knows
begin to answer our broken world's woes?

FIFTEEN

DEBT TO SOCIETY

Grace and Reconciliation in Establishing Shalom

If only it were all so simple! If only there were evil people
somewhere insidiously committing evil deeds, and it were
necessary only to separate them from the rest of us and destroy
them. But the line dividing good and evil cuts through the
heart of every human being. And who is willing to destroy a
piece of his own heart?[1]

ALEKSANDR I. SOLZHENITSYN

The doctrine of original sin is the only empirically verifiable
doctrine of the Christian faith.[2]

REINHOLD NIEBUHR

When Jesus taught His disciples to pray, He taught them
to ask their Father in heaven to forgive their sins.
When His disciples asked Him how many times
they ought to forgive when someone sinned against them, He said
seventy-seven times (Matthew 18:22).[3] Think about that: Jesus is
telling me that if my neighbor sins against me—maybe stealing my

newspaper before I wake up or lying about me around town—I should forgive him, over and over.

But is sin the same as injustice? Perhaps we should forgive sins, like pride and selfishness, but we don't have to forgive injustices that are committed against us?

In Scripture we see that sin and injustice go hand in hand. God says that when we commit injustice, we sin, and sin is an injustice because it rebels against God's intended *shalom*. In Amos 5:10–12, God condemned those who "detest the one who tells the truth," telling them:

> "You levy a straw tax on the poor
>> and impose a tax on their grain.
> Therefore, though you have built stone mansions,
>> you will not live in them;
> though you have planted lush vineyards,
>> you will not drink their wine.
> For I know how many are your offenses
>> and how great your sins."

Notice what the people had done: they had taxed the straw the poor needed for their animals and taxed the grain they needed to feed themselves. God judged them for this serious sin.

Amos isn't the only place we read about this connection. Ezekiel 16:49 has this to say about the relationship between sin and injustice. "Now this was the sin of your sister Sodom: She and her daughters were arrogant, overfed and unconcerned; they did not help the poor and needy."

We can trace this theme in Micah and Deuteronomy, to name two other examples, and in Isaiah 1, God connected His condemnation of sin with Israel's failure to "do right" and "seek justice." What Isaiah meant by these phrases was to "defend the oppressed. Take up the cause of the fatherless; plead the case of the widow" (v. 17).

Throughout the rest of Isaiah's sixty-six chapters, the theme continues: injustice is equated with sin. Sin creates debt, and that debt must be paid.

BENT CREATURES

In C. S. Lewis's science-fiction novel *Out of the Silent Planet*, he modeled the main character, Ransom, after his close friend J. R. R. Tolkien. Ransom leaves Earth and finds himself on Mars among indigenous people groups who have never known sin and, therefore, have no word to describe sin.

The ruler of the planet, Oyarsa, refers to Earth as the "Silent Planet" because (as a result of the fall) light and song are no longer broadcast from it. Contrasting his own people's sinless lives with Ransom's life, he says, "I see now how the lord of the silent world has bent you."

Often, sin is a corruption or debasement of what is good. It may even share a similar appearance at the beginning, yet its end is not focused on God's shalom. Oyarsa, summarizing the consequences that result from humanity's *bentness*, says, "a bent [human] can do more evil than a broken one."[4]

When we're broken, we know we need help. When we're bent, we can assume everything is fine. We can believe that being close enough to good is good enough.

I've always thought Lewis's description of the effects of sin as bending or warping us is profound in its simplicity. We were created to be one way, to live in the direction of God. Sin mars us, defaces and twists us. We are bent—not the way we are supposed to be.

We were created for relationship, but we see only ourselves.

We were created for dependence and to walk by faith, yet we seek independence and to walk by sight.

We were meant to live in a right relationship with God and a right relationship with others, but we find ourselves hopelessly out of line with both.

Justice is the state that exists when there is equity, balance, and harmony in relationships and in society. Injustice is the state that exists when unjust people do violence to peace and *shalom* and create inequity, imbalance, and dissonance.

Like bent arrows, we miss the mark we are meant to hit.

CONTINUING DEBT

Relationships are meant to be characterized by *shalom*—by justice, fairness, harmony, and flourishing. All of us are in relationships, even if we live alone in a cabin in the woods. We were raised by one or more people, we were taught by people, we want to be closer to or more distant from certain people, and so on. We are even in relationship with ourselves—who we were, are, and want to be. There are other fields of relationship: to the environment, to the past, to animals, to future generations, to authors, and to our vocations, just to name a few.

We are relational beings. At some point, every relationship incurs debt. Relational debt is the gap between what is meant to be and what actually happens. In the case of my relationship with

God, this is easily seen as sin. For example, I am meant to trust God and live by obedience, so when I disobey something God is asking of me, I incur a relational debt with God. I offend God and owe the difference of what was supposed to have been rendered to God, but wasn't. That gap is debt.

We even acquire debt unintentionally, but it is debt nevertheless. If I buy a product that was made by a child slave, my money helped keep that child imprisoned. My ignorance of that fact cannot change the reality of the child's experience. I commit injustice, I incur debt, I sin.

Any sin that occurs degrades a relationship, whether between individuals, groups of people, or people and God. If injustice causes relational debt, how is the debt paid back? We typically answer this two ways.

The first is *punitive justice*. This is eye-for-an-eye punishment, the demand that a wrong be righted by inflicting equal wrong upon the wrongdoer. It brings about fairness and equality by inflicting a commensurate suffering or pain on the person who caused it for the victim. Some states still punish murder with the death penalty, for example, taking the life of the murderer as payment for the life of the victim, while other states punish murder with a figurative death, ensuring that the murderer spends the rest of his life in jail. Either way, the idea is that a punitive action makes the person who committed an injustice pay a debt through punishment. Picture a two-sided scale: the original wrong weighs down one side, and for the scale to be brought back into balance, the wrong must be offset by an equal punishment.

As a fascinating aside, America has fewer than 5 percent of the world's population, but it has nearly 25 percent of the world's incarcerated people! More than two million Americans are incarcerated (and another five million are on probation or parole), giving America the highest per-capita incarceration rate in the world—more than seven people out of every thousand.[5] No wonder we so often identify justice with definitions that center on criminal justice and punitive responses.

This is partly an issue of racial justice. "There are more African Americans under correctional control today—in prison or jail, on probation or parole—than were enslaved in 1850, a decade before the Civil War began."[6] As Michelle Alexander has written, "the fate of millions of people—indeed the future of the black community itself—may depend on the willingness of those who care about racial justice to re-examine their basic assumptions about the role of the criminal justice system in our society."[7]

The second solution to relational debt is *reparative justice*. This method focuses on repayment. Suppose I steal from a business and am subsequently caught and convicted. I spend a year in jail, and when I get out I go on with my life, never compensating the business for my crime. Punitive justice has been served, but is the business better off? Simply "doing time" cannot be a sufficient application of justice, which is why in reparative justice, a wrongdoer makes amends to the person or people who have been wronged. This can take the form of money, time, or some other type of assistance.

An organization that exists to promote reparative justice, and not simply punitive justice, is Prison Fellowship International. Like other groups that advocate a biblical view of justice, PFI—whose motto is *beyond crime and punishment*—seeks to restore dignity to both the offender and the victim. The root of the word *reparative* means to "make ready again," so in the case of theft, that might involve the offender working to repay his victim *and* beginning to restore the trust he violated.

There are certain injustices, however, that appear intractable or where reparation seems impossible. It is one thing for a thief and his victim to meet together for the purpose of reparation and restoration, but what in the world can transform the relational debt between an abused child and the abuser? What can restore just relationships between the members of two ethnic groups involved in a genocide? Simply put, what happens when punitive or reparative justice can't bring about full restoration?

ONLY GRACE

Célestin Musekura knows both the pain of genocide and the difficulty of forgiveness. A Rwandan Hutu, he lived through the Rwandan Genocide between April and July 1994, experiencing a raw form of evil that few people can imagine. In the reprisal attacks that followed in the next four years, members of his family were murdered. He received multiple death threats because of the reconciliation work he pursues.[8]

For a man like Célestin, there is no possibility of justice being peripheral or optional. Indeed, he has given his whole adult life to the quest for justice, earning advanced degrees in theology and specializing in communal forgiveness, becoming one of the world's most respected voices on reconciliation and forgiveness. He founded African Leadership and Reconciliation Ministries (ALARM),[9] whose mission is primarily grassroots and sustainable peace-building, as well as conflict resolution, forgiveness, human rights advocacy, trauma counseling, and justice initiatives.

"Americans tend to think that punishment is the only way to satisfy justice," said Célestin at my church recently, "when in fact punishment is only one of several ways to satisfy it. The evil must be punished, but the goal is not just to punish the perpetrator; the goal is to restore the community."

But how? How can relationships be restored?

My friend answered plainly, "There is no justice without forgiveness."

But *how*? How can someone like Célestin forgive? He has witnessed, and been a victim of, some of the most spectacularly evil events imaginable. Surely he should emphasize forms of justice that are primarily punitive. After all, who deserves to be punished more than people who willingly chose to murder their fellow citizens—usually with a machete, always face-to-face—men, women, and children whose only crime was being born into a different tribe? Yet Célestin said, "There is no justice without forgiveness."

Could you forgive such things? Injustice tears the fabric of shalom and community, and sometimes we cannot imagine how the shredded threads can possibly be restored.

I want to tell you the rest of what Célestin said.

"There is no justice without forgiveness, and there is no forgiveness without justice. Before I forgive something, I have to judge it as evil."

There it is, stark and troubling. Justice cannot simply be punitive or reparative; it must involve forgiveness. Yet to truly forgive we must look into the face of evil. We must know exactly what it is we are forgiving.

Why not simply lock up or hang the leaders of those murderous gangs? Why not clear the streets of Rwanda of everyone who ever swung a machete or tossed a burning torch into a home?

Célestin won't have it. "Justice without forgiveness sets up the process of more revenge.... The desired result of forgiveness is that you will reconcile." It is possible to forgive without reconciliation, but reconciliation is the ultimate goal.

Forgiveness is a choice that happens within us. However, when we believe that forgiveness and reconciliation must happen simultaneously, we oversimplify a process that is painful and often prolonged. The victim of injustice isn't expected to transform, in an instant, from deep wounds to a trusting relationship with the perpetrator.

Reconciliation is needed as a category in order to describe the lengthy, difficult process by which injustice can be rebuilt into full shalom. Reconciliation happens in the context of personal and communal relationships, and requires trustworthy behavior over time. Such reconciliation doesn't always happen, but it remains the ultimate goal of forgiveness.

But . . . *how*?

Grace. Grace, manifested as love, is the only way to both erase the debt of sin and injustice *and* restore relationships through reconciliation. As Proverbs 10:12 puts it, "Hatred stirs up dissension, but love covers over all wrongs." It must be grace, for we cannot do it on our own. Working toward a just society requires more than doing justice—it requires a willingness to forgive and be reconciled in the presence of pain and injustice.

Grace interrupts the hopeless standoff between what is and what ought to be.

"The divine seed and gift of grace in our lives serves as a catalyst," Célestin wrote to me, "in encouraging us to grant others the same grace granted to us . . . and therefore the grace to truly forgive comes from God."[10]

Only grace fully cancels the debt we owe. We are bent people. We miss the mark, and only grace can restore relationships to their intended shape.

Célestin urges people in need of forgiveness, and who need to forgive, to focus "on the restoration of relationships whereby the oppressed begins to give grace and empathy to the perpetrator and to consider a possibility of change and transformation. Grace is essential in reconciliation."

Justice requires the grace we get and the grace we give, because only God's grace can make us just, and only grace can empower forgiveness.

Jesus asks us to forgive, not seven times, but seventy-seven. It's impossible for us, in our own power, to forgive so freely and so frequently. True forgiveness requires grace.

This is the ultimate goal of justice: not only that debt is paid, but that relationship is restored. That is why Célestin says, "Justice without grace is like an atmosphere without air."[11]

> Above all, love each other deeply,
> because love covers over a multitude of sins.
>
> 1 PETER 4:8

ECCLESIASTES

By Matt Smith

M eaningless—everything is meaningless."

The Teacher paused and stared at us while we sat silent, openmouthed and astonished. Could it be true? Then he turned, and in a room of a hundred men he looked at *me*.

"Trust me," he said, his boney finger pointing, "it's not a woman. It's not all the women. It's not money. It's not success or power. It's not what you think you want. It's not that at all. Run after them! Go ahead! But know this . . ."

His voice caught and he fell to his knees. He cupped his hands like Father Abraham praying, his eyes now level with mine.

"I pity you. You are the fish caught in the snare. You are the bird stolen from air. You are the one trapped by these times. You are each soul who must walk the line."

"Teacher!" I startled to my feet. "Is there no hope?"

"My boy, my boy . . ." His hands dropped to his lap. "Hear me, for this is all I have. Keep God close. Do what he tells you. Everything else is meaningless."

He stood and left the room.

I remained standing, silent, considering that the King himself had pleaded with me, baring his heart for me to see.

SIXTEEN

EENY, MEENY, MINY, MOE

How Justice Surfaces the Need for Grace

The future is always at stake in how we understand the past.[1]

ANDREW DELBANCO

Only when we have come to realize that God's love is freely bestowed do we enter fully and definitely into the presence of the God of faith. Grace is not opposed to the quest of justice nor does it play it down. On the contrary, it gives it its full meaning. God's love, like all true love, operates in a world not of cause and effect but of freedom and gratuitousness.[2]

GUSTAVO GUTIÉRREZ

ELMINA

I don't believe we can talk about justice without talking about grace. The two are intricately linked. Our pursuit of justice should be motivated in large part by our awareness of and gratitude for grace. The experience that best illustrates this for me is my visit to Elmina Castle, a slave fortress in Ghana.

Elmina was a Portuguese and then Dutch slave-trading port located on the Gold Coast in modern-day Cape Coast, Ghana. Elmina Castle is situated on a strategic outcropping with a commanding sweep of the ocean. It's a fortified stronghold that once had a moat and a drawbridge; some of the cannons that pointed seaward and inland remain to this day. By the start of the eighteenth century, thirty thousand slaves on their way to the Americas passed through Elmina annually.

While there, I took a walking tour with a guide, and something he said surprised me. I'd come to study the transatlantic slave trade for a college course I was preparing to teach—but instead of being drawn into the horrors of slavery, my guide drew me into the horrors of sexual violence.

He explained how female slaves and prisoners would be brought out into a small courtyard at the heart of the castle. The governor's quarters were directly above the courtyard, and he would step out onto a walkway from which he could survey the women and girls. Then he would choose a sex slave for the night.

Standing inside a physical symbol of the transatlantic slave trade in general, I found myself more and more affected by the particular horror of individual women and girls being raped, decade after decade after decade. I asked the guide every question I could think of as I struggled to understand this human side of slavery that I'd lost in the big picture of slave ships, abolitionism, and the American Civil War.

My host had arranged for me to meet a local scholar later that afternoon, who had earned a doctorate in England in the history of the transatlantic slave trade on the west coast of Africa. Over the years, I have learned not to take everything I learn from tour guides at face value, so when I peppered the scholar that afternoon with questions and the subject of gender violence came up, I asked him if there was any hard evidence of various governors abusing slaves, or whether it was based purely on oral tradition.

View of the Courtyard from the Governor's Quarters,
Elmina Slave Fortress, Cape Coast, Ghana

He answered by explaining how crucial and powerful oral tradition was, and that the reality of gender violence at Elmina Castle was well attested by an avalanche of similarly painful stories. He added that such stories were further verified by certain data points. "First," he said, "the number of mulattos, or light-skinned Africans in that region, also gives evidence for the use of slave women as concubines." *Mulatto* is a Spanish or Portuguese word from the sixteenth century meaning "offspring of a European and a black African."³

Anthropologists have shown a strong mixing of the races from the white Europeans who would have been in that area during the time as slave traders. The scholar said, "In this region, considerably more than the rest of Ghana, you can see an amazing variance in skin color."

He went on to talk about what he called "stone houses." During the transatlantic slave trade, the locals didn't build stone houses, opting instead for other traditional materials. The Europeans, however, built stone houses, many of which are still standing today, often for women they had impregnated. They would provide these houses to help ensure their children would be safe and provided for. In the Europeans' eyes, the women were savages to be exploited, but the children, owing to their fathers, were half-civilized and half-Christian—and therefore worth something. In fact, many of the first Christian missionaries to the region were called to Cape Coast as educators or schoolteachers for the illegitimate children of the slave traders.

I was simultaneously fascinated and appalled. I asked this scholar if there was any written evidence of this sexual exploitation. He replied that the written records were thin, but that occasionally something would show up in a diary or a journal. "There was one journal I came across," he said, "from a Portuguese soldier while I was studying for my doctoral dissertation. It told the story of a song they would sing, a rhyme the men would use in choosing who they were going to take to sleep with. Basically they were going to sing the song and point from woman to woman, and when the song ended, that would be the woman they would choose."

He then began to sing the song in what I assumed was Portuguese, and the familiar cadence of its opening sounds immediately caught my ear and transported me to my own childhood and what I took to be the same song I used to sing on the playground, picking sides for a game of baseball.

> Eeny, meeny, miny, moe
> Catch a tiger by his toe
> If he hollers, let him go
> Eeny, meeny, miny, moe

Somehow, it seemed, there had been an early variant of this rhyme, or a rhyme with similar beginning sounds and purpose, used as a way for European men to pick which African woman or girl they were going to rape.

I could scarcely believe it.

That night I began researching what else I could find on the history of "Eeny, meeny, miny, moe." I didn't discover many written leads, but I did discover different oral traditions leading back into a variety of countries. Perhaps the best-attested history of the song is its use in the American South—another piece of the historical puzzle I'd been missing.

"Eeny, meeny, miny, moe," in the South, contained a racist term for blacks instead of the word *tiger*—a fact so well-known in some African-American communities that a lawsuit was brought against Southwest Airlines by two women because a flight attendant, preparing for take-off, sang "Eeny, meeny, miny, moe, please sit down—it's time to go!"[4] Her song, though seemingly harmless, obviously touched deep and painful memories.

Several months after my trip to Ghana, I was in the Museum of the African Diaspora in San Francisco, talking to one of the curators. I began to relay what I'd learned about the song at Elmina Castle, and before I could get far, she interrupted—"Oh yeah, 'Eeny, meeny, miny, moe' . . . I know what that one's all about!"

What remains so powerful to me is the subtle but undeniable connection between myself as a young boy on the playground, racism in the South, and some of the most horrific violence in the transatlantic slave-trade era.

If something as innocuous as a childhood rhyme can be connected to violent injustice, how many other injustices do I trip over every day? How many products do I see at the store that have a story of injustice behind them? How many people do I drive by on street corners, begging or waiting for day-labor jobs, who have stories that are more connected to me than I realize?

"Eeny, meeny, miny, moe" taught me that the world is both smaller and less neutral than I'd previously believed. The more we know about how history is rife with injustice, the more it begins to feel as though we can never be completely innocent or fully just. And we don't have to travel across the ocean to a former slave castle for these sorts of realizations—they can happen near the places we live.

THE GENTRY

I enjoy walking around renovated neighborhoods in Portland, Oregon—neighborhoods like the Pearl District—and soaking in the sights and sounds.

Urban renewal is happening in cities and towns across America. As in Portland, decaying buildings in traditional, historic downtowns are being purchased and repurposed. An old warehouse may become an art gallery with second-story loft apartments, or condemned row houses may be torn down to make room for new, retro-styled homes and upscale boutiques. Crime rates often plummet, and increasing numbers of shoppers and tourists enjoy walking on streets they would have formerly avoided.

We can grab high-end coffee in one of the brand-new coffee shops, walk around on perfect brick sidewalks, and enjoy the sculptures and landscaping. In doing that, it's easy to forget that in the process of urban renewal, an entire existing community is gradually but inexorably displaced.

That's why city officials don't like to use the other word for urban renewal. *Gentrification*. The term comes from the word used to describe the social class of people just below the nobility in England: the *gentry*.

"[Gentrification is a process] that slowly pushes the poor, or the folks who didn't have a lot of resources, out of that space," said Leroy Barber, president of Mission Year.[5]

The real story is never as simple as the official one. When certain gains are made in a neighborhood, they nearly always come with a cost. Often the gains important to a local government are gains for the middle- and upper-class citizens, or what might be called "the gentry." Those advances in comfort, accessibility, and opportunity frequently at the expense of the poor, the disadvantaged, or the destitute.

When we're strolling past shining store windows in a gentrified neighborhood, we can easily miss or ignore the human history of the place we're standing—not to mention the fact that we're linked to people we may never see or know who have been disenfranchised or displaced.

It's messy. We're caught deeper in the web of society, for both good and bad, than we realize.

WHAT'S WRONG WITH THE WORLD?

G. K. Chesterton was once asked by an editor to write a piece on the theme "What's wrong with the world?"

His response was simple: "I am."[6]

Dallas Willard wrote in the classic *The Spirit of the Disciplines*, "We delude ourselves about the sustaining conditions of people's evil deeds because we wish to continue living as we now live and continue being the kinds of people we are. We do not want to change. We do not want our world to be really different. We just want to escape the consequences of its being what it truly is and of our being who we really are."[7]

The more we try to be just, the more aware we become of our inability to be perfectly just.

We can't even do all the good things we want to do—and what about the countless injustices we don't even know about? What about those that are systemic, institutional, generational . . . injustices far bigger than our small efforts?

What about the connections our actions have to people who are hidden from us? We tend to only see our successes or the easy victories. But what about the messy side of our efforts and our failures?

Danae Yankoski, writer with Francis Chan of the best seller *Crazy Love*, addressed this in a unique and amazing way at the first Justice Conference. She shared a story of what she and her husband, Mike, had been trying to do to live out justice in an intentional and sacrificial way. She finished with two words.

"We failed."

Those were two of the most shocking words anyone could have expected from a conference speaker—and the two most encouraging.

Yankoski's admission that justice is difficult and that we don't always succeed allowed everyone to breathe a sigh of relief. She gave them permission to attempt good things without the tyranny of perfection. Admitting failure but continuing to seek justice is an example of how walking humbly and doing justly go hand in hand.

It is impossible to navigate the world without stepping, somehow, into a system of injustice, however small or subtle. We can't walk across the lawn without breaking a blade of grass.

That's where grace comes in. Our pursuit of justice both surfaces the need for, and is made complete by, grace.

COVERED AND SUSTAINED

Grace covers us by putting us in right relation with God. Even though we are guilty of injustice, even though we have participated in systems of injustice, and even though we've broken our share of grass blades, grace covers us. It allows the unjust to stand next to a just God as if we are just. It covers our sins and reconciles us to God.

Grace also sustains us, giving the strength, energy, and confidence before God and the world to pour out our lives for others. This same idea was expressed by Paul when he talked about what it takes to continue serving—Second Corinthians 4:1 says, "Therefore, since through God's mercy we have this ministry, we do not lose heart." Knowing that, through grace, we are in right relation with God, we are energized for the fight against injustice.

Grace both covers and sustains us. We must work to unite these two ideas about grace, or we can become unbalanced in our perception of our own righteousness.

If we think grace was only intended to cover us, rather than also sustain us, we start to think "Amazing Grace" was written just for us. We forget the sustaining power of grace that was given to energize and motivate us to change the world. Covering grace without sustaining grace can make us consumers of grace. As if grace were a product, we keep it for ourselves.

If we think that grace was only intended to sustain us, rather than also cover us, we don't take seriously enough the messiness of life, our own weaknesses, and the mystery of God. We can become triumphalist in our justice efforts, thinking we can literally fix the world and solve all its problems. We overestimate our own significance, while at the same time underestimating how intractable sin and some issues of injustice really are.

When we unite these two halves of grace, covering and sustaining, we begin to understand what God's grace is meant to be and do, and we avoid erring on either side.

Paul emphasized again and again to the Corinthian church the power and necessity of grace.

And God is able to make all grace abound to you, so that in all things at all times, having all that you need, you will abound in every good work. (2 Corinthians 9:8)

But by the grace of God I am what I am, and his grace to me was not without effect. No, I worked harder than all of them—yet not I, but the grace of God that was with me. (1 Corinthians 15:10)

Therefore we do not lose heart. Though outwardly we are wasting away, yet inwardly we are being renewed day by day. (2 Corinthians 4:16)

Grace renews us, and that grace is not without effect—because of grace we can abound in every good work.

Imagine you are a firefighter in 1871, standing in the street near a ferocious house fire. You and the other firefighters form two long lines from the nearest water source to the house, passing buckets full of water up one line to be dumped on the fire, then back down the other line to be filled again.

In a bucket brigade, you reach to one side to receive the bucket, then pass it to the next person on the other side. Slowly, bucket by bucket, the fire is extinguished.

That is how grace works. We come to God for forgiveness and restoration, knowing that we are unjust people contributing to an unjust world. As we receive God's grace, we pass it to the next person, adding our chapter to God's grand story of renewal and restoration in His world.

HUMBLE RESOLVE

Galatians 6:9 says, "Let us not become weary in doing good, for at the proper time we will reap a harvest if we do not give up."

Injustice is a cold, unrelenting reality. It can be tempting for us to use our comfort to ignore injustice or rationalize it away. But God would have us join His work. As Timothy Keller has written,

> If a person has grasped the meaning of God's grace in his heart, he will do justice. If he doesn't live justly, then he may say with his lips that he is grateful for God's grace, but in his heart he is far from him. If he doesn't care about the poor, it reveals that at best he doesn't understand the grace he has experienced, and at worst he has not really encountered the saving mercy of God. Grace should make you just.[8]

May we not grow weary in doing good or in doing justly, but

move forward with a humble resolve, motivated by gratefulness for the grace that both covers and sustains us.

> Let us not become weary in doing good,
> for at the proper time we will reap a
> harvest if we do not give up.
>
> GALATIANS 6:9

INTERLUDE

TENDER

By Judith H. Montgomery

To start this morning's fire, I've laid
news of the world I cannot bear to read—
shredded paper spread across the wood-

stove grid that soon will raise the flame.
Then a slim hand of kindling tented over
forest moss that rises to the match.

A hiss, and first flame curls, tasting
needles, white wood shavings, rising
to a roar when I twist shut the glass-

faced door: the secret's in the drawn-in
draft, the oxygen that also feeds the fire.
When the flames have leapt and twined,

I'll take the smallest, dry-split log you've
left me, set it at the hot heart. A second,
a third, then as the cured wood catches,

the largest chunk—each piece of juniper
and ash printed by your axe, and perhaps,
as I imagine, by drops of sweat that fell

as your constant arms rose and descended
precisely with the blade, each stroke an
offering to this, and to our other fire.

Because I crave both warmth and light,
I will not leave this blaze to burn alone:
any fire can collapse from lack

of nourishment and sink back into dull
cold ash, or run red out of bounds
and torch the house it's meant to warm.

We tend to one another, or we burn.

This poem, first published in *Poet Lore*, was written on March
19, 2003, upon the start of the Iraq War.

SEVENTEEN

LEARN TO CHANGE
THE WORLD

Education and Knowledge in the Pursuit of Justice

Education is not the filling of a pail, but the lighting of a fire.[1]

WILLIAM BUTLER YEATS

Next in importance to freedom and justice is popular
education, without which neither freedom nor justice can be
permanently maintained.[2]

JAMES A. GARFIELD

When Thomas Jefferson was a young politician, he led a
successful effort in the Virginia General Assembly to
ban the import of slaves into Virginia.[3] When the final
language of the Declaration of Independence was being hammered
out in 1776, Jefferson argued for passages condemning elements of
the slave trade; they were eventually edited out.[4] Later, as a delegate
from Virginia to Congress, Jefferson advocated for an end to slavery in the nation's territories, though it never became law.[5]

Yet, throughout his life, Jefferson owned slaves and represented a government whose official laws supported the continuing existence of slavery.

Don't we often want life to be less messy than it really is? We want to lionize Jefferson as a heroic figure in our nation's history—until we want to demonize him for considering other humans to be mere property.

In hindsight, Jefferson seems to have caved to what he considered pragmatic realities. He failed to extend his understanding of natural rights and liberty into his core convictions. Perhaps he assumed that if he continued to attack slavery, it would cost him too much political capital. Perhaps he was afraid of the consequences in his own life. Accommodating may have seemed like the wisest course of action.

I remember considering Jefferson in graduate school and thinking, *Man, if there was slavery today,* I'd *do something about it. I wouldn't be like Jefferson and ignore it.*

The great irony didn't strike me until later in my education: the Trans-Atlantic Slave Trade Database puts the number of slaves imported to the Americas between 1501 and 1866 at around 12 million,[6] while the number of people held in slavery today worldwide is estimated to be between 20 and 27 million, more than at any time in world history.[7]

Slavery is a far bigger problem now than it was in Jefferson's day.

At the same time, we also have more mechanisms at our disposal to advocate on behalf of slaves than any generation before us. For example, in the 1800s it would have taken weeks for an abolitionist to go from the North to the South by wagon, whereas we can fly to the other side of the planet in half a day. It's easy to throw stones at people in the past, condemning them for what they didn't do. It's much harder to take stock of ourselves in the present, and ask ourselves, in light of our greater resources, what we're willing to do.

We read about Thomas Jefferson and think, *What a hypocrite—authoring the Declaration of Independence while owning slaves!* The question, what would I have done about slavery if I were Thomas Jefferson? may be answered easily. The larger question is, what am I doing about slavery *now*?

In my role as an educator, both at Kilns College and when I speak at conferences and retreats, I try to use education to call people into a fuller understanding of our present reality—a reality that is often shaped by past events in profound ways. Cultivating a lifelong habit of learning is one way we can avoid simplistic characterizations of the past. Such characterizations often do little more than assuage our own guilt. And education can help us perform the twin tasks of evaluating our lives and understanding how we ought to live.

KNIT TOGETHER

When we are confronted with the need for justice in the world, it is important to navigate between being overwhelmed and underwhelmed.

When a problem overwhelms us, we can become fatalistic. We can believe there is no way for us to make any real difference, so why try? When a problem underwhelms us, however, it can engender a false sense of simplistic possibility, leading us to believe that our desire to change the world is all it takes to change the world. Neither extreme is helpful. What is called for is a careful understanding of what the cause of justice is and what it requires of us. Education and knowledge are excellent ways we can build our capacity to accomplish lasting good.

Jeff Johnson's story demonstrates this. I met Jeff when he began an ongoing relationship with Kilns College, helping design justice curriculum. He's currently studying for a master's of divinity, focusing on justice issues, at Princeton Theological Seminary, as well as running the South African nonprofit he founded, Themba International.

Jeff grew up in Bend, Oregon, enjoying a comfortable and insulated life. It wasn't until his senior year in college that he first confronted devastating injustice. During a semester abroad in South Africa, he met a young mother who changed the course of his life.

The mother of two small children was stricken with AIDS. Because of her weakened condition, she could no longer travel to work, and she had lost her job. No job meant she could no longer afford bus fare to receive treatment at her local clinic.

"I sensed her tears were being shed for a future she would never see—a future in which her children could not afford school fees or food," remembers Jeff, "a future in which her children wouldn't receive the love of their mother."

Jeff felt paralyzed and hopeless. In his desperation, he cried out to God, "Where are You in all of this?!"

To this day, Jeff is haunted by God's response.

"Jeff, where are *you* in all of this?"

Less than a year later, Jeff gave up his plans for graduate school and traveled back to South Africa, trying to live out justice in the communities that had forced him to reevaluate his life. His time there gradually led him to found Themba International, which seeks to enact justice in the developing world through fashion. By training women in Jeffreys Bay, South Africa, to sew, design, and construct garments, Themba is investing in the lives of those on the margins by providing meaningful and lasting employment.

Jeffreys Bay, in the Eastern Cape province, is one of the top travel destinations for surfers in the world, as well as the site of a Billabong factory and an event on the professional surfing tour. This glamour exists side by side with generational poverty, informal settlements, and ramshackle living conditions. In that context, Themba works to extend justice and dignity into the lives of its employees, helping them participate in building resiliency and self-determination into their communities.

"My priorities have changed," reports Jeff. "Society tells me to pursue pleasure, wealth, and power, but God is teaching me to become relentless in my pursuit of mercy, humility, love, and justice." This new pursuit has taken Jeff back to graduate school, where he hopes to build his capacity to be more compassionate and faithful in his desire to follow God's calling.

"I'm just a single thread in the garment of humanity," Jeff reflected recently, "but I'm connected to something so much greater and more beautiful than my solitary life. I thank God for what He is showing me—that we are knit together."

Jeff says it reminds him of what Martin Luther King Jr. once said—words that inspired the mission of Themba: "All [people] are caught in an inescapable network of mutuality, tied in a single garment of destiny. Whatever affects one directly affects all indirectly. I can never be what I ought to be until you are what you ought to be, and you can never be what you ought to be until I am what I ought to be."[8]

Perhaps, like Jeff, you have been called to a life of vocational justice, or for the first time you are becoming aware of the need for justice. Wherever you are in your journey of pursuing justice, awareness and engagement can only take you so far.

Every journey toward justice begins with *awareness*—when we're awakened to the lack of quality education in many inner cities, or the issue of clean water in sub-Saharan Africa, we feel compelled to engage. Awareness, although not the whole story, is a good thing, which is one of the reasons I believe in The Justice Conference and other movements that help raise awareness regarding justice.

Engagement happens when we decide that rather than sitting around feeling bad about injustice, we're going to get up and do something about it. This decision quickly carries us to the next step: recognizing our *need for greater capacity*. It doesn't matter how much passion we have if we don't have the skills or the information to be effective.

This is where *education* enters the picture, for education *develops our minds and builds capacity and engagement* in us.

Any novice fisher who tries to cast a fly rod without first learning the technique will be ineffective at best—and dangerous at worst. To be successful at fly-fishing, the fisher must first grow his capacity and capability. Similarly, we need to grow our capacity and capability to practice justice.

Since all people are knit together by the *Imago Dei*, we cannot allow ourselves to become overwhelmed by injustice and sit on the sidelines. But neither can we allow ourselves to be underwhelmed by injustice, trying to fix everything either by ourselves or without the necessary wisdom and knowledge. If we want to change the world, we have to be equipped; we have to grow; we have to learn *how* to change it.

A GROWING COMMUNITY

"Education is the most powerful weapon which you can use to change the world." This statement is attributed to Nelson Mandela, and it describes why, in 2008, we founded Kilns College in Bend, Oregon.

Kilns is a unique startup—a community of learners united around a single purpose: understanding and teaching how to live out God's call to justice. What we're about is an educational experience that is laser-focused on building students' capacity and equipping them to give their lives away. Some schools define success by how many graduates they place in jobs at Fortune 500 companies; we want to place our graduates wherever God is calling them.

My vision of an excellent educational experience is this:

An affordable college whose faculty are devoted to inspiring and equipping its students through educational excellence, dialogue, service, and identifying and developing gifts and talents.

A welcoming community in which fellow students mutually support each other and live life together as friends and confidantes.

A creative collaboration between individual passions and God's wisdom and calling.

We started small: just four night classes to allow people with nine-to-five jobs to enroll, and a handful of part-time students. As I write this, however, Kilns offers several dozen classes and four distinct degree options—each designed around the passions of the individual student.

Education is a vital piece of pursuing justice over a lifetime. When Jeff Johnson was confronted by injustice in South Africa, he took time off from college and canceled the plans he had then to attend graduate school. However, as his engagement with justice deepened, he understood that further schooling was exactly what he needed to be further equipped.

Sometimes the most urgent problems are the ones requiring the most study.

LEARNING IN WARTIME

We are challenged constantly by what's been called the "fierce urgency of now." Statistics are batted around. Celebrities take up causes and jet to all corners of the globe. Every new injustice we hear about is billed as the one cause we should act on.

Can we really say that education or learning is valuable when presented with a list of emergencies? I'd be troubled if I saw a paramedic open a medical book at the scene of a head-on collision. Isn't the time for learning behind us, and the time for action at hand?

One of the first things we want in a professional—whether a doctor, lawyer, teacher, or plumber—is education and experience. Yet one of the first things we expect from ourselves is action.

The professions I listed are all complex, and we agree that training and education are critical to their success. How equally complex is fighting injustice in our communities and across the world! Shouldn't we *expect* to need education if we attempt such a complicated and messy undertaking?

Many people striving to give their lives away understand this and have chosen to educate and train themselves. Doctors, agricultural scientists, policy lobbyists, police officers, immigration lawyers, trauma therapists—all of these have invested time and money and considerable energy into preparing themselves to serve.

Education can do more than teach us to care about injustice— it can equip us to do something about it.

During World War I, C. S. Lewis left Oxford University to join the British Army. Universities faced the very real question of why students would stay in school and study while their friends fought in the trenches.

Years later, on October 22, 1939, Lewis lectured at St. Mary the Virgin Church, Oxford, on the necessity of education in wartime. This lecture later became an essay titled "Learning in Wartime."[9] In this essay, Lewis suggested that we misunderstand present wars, injustices, national debts, and other crises as *new* situations that make the pursuit of education less worthy or important, while in reality there are always situations that seem to be urgent and that battle for the focus of our souls. A literal war—or the felt need of a particular injustice—will simply make this ongoing reality feel more pressing.

In that context, he diagnosed three impediments to education:

Excitement: we can feel the need to respond to the latest crisis, but Christians are called to pursue the task at hand to the glory of God and to be fully present with what is set before us. Sometimes that task is education.

Frustration: we live in awareness of time's constraint, but refusing to start for fear we won't have time to finish is not the right response. Instead we are to focus our energy on today, since that is all we are promised.

Fear: war reminds us of our mortality and our ability to suffer[10]—and this is proper. War should sober us to the work at hand and prepare us to pursue our calling with courage instead of cowardice, even if that calling is education.

Education is a means, not an end. We don't enroll in formal education ad nauseam as a way of escaping life. Rather, we educate ourselves in order to become equipped to respond wisely to God's calling. As French theologian Bernard of Clairvaux said, "There are those who seek knowledge for the sake of knowledge; that is Curiosity. There are those who seek knowledge to be known by others; that is Vanity. There are those who seek knowledge in order to serve; that is Love."[11]

CELEBRITIES AND SAINTS

The late Librarian of Congress Daniel Boorstin was the first to define a celebrity as "a person well known for well-knownness."[12]

There is a chasm between saint and celebrity. One requires character, while the other mere popularity. Discipleship is what builds our character, and it's the work of a lifetime. We can become an overnight celebrity, but never an overnight saint.

Justice has become a fad in some circles, a personal brand we can use to accessorize our personality. This is a way of twisting justice into our own personal "celebrity"—being known for what we say we're *for*, not for who we actually are or what we're actually doing.

The heart of justice is something much deeper than fashion or celebrity. Justice is a long-term commitment, and it requires long-term learning, growth, and discipleship. It is, in the words of Eugene Peterson, "a long obedience in the same direction."[13]

Justice isn't well-known for well-knownness. In fact, justice may never even be known or celebrated. When it is, however, it points back to God, the source of goodness, as a mirror reflects the sun.

There is no end to the value of learning. Like health, if some is good, more is better. This doesn't always happen in a formal, institutional setting such as a classroom, but it should always happen. As George MacDonald wrote, "It matters little where a [person] may be at this moment; the point is whether he [or she] is growing."[14]

INVESTMENT

As I speak with people about justice, I sometimes hear a variation on this desire: *I want to be a modern-day William Wilberforce. I'm going to end slavery in my day.*

Perhaps, instead of wanting to *do* like Wilberforce, we should spend more of our energy trying to *be* like Wilberforce.

Wilberforce began thinking and praying about the abolition of the slave trade in the 1780s, first bringing up the issue in Parliament in 1787 when he was twenty-nine.

On July 26, 1833, Wilberforce was told that a bill would certainly pass that would abolish slavery in the British Empire. Three days later, Wilberforce died. He was seventy-three.

Wilberforce was constant and measured in his resolve to end slavery. He dramatically changed the world. He is widely credited with being a major force in ending the slave trade and abolishing slavery in the British Empire.

Do you believe he regretted giving his life to a cause that took a lifetime to achieve? I don't.

Justice doesn't have a finish line, and neither does education. We never reach a point where we cannot learn, where ceasing to learn would make us, or our world, better. It takes perseverance to walk the road of justice, and we cannot know where or when—or if—it will end for us.

Nicholas Wolterstorff, a professor of theology at Yale, stated, "We [institutions of higher education] must not just teach *about* justice—though we must; I mean we must teach *for* justice. The graduate whom we seek to produce must be one who *practices* justice."[15]

Do you want to change the world?

In a cultural climate where it's far easier to cast stones and critique, let's instead choose to engage.

This isn't something we accomplish overnight. It's not about one-time actions, but about our calling. It's not about single events, but about a lifetime of faithfulness. Learning to change the world is rarely easy or convenient—it can be complex, costly, and messy. With so many injustices confronting us at home and abroad, these times can seem overwhelming . . . but they don't have to overwhelm us. Let's not let what we cannot do interfere with what we can do.[16]

What will we decide to do with the time and opportunities we've been given? It isn't enough to *say* we want to change the world. To change the world requires knowledge and skill, as well as dedication, which is why the motto of Kilns College is *learn to change the world.*

> And let us consider how we may spur one another on toward love and good deeds.
>
> HEBREWS 10:24

CREATION AND CONSERVATION

A conversation with Tom Rowley, executive director of A
Rocha USA, a Christian conservation organization working in
nineteen countries on five continents to mobilize a response to
the ecological crises we face today (www.arocha-usa.org). He
has worked with the National Rural Development Partnership,
the President's Council on Sustainable Development, and the
Organization for Economic Co-operation and Development.

Some suburban or urban Christians might think that creation is "out there" and therefore isn't something they can do much about.

The main mistake there is forgetting that *we* are part of creation—
all of us, all the time! The environment isn't something "out there"
or something that only shows up in national parks. God's creation
is everything God made, like air and water and trees and people.
So creation is all around us, even if it's water coming out of a tap in
Chicago. You absolutely don't have to go somewhere else to know
and care about the environment.

How did we lose our way in caring for creation?
I look at it like a series of falling dominoes. At creation, everything

was in a state of shalom. But sin broke our relationship with God, then with ourselves, then with others, then with nature. We can't set the dominoes back up in reverse order, and we can't leave out one of the dominoes. If the problem is holistic, the remedy must be as well. If brokenness carries through all our relationships, restoration must as well. We've got to begin with a right relationship with the Creator if we want to restore right relationships in creation.

Some wonder how we can justify investing in creation care when tens of thousands of kids die each day from starvation and poverty.

It's a false dilemma. It's true that we're limited in what we can pay for and what we can pursue. If I have a hundred dollars, I can't give a hundred dollars to food aid *and* a hundred dollars to reforesting the barren land that helped precipitate that food crisis. But I should pay attention to both. The solutions have to be integrated or else they'll be isolated Band-Aids. God doesn't give us the choice to care about only certain things He cares about—He isn't an either-or God; He's a both/and God! We're supposed to care about *everything* He cares about.

Can you share an example of what you're working toward?

We worked in a part of Kenya where there used to be massive coastal forests, but over the years the forests had dwindled to a fraction of their former size. The people wanted to send their kids to school, and one of the only ways they had to make money was cutting down the trees and converting them into charcoal to sell. In an effort to help their kids, they were actually hurting their own futures. We helped them create an ecotourism industry so they could make money from protecting the trees. Now creation is being protected, the kids are being sent to school, and the people are beginning to control their own economic destiny. That's an example of environmental injustice that's starting to look a lot more just.

Some wonder why we should be out caring for creation instead of out sharing the gospel.

What we find is that when we send out a team to help Trout Unlimited to care for streams, for example, we're taking the church out into the world. Most of those folks aren't coming through the doors of our churches. Truth be told, they often care more about creation than God's church does, and when we get out there and work beside them, that's a strong witness—to both of us! We can take advantage of chances to witness *and* do justice as we begin doing what God told us to do, which is to be stewards of *His* creation.

What are some good first steps or first practices for Christians who want to care for creation?

Get to know the place you live. Learn about your watershed, the trees in your region, the birds. Steven Bouma-Prediger says, "We care for only what we love. We love only what we know. We truly know only what we experience."* Then he talks about how we're destined to overuse or abuse creation if we only have a surface knowledge of it. When we talk about "the environment" in the abstract, we understand very little about it. It's hard to care. But when I learn that the tree in my yard is a juniper and the birds who come to feed are Oregon juncos and house finches and California quail, I'm a lot closer to a right relationship with

---

* Steven Bouma-Prediger, *For the Beauty of the Earth: A Christian Vision for Creation Care*, 2nd ed. (Grand Rapids: Baker Academic, 2010), 21.

creation and I have a deeper sense of awe for the Creator. The best part is that learning about God's creation and caring for it isn't a duty—it's a blessing. We're meant to enjoy it and enjoy the Creator in the process.

What are some hopeful practices or signs of life?

I see people beginning to reconnect to *place*. We all belong to a place where God has put us. Paul wrote to the church at Galatia, at Corinth. The church, I think, is a people set in a place and called to care for that place—for all the people and plants and animals in that place. Reconnecting to place is the first step in bringing shalom back to a place.

At A Rocha, we like to follow the model of Nehemiah—to help people build their section of the wall, right where they live, and connect it to something larger.

EIGHTEEN

GIVE YOUR LIFE AWAY

Why It's Better to Give than Receive

Look for yourself, and you will find in the long run only hatred, loneliness, despair, rage, ruin, and decay. But look for Christ and you will find Him, and with Him everything else thrown in.[1]

C. S. LEWIS

When you give your life away, you get it back enhanced.[2]

WALTER BRUEGGEMANN

Remember my friend Marcel Serubungo? He is a pastor who works with World Relief in his hometown of Goma, Congo, located in eastern Congo, which has, for decades, been one of the most violent places on the planet.

When a team from Antioch first met with Marcel in Congo, he made the comment, "If you do not commit suicide—like we have committed suicide—then do not come to the Congo." His powerful statement led us to adopt the phrase "Give your life away," which drives much of our thinking at Antioch.

It's not a cliché to be repeated by masochists or frowning

Christians devoid of joy. Rather, it captures an invitation Jesus gives to all people.

The truth is, we are *all* giving our lives away—the only question is, to what?

We spend ourselves on television, money, power, sex, leisure, adventure, and fame, but as Jesus taught, these things cannot give us life in return. They are a bad investment. If we look for life by spending ourselves here, we look in vain.

Jesus said, "Whoever does not take up their cross and follow me is not worthy of me. Whoever finds their life will lose it, and whoever loses their life for my sake will find it" (Matthew 10:38–39). Jesus invites us to give our lives to Him. Not flippantly, but faithfully—as those who want to find life badly enough to pursue it even through trials.

The objects of consumer culture, ironically, consume us. Conversely, in giving our lives away to God by serving others, laboring for justice, and loving sacrificially, our lives are given back to us.

Recently, as Marcel shared a meal with my family, I asked him to tell me more about what he'd meant by his comment on committing suicide. After pausing to reflect, he elaborated in his characteristic measured pace. He talked about getting on his knees before each difficult trip and giving his life to Jesus, whether he returned or not. He told us that when his family hears about trouble in a region where he's working, "they don't eat that day."

That's Marcel's way of saying they pray and fast as if his life depends on it.

As hard as it sounds to talk about "committing suicide," I believe this is an image for the way every Christian is called to give his or her life to Christ—to give their lives away—knowing that only Christ can give life back.

DIE BEFORE YOU DIE

One of the best things I've read in Dietrich Bonhoeffer is his plain reminder, "When Christ calls a man, he bids him come and die."[3] It's one of the most elemental statements of this simple truth: for Christians, having all of our needs, wants, and wishes met in this life is not the chief end. We were made for another kingdom.

Jesus seems to be calling us to something very different with His invitation "Take up your cross, and follow me" (Matthew 16:24 NLT).

You don't take up a cross unless it's to die.

That means sacrifice. Think of how Jesus confronted the rich fool in Luke 12—not to ridicule, but in the hope he'd loosen his grip on his material security and respond in faith.

I've heard it said that it's easy to agree with John the Baptist— "[Jesus] must increase, but I must decrease"—when you're in full retreat and don't have much going for you (John 3:30 ESV). Can we say this, however, when all the advantages are flowing our way?

It's a question I ask myself often, and I don't always like the answer.

Can we give away stuff after we start to receive a lot of it? Are we able to follow Christ with open hands when we're offered an easier way? Perhaps that's the crux of the difference between the American Dream and the call of Jesus: Jesus requires us to have enough faith to choose to die at the moment our culture offers us life.

Do we truly believe that giving our lives away is the only way to have true life?

Do we have faith enough to die before we die?

HUMAN RIGHTS AND BROKEN EGGS

Many Americans, like me, usually live in a relatively just and fair cultural bubble, often oblivious to many injustices surrounding the community or embedded in its history.

Once, while teaching a course on the history of human rights, I tried to illustrate on the first day of class the give-and-take nature of a just society. To do this, I asked two volunteers to toss an egg back and forth. The illustration was that in a just society, justice flows naturally and easily, from one to the other. It is as much *take* as it is *give*. We have rights and responsibilities, but we don't mind giving because of what we get back.

Hidden in my hand was a second egg, which I planned to break on a stool to shock the class and change the metaphor. Pursuing justice, or cleaning up the broken egg, is less about getting something and more about a commitment to roll up our sleeves and get dirty. When we engage injustice, it may not seem as if we'll get much in return.

I didn't realize that all I needed to do was gently drop the egg to break it. Instead, I slammed it on the stool with so much force that it sprayed yolk across the three girls sitting in the front row. But everyone got the analogy . . . except the girls covered in egg.

Luke 6:32–34 says, "If you love those who love you, what credit is that to you? Even sinners love those who love them. And if you do good to those who are good to you, what credit is that to you? Even sinners do that. And if you lend to those from whom you expect repayment, what credit is that to you? Even sinners lend to sinners, expecting to be repaid in full."

When our daily environment is rich with justice, we can forget the value and importance of it. We can fall into the trap of thinking that the rest of the world must be doing okay also, without our help. All we see is the comfortable give-and-take of the relatively just society in which we go to work and raise our families.

I had several friends in high school who were on the football team. When they went to parties on Friday nights after football games, they'd often end up committing some kind of vandalism. High school kids at a party can vandalize if they have no concern for the house. They'll destroy it themselves or let others destroy it without a second thought.

Christians can't be vandals. Instead, they act as stewards and protectors and with concern for the world's overall well-being.

We are responsible agents in this, our Father's world. Philippians 2:2–4 says, "Make my joy complete by being like-minded, having the same love, being one in spirit and of one mind. Do nothing out of selfish ambition or vain conceit. Rather, in humility value others above yourselves, not looking to your own interests but each of you to the interests of the others."

If we aren't giving our lives away, the world won't flourish—and neither will we. That's why I set out to write this book—not to talk about justice for the sake of discussion, but to talk about it as a bridge to God, full life, and happiness. What we find is that justice, obedience, and right living affect all other things. They are gifts that transform the giver. They are acts that shape the one acting.

Pursuing justice affects the relationship between God, ourselves, and the people with whom we enter into relationship. It's a triangle. Change one point and you change the other lines and angles.

Our lives are bound up with the lives of others. Our joy is bound up with the joy of others.

IS GIVING REALLY BETTER?

Paul, bidding farewell to the Ephesian elders in Acts 20:35, said, "In everything I did, I showed you that by this kind of hard work we must help the weak, remembering the words the Lord Jesus himself said: 'It is more blessed to give than to receive.'"

Is it really better to give than receive? The answer comes in the following promises:

> A generous person will prosper;
>> whoever refreshes others will be refreshed. (Proverbs 11:25)

> Cast your bread upon the waters,
>> for after many days you will find it again. (Ecclesiastes 11:1)

> "His master replied, 'Well done, good and faithful servant! You have been faithful with a few things; I will put you in charge of many things. Come and share your master's happiness!'" (Matthew 25:21)

> A man reaps what he sows. (Galatians 6:7)

The paradox of giving life away is that we can't give without also receiving. It is like exhaling and inhaling. To do the one brings about the other. It's God's comic irony that we can never out-give Him or His blessings. "Good will come to those who are generous and lend freely, who conduct their affairs with justice," says Psalm 112:5.

Giving your life away is an investment. Sometimes I like to joke that I'm simply being smart with how I invest my life, since God promises that giving away my life is actually the greatest form of receiving. *Give your life away* defines how I seek happiness—not in selfishness, but in service and sacrifice.

Remember Isaiah 58?

> "If you keep your feet from breaking the Sabbath
> and from doing as you please on my holy day,
> if you call the Sabbath a delight
> and the LORD's holy day honorable,
> and if you honor it by not going your own way
> and not doing as you please or speaking idle words,
> then you will find your joy in the LORD,
> and I will cause you to ride in triumph on the heights of
> the land?
> and to feast on the inheritance of your father Jacob."
> For the mouth of the LORD has spoken. (vv. 13–14)

If we learn to worship—to give our lives fully to God and others—our lives will become arguments for finding goodness and gladness in God.

True happiness, a state of joy and contentment, comes not in pursuing pleasure as an end, but in giving our lives away. Matthew 19:30 says, "But many who are first will be last, and many who are last will be first."

It truly is better to give than to receive.

JESUS AND JOY

The problem with talking about happiness is that the conversation is soon swallowed by myriad voices promising quick fixes, self-help, and immediate gratification.

However, *not* talking about something important is very different from providing a *corrective*. If our version of love became deficient, the correct answer would not be to stop talking about love, but instead to provide a healthy theology of love.

That's why providing a healthy theology of joy and happiness that is rooted in God is vital. Some will wonder if finding joy in doing an act of goodness or justice pollutes the purity of the action.

It doesn't.

If we help a neighbor, and he or she thanks us, we often say, "My pleasure!" That isn't a lie; it truly is our pleasure and privilege to help someone. So connecting joy with service is a natural way to think about how we already behave.

I began this book by telling the story of what I learned in visiting a nursing home on a regular basis as a new Christian. Pure love is love that gives even when the other person cannot give something back. What I learned over time is that pure love inevitably carries with it joy. I'm happiest when I'm showing love to others.

Now, as I struggle to continue giving my life away and to call others to a life of sacrifice, I'm learning to trust the twin motivations in my mind—doing good and receiving joy. Psalm 45:7 says, "You love righteousness and hate wickedness; therefore God, your God, has set you above your companions by anointing you with the oil of joy." Hebrews 1:9 applies that psalm to Jesus, about whom

God says, "You have loved righteousness and hated wickedness; therefore God, your God, has set you above your companions by anointing you with the oil of joy."

Not only can we see joy as a natural crown for righteous and just living, but in Hebrews 12:1–3 we can discover something paradigm altering:

> Therefore, since we are surrounded by such a great cloud of witnesses, let us throw off everything that hinders and the sin that so easily entangles. And let us run with perseverance the race marked out for us, fixing our eyes on Jesus, the pioneer and perfecter of faith. *For the joy* set before him he endured the cross, scorning its shame, and sat down at the right hand of the throne of God. Consider him who endured such opposition from sinners, so that you will not grow weary and lose heart. (emphasis added)

We sometimes think Jesus pursued His calling with stoic resolution, but the writer to the Hebrews implied there was an added motivation.

For the *joy*.

The author of Hebrews chose his language carefully, using words in parallel to reinforce meaning. In verses 1 and 2 of chapter 12, the writer used the same Greek word, *prokeimai*, to modify the race and the joy. They were translated *marked out* and *set before* in English, but the Greek word means "I am set before, am already there." This gives the sense that our race is akin to Jesus' suffering, and His joy, like our joy, accompanies the journey. It is an ongoing, present, *and* future joy. Jesus was motivated, even in sacrifice, by joy.

We often hear these verses used as an exhortation to run the race of life in order to earn a heavenly reward. What it seems this passage actually proposes is that when we follow Christ's example and run the race, *we are already in the presence of joy.*

Jesus pursued the path of sacrifice motivated by and fully aware of the joy inherent in that path. Likewise, when we choose to give our lives away, we do so motivated by that same knowledge—that our deepest fulfillment and, yes, *joy,* comes as we walk the path of sacrifice marked out before us.

When we look for life, we don't find it. When we give our lives away for His kingdom's sake, we find them—and joy is the fitting reward of just living.

Giving is made complete by joy. As a father, when one of my daughters voluntarily chooses to forgo her own desires in order to serve her sisters, it never fails to elicit a joyful blessing of approval from me. God responds the same way when we forgo our desires and serve others, which is why Paul can say in 2 Corinthians 9:7 that everyone "should give what he has decided in his heart to give, not reluctantly or under compulsion, for God loves a *cheerful* giver" (emphasis added).

What a paradigm-altering truth: obey cheerfully!

It's not only giving that God loves. It's giving in a spirit of appreciation, sacrifice, and an already-present joy that God loves.

Martin Luther once pointed out the ironic absence of godly happiness from the life of Christians, stating, "Too many Christians envy the sinners their pleasures and the saints their joy, because they don't have either one."[4] Yet Jesus, who authored and perfected our faith, died for us motivated by joy. Joy is the natural outcome of selflessness.

THE ULTIMATE VISION

Remember the Latin word *beati*, which gave the Beatitudes their name? That word is also where medieval theologians derived the concept of the "beatific vision." The beatific vision is the view of heaven and what we will behold when we stand before God. It implies the greatest degree of blessedness and happiness we will experience. For Saint Thomas Aquinas, the beatific vision— unmediated or direct face-to-face relationship with God—was the end wherein his happiness would be fully realized and complete. Saint Cyprian described it this way: "How great will your glory and happiness be, to be allowed to see God, to be honored with sharing the joy of salvation and eternal light with Christ your Lord and God . . . to delight in the joy of immortality in the Kingdom of Heaven with the righteous and God's friends."[5]

Happiness, far from being a distraction in our view of God, is bound up in our view of God. I can no more extract my sense of awe from seeing a sunset than I can extract my sense of happiness from doing good, obeying, and being in the presence of God.

Bonhoeffer understood what happiness looked like, even in the midst of suffering.

This is the way the Beatitudes are given in Luke. Here nothing is said about the "poor in spirit" (Matthew 5:3) or "hunger and thirst for righteousness" (Matthew 5:6), but "blessed are you poor, you hungry, you who cry," as we know you to be in this world. Blessed are you Lazaruses of all times, for you will be comforted in Abraham's bosom. Blessed are you rejected and disdained, you victims of society, you jobless men and women, you crushed and ruined, you abandoned and forsaken who have suffered violence, rape, and abuse, you miserable in body and soul. Blessed are you, for God's joy will come over you and rest on you forever. This is the gospel, the good news of the new world that is breaking in, the new order of things that is God's world and God's order. "The deaf hear, the blind see, the lame walk, and the good news is preached to the poor" (Luke 7:22).[6]

God's joy will come over us and rest on us forever. To arrive at God is to arrive back home—and the happiness of heaven cannot be taken away.

FAITH'S BIG GAMBLE

A duty toward obedience is a duty toward happiness. Each command or leading of God is directed toward our greatest good and our greatest happiness—as well as the greatest happiness of others. It may require a delay of gratification. We may endure temporary pain. Perhaps we will even lose our lives. Yet this is for a greater and lasting joy.

Faith's big gamble is that in giving up one's life completely, we hope to receive back our life, both now and eternally.

Two days before I finished the manuscript for this book, I was talking to Dr. John Perkins on the phone at a café where I was grabbing some oatmeal. The year before he'd told me, "I want to be a Barnabas.[7] I want to encourage the next generation of people who are involved in justice and help get them connected to each other."

The picture of Dr. Perkins—who has been a civil rights leader for half a century—taking on a focus of serving, pouring himself out for, and encouraging others, has stuck in my mind as a living example of what it means to give your life away.

Maybe I needed some of that encouragement. As he spoke, I furiously scrawled notes on both sides of a receipt I had with me. In our conversation, he pointed me toward a verse I hadn't yet thought about in the context of justice: Matthew 6:33, which says, "But seek first his kingdom and his righteousness [*dikaiosune*: being right with God and with others, justice], and all these things will be given to you as well."

I asked what made him think of that verse. "Society doesn't meet this with enthusiasm, Ken, but when we will to do His will, He *will* bring the opportunities. We need to focus on His will with whatever time we have left," he told me. "Seek first His kingdom and His righteousness, and all will be given."

SEEK FIRST

We did a sermon series at Antioch a number of years ago about what it looks like to give your life away. The short answer is that it looks different for every man, woman, and child. When it comes to *how* God wants us to give our lives away, *there is no formula.*

To discern the path God would have you walk, begin with repentance. Lament the problem of pain and the ache of injustice in the world. Ask God to lead you, and listen long and intently for His answer. Be willing to obey unreservedly, no matter how big or small, no matter how heroic or mundane the task God sets before you or the path God calls you to walk.

At The Justice Conference, we highlight *creative advocacy*—the process by which artists use their unique gifts to help vulnerable

people and tell the story of justice in the world. Such artists are following God's leading and trusting that giving away their time and
talents is the path by which God is directing them toward joy.

I have an electrician friend, Jim, who is often seen sipping black
coffee outside a local coffee shop, wearing jeans, a flannel button-
down, and a tan Carhartt vest. Like most in his generation, he is
unassuming and honest, a hard worker who has spent the larger
part of his life developing a successful family business.

Jim isn't the typical poster boy for justice, but he has developed a life deliberately marked with compassion and generosity.
Jim regularly offers himself as an electrician to help those in need,
donating his time, and often materials, for local nonprofit repair
and installation needs.

Jim and his wife live with their finances in open hands. Every
month or so Jim comes into the church office to drop off a wad of
large bills, saying, "I got a few extra jobs . . . See if there's someone
who could use this to get them through the month."

Jim has developed a lifestyle of justice in which he constantly
gives himself away by being generous with his skills and his
resources. He is filled with joy.

Jim gambled on faith, and he won big.

What are *we* waiting for?

A BLESSED DEFEAT

As I mentioned earlier in this chapter, Jesus said, "Whoever
does not take up their cross and follow me is not worthy of me.
Whoever finds their life will lose it, and whoever loses their
life for my sake will find it" (Matthew 10:38–39). I also quoted
Proverbs 11:25, which says, "A generous person will prosper;

whoever refreshes others will be refreshed." Now let me put these verses in terms of the golden rule and an electrical analogy from my engineering days.

When a circuit is open, nothing can flow through it. If a circuit is closed and complete, the electricity moves through it and the power turns on. Practicing the golden rule completes a circuit with God; blessing moves through it and the power turns on.

If we are willing to risk all to follow our God, we can expect to find nothing less than the fullness of joy in the process. But when we wait in apathy, the "circuit" remains open, and some of the presence and power of God we're offered in this life cannot flow.

It is counterintuitive to die in order to live, but as Jesus said, "What good will it be for someone to gain the whole world, yet forfeit their soul?" (Matthew 16:24–26). Jim Elliot, a missionary who was killed in Ecuador, is well-known for having paraphrased Jesus' words, saying, "He is no fool who gives what he cannot keep to gain what he cannot lose."

Finding joy does not mean we will have it easy. We won't always be comfortable or experience a pain-free life.

What finding joy *does* mean is knowing with certainty that we are inside of God's will. It means experiencing a satisfaction and fulfillment independent of particular pleasures. It means, ultimately, that we're truly living the life we were meant to live—even if that life is cut short.

SEEDS OF HOPE

The kingdom of God is an upside-down kingdom. It beckons us to gamble all, to trust radically, to come and die so that we might live—to give our lives away. Giving life away is a paradox. It's losing so we can win. It's giving so we can receive. It's risking for security. It's faith. The kingdom of God means *living that tension*.

Delayed gratification is not denial of gratification. For the joy set before him, Jesus endured the cross. For the joy set before us, we, too, can endure suffering.

Recall how we imagined Jesus in the introduction, sitting on a rock, with His disciples gathered in a loose ring. He's looking around, searching for a way to *somehow* get through to them. He stands, walks to the edge of a nearby field, and plucks a head of wheat. He rolls it between His rough palms and blows away the chaff. Holding a single kernel up to the light, He looks at His friends.

"Unless a seed falls to the ground and dies," He says, "it remains only a single seed. But if it dies . . ." He tosses the seed into the field and locks eyes with the disciples one by one before driving home the point. "If it dies, it produces many seeds."

When we die to ourselves—when we give our lives away—God takes our lives and uses them to bring new life and restore creation and goodness.

In a broken world full of inequity and injustice—from human trafficking to racism to gender violence, and from gossip to consumerism to petty anger—can we *really* treat our lives as God's? Can we redeem and energize the concept of justice and embrace the fullness of God's plan for creation? Can we expect to find true life and happiness in obeying Him as we seek to give our lives away for others?

I believe we can. I believe we *must*.

And I believe that's what this life is about.

You love righteousness and hate wickedness;
> therefore God, your God, has set you above your companions
> by anointing you with the oil of joy.

PSALM 45:7

NINETEEN

LIVE AND DIE FOR BIGGER THINGS

The average man does not know what to do with his life,
yet wants another one which will last forever.[1]

ANATOLE FRANCE

Every man's life ends the same way. It is only the details of
how he lived and how he died that distinguish one man from
another.[2]

ERNEST HEMINGWAY

Many of us desire a more radical faith, but we can't stomach the idea of giving our lives away. We wait and wait for God to tell us one action, one specific task, and we won't move until we hear it. While we wait for God to call us, however, we do nothing. The abolitionist Frederick Douglass diagnosed the fallacy in waiting for the perfect moment to pursue justice:

The whole history of the progress of human liberty shows that all concessions yet made to her august claims, have been born of earnest struggle. . . . If there is no struggle there is no progress. Those who profess to favor freedom and yet depreciate agitation, are men who want crops without plowing up the ground, they want rain without thunder and lightning. They want the ocean without the awful roar of its many waters.[3]

What captures me about Douglass's statement is the necessary connection between pursuit and the ends we hope to achieve.

People like those Douglass described remind me of the guy on my high school baseball team who would let twenty pitches pass in batting practice before ever swinging the bat. No matter how wise it may seem to ignore pitches you don't want, you'll never learn how to hit by merely watching.

There's a difference between a specific *calling* from God and His *general call* to humanity. Both are equally binding, but the specific call—hearing our names and being told exactly what to do—is much more appealing in our individualistic culture.

Yet while we wait to hear our names called, God's moral authority continues to rest in His general calling, always inviting us and always expecting us to follow and obey.

Jesus calls us to follow. He calls His followers to love. In His kingdom the harvest is plentiful, He said, but the workers are few.

We don't always need to see where the road leads—we simply need the faithfulness and commitment to take the next few steps in front of us.

ALL ON FIRE

William Lloyd Garrison, born in 1805, was a prominent American abolitionist and social reformer. He is best known as one of the founders of the American Anti-Slavery Society and the New

England Anti-Slavery Society, where he promoted immediate emancipation of U.S. slaves. Garrison was also a prolific journalist, later becoming the editor of his own abolitionist newspaper, *The Liberator.*

In one of the weightier biographies on Garrison, Henry Mayer described a conversation between Garrison and his friend Samuel May about Garrison's extreme nature. I'm going to quote it at length because it is so powerful. Mayer wrote:

> Yet even Samuel May, who understood more than most the dramaturgy of Garrison's editorship, once entreated him to be more temperate. While out for a walk in early spring, Garrison listened "patiently and tenderly," May recalled, as the older man rehearsed the concerns of their more timorous friends. Then, however, Garrison exploded, insisting that he would only soften his language "when the poor downtrodden slaves tell me that I am too harsh."
>
> "O, my friend," urged May, "do try to moderate your indignation and keep more cool; why, you are all on fire."
>
> Garrison stopped walking and looked straight at his beloved friend. He laid his hand upon May's shoulder with "a kind but empathetic pressure" and, speaking "slowly, with deep emotion," said:
>
> "Brother May, I have need to be *all on fire*, for I have mountains of ice about me to melt."
>
> The two friends stood there in the street, silent for a moment, and May could feel the pressure on his shoulder long after Garrison had withdrawn his hand. "From that hour," May wrote forty years later, "I have never said a word to Mr. Garrison in complaint of his style."[4]

I love that phrase—*all on fire*. Samuel May was speaking about the indignation his friend William Lloyd Garrison felt about slavery. It was an indignation felt so deeply that it was evident on the outside. I see in that phrase a picture of a life consumed with purpose.

What would you lose everything for? Is there something bigger to give your life to? My friend Marcel said, "If you haven't committed suicide, like we've committed suicide, then don't come to Congo." In other words, until you are ready to give your life away, you are not able to help.

Unless we've chosen to sacrifice our life to serve the most vulnerable, we shouldn't pretend to be *all on fire*. As Jesus said in the Sermon on the Mount, "Let your light shine before others, that they may see your good deeds and glorify your Father in heaven" (Matthew 5:16).

PASSION

Antoine de Saint-Exupery once wrote, "If you want to build a ship, don't drum up people to collect wood and don't assign them tasks and work, but rather teach them to long for the endless immensity of the sea."[5]

Saint-Exupery was writing about passion, and passion and suffering are married.

Studying the history of the word *passion* shows that it referred to *suffering* long before it took on the sense of *strong desire* we often associate it with today. In fact, it actually originally referred specifically to the *suffering of Jesus on the cross*.[6]

Passion and suffering are married at the cross. They are married in love. They are married in every situation in which we lean into suffering and sacrifice as Jesus did.

Jesus' passion was the ultimate expression of giving His life away. His passion was the ultimate pursuit of joy. And His passion—His suffering in order that we may receive grace and joy—was the accomplishment of justice.

Justice isn't served best by guilt or pride or an overblown sense of duty or obligation. Rather, justice is kindled and unleashed when our joy, empathy, and passions carry it forward.

We try to follow Jesus and remain just another face in the crowd, neutral and safe, rather than following Jesus and becoming more like Him: in the crosshairs, divisive, persecuted. But as Garrison said about his approach to printing his abolitionist newspaper, "There shall be no neutrals; men shall either like or dislike me."[7]

Jesus' disciples learned this lesson over time. They went from arguing about privilege and power in what they thought was His earthly kingdom to becoming martyrs for the coming kingdom. And while they lived, they "turned the world upside down."[8]

Have we?

In pursuing justice, we don't need a formula, but a desire to see love reign. Not a list of wrongs to right, but a hunger for the joy that comes in giving. Not simply a cause, but a calling to live and die for bigger things. Can we truly call each other to a life of passion? To a life of deliberate sacrifice and self-denial? To a life of moral happiness instead of cheap pleasure?

Are we all on fire?

EVERYDAY JUSTICE

I was at a coffee shop recently and asked a friend for a deep word or topic.

"Greed," she replied.

It wasn't quite what I expected. From our conversation, I had been expecting something like *selfishness* or *consumerism*. As I considered her response, though, it struck me that each of us uses different words to deal with the same spiritual issues.

Lurking beneath our issues, our topics, our struggles, is sin. Liberals sometimes underestimate sin, just as conservatives sometimes stereotype it. Yet there it is, the definition of all the things I wish I did but don't, and all the things I wish I didn't but do.

Sin is captured best for me in Philippians 3:19. Listen to this language and the picture it conveys of sinners: "Their destiny is destruction, their god is their stomach, and their glory is in their shame. Their mind is set on earthly things."

Their destiny is destruction.

Their god is their stomach.

Their glory is in their shame.

Sin is appetite and idolatry intertwined, the celebration of selfish living. Whether it's greed, selfishness, consumerism, lust, gossip, competition, or nearly any other symptom of sin, it all begins with sin itself, alive in our bellies. It begins with appetites that overwhelm faith.

Whether we downplay sin or focus only on behavior, eventually we come back to having to deal with the thing itself: Sin, and our need for a cure—captivity, and our need for salvation.

The gospel radiates good news precisely because there are some shackles only it can unlock.

CALLING AND GIFTING

People all over the country are waking to the fact that justice isn't just another good cause for fanatics or those who chase fads. Justice is a necessary part of God's call in the Christian life. The call to follow Christ invites us into a sacrificial way of loving that will transform all of our relationships.

Truth corresponds to what is, justice to what ought to be.

Both truth and justice are lenses for seeing what is real and what matters. As such, justice isn't something we look at, but a paradigm we look through and enter into. We don't pursue justice alone, but rather join with all those who love God and would see His goodness reign. We carry our own biases and blind spots, our own agendas and comfort zones, but grace makes us just, and if we choose, we can grow together in love.

As a new Christian, I sat in college ministries at Clemson and heard various guests come in week after week to share their testimonies—missionaries, leaders, athletes, and more. Each person had an amazing story of seeing God move in just the right way at just the right time.

One night, I looked around at all of my fellow students, watching the faces of college men and women listening intently to a story of God's grace and power. I realized then that there are two kinds of people in this world: those who tell amazing God stories and those who listen to them—those who have seen God move in power and those who wish they had.

I decided at that moment that I wanted to be the kind of person telling the God stories, to God's glory.

I want to live a life in which I risk big things, in which I'm willing to follow God into any challenge. That's the only way to have plenty of stories to tell of how God showed up, moved mountains, and opened doors. I want this for my family. I want this for my church. I want this for you.

The cynic will attack, saying, "You can't really change the world. It's impossible." But as I used to say when we first planted

Antioch, "I'm looking for a few people idealistic enough to believe we can still change the world . . . because if it was impossible to change the world, God wouldn't have told us to try."

We weren't created by a fatalistic God; we don't follow a fatalistic Savior. World-changers surround us. Some are well-known to all, like Mother Teresa. Some are known only to you and a few others, like the teacher who inspired you or the parent who sacrificed so much so you could have more. Others are anonymous in this life, but their contributions remain.

The world changes every day in both big and small ways. I want to watch where God is moving and join Him there. There will always be injustice and sin, but even though we can't fix the world, we can certainly change it. When we planted Antioch, I believed this. I still believe this.

What has changed, however, is what the idea of living and dying for bigger things has come to mean.

It's less heroic now, and more fundamental. Living and dying for bigger things is an idea that now lives in my everyday world. It shows up in my patience with my children. It exists in the values I'm willing to live for and in how I make my decisions and lead my family and church. It changes how I spend my money and my time. It frames the questions of what I'm willing to do and what I'm willing to refrain from doing.

As I've learned the breadth and necessity of justice, I've come to see it as a ready sentry between myself and the daily life before me.

Justice is about my relationships here and my compassion there.

Justice is about knowing God as much as it is about serving God.

Justice has become both a daily necessity and an impossibility.

Justice makes immoral pleasure distasteful and grows a deep and abiding happiness.

Justice leads me into a way of living by faith that is beautifully awkward.

Justice highlights the amazing grace of a God who allows me to stand before Him as if I was fully just.

Jesus says that in seeking my life I will lose it, but in losing life—for His sake—I will find it. I have digested those words. I have proved them with the experiment of my own life. I have discovered happiness and joy in the paradox of giving my life away, just as I am learning to live and die for bigger things.

> Better a little with righteousness
> than much gain with injustice.
>
> PROVERBS 16:8

A PRAYER

Written for the inauguration of The Justice Conference
February, 2011

God,
Lead us to hear the cry of the vulnerable and oppressed,
lead us to care for the weak and needy,
and lead us to see others as brothers and sisters.
Help us appreciate goodness, love simply, and not hide
hypocrisy with rhetoric.
Let us embrace justice and mercy.
Grant us humility,
supply us with enough faith to give our lives away,
and bless us with strength when we grow weary.
Lord, let the knowledge of Your love
    fuel our commitment,
    inform our passions,
    stir our gratitude,
    and help us transform the world.
For You and Your glory—amen.

INTERLUDE

PICTURING JUSTICE

The top twenty-five words in *Pursuing Justice*,
as pictured by www.wordle.net.

ACKNOWLEDGMENTS

One of the challenges in telling your story is that it includes countless other voices, experiences, and insights. All the people profiled in this book by name gave permission for their names and stories to be used. These people have helped shape me in the area of justice. Their stories overlap my story. I am grateful for their contributions to this manuscript and to my life.

I owe special thanks to many friends and colleagues who have helped me grow and process my thinking about justice and theology: my philosophy and theology professors, Bill Chiaravalle, the faculty at Kilns College, Ed Underwood, Gerry Breshears, and Don Golden and Stephen Bauman at World Relief.

To the people of Antioch in Bend, Oregon, you are my picture of all that can be good in a local church and what sacrificial love can look like.

To Caitlin Querio, Erin Lytle, the staff at Antioch, and my family who have tolerated me during this project, thank you.

To the professionals at World Relief who daily give their lives away to stand for the vulnerable, thank you for teaching me about relief and development, genuine commitment and compassion, and for believing in me.

To Keith Wright and the folks at Food for the Hungry for their collaborative spirit, support on this project, and the impact they're making around the globe.

Special thanks to David Jacobsen, Ben Larson, and Caitlin Querio for your labor and energy in writing this book.

For editorial and research assistance, I am indebted to Antioch interns, including Michelle Struwing, Gordon MacPhail, Mariah Truax, Tabitha Sikich, Spencer Trefzger, Chad Mustain, Heather Mustain, and Levi Polus, as well as to Tamara Wytsma, Matt Smith, Amos Caley, Jeff Johnson, Megan Griffith, Linda Van Voorst, Melissa McCreery, Ann Mara, Derek Brown, Don Dunscomb, Keith Wright, my parents, my sister, and the dozens of other readers who volunteered their time and energy to make this book better.

I was blessed by the creative talent and artistic contributions to this manuscript by Paul Crouse, Natalie Puls, Dan Seward, Jessie Fleury, Micah Bournes, Matt Smith, Judith Montgomery, Cathy Warner, Nate Salciccioli, David Jacobsen, Jerod Wanner, Alex Davis, Tamara Wytsma, and Daniel Fan.

For intensive editorial reading and comments, I am indebted to Rick Gerhardt, Linda Van Voorst, Gerry Breshears, Mike Caba, and Jonathan Wilson-Hartgrove.

Thanks to my agent, Don Jacobson, and the team at DCJA, for taking this book on and finding it a home.

Thanks to Matt Baugher, my editor Adria Haley, and the rest of The Baugher Group at Thomas Nelson for believing in this project.

And to all those who have spoken or presented at The Justice Conference, or contributed to AskQuestions.tv, thank you for the challenge and encouragement your voices are to me. (You can learn more from many of these people at www.askquestions.tv.)

This is an ongoing conversation that requires many perspectives and voices. If you'd like to lend your voice to the conversation, you can e-mail me at kjwytsma@gmail.com.

NOTES

Introduction

1. Henry Daivd Thoreau, *Walden* (Boston: Houghton Mifflin Co., 1995), 87.
2. You can read this story in John 12.
3. Wendell Berry, "The Mad Farmer Poems" (Berkeley, CA: Counterpoint, 2008), 12.

Chapter 1

1. Ashton Applewhite, Tripp Evans, *And I Quote: The Definitive Collection of Quotes, Sayings, and Jokes for the Contemporary Speechmaker* (New York: St. Martin's Press, 1992).
2. Daniel Webster, The Great Speeches and Orations of Daniel Webster (Boston: Little, Brown & Co., 1886), 533.
3. http://www.hagiasophia.com/.
4. Francis Schaeffer, *A Christian Manifesto* (Wheaton, IL: Crossway, 2005), 17.
5. Dr. Walter Brueggemann, The Justice Conference interview, 2012, https://vimeo.com/39386352.
6. Author David Ford puts this radio address in April 1933. David Ford, *The Modern Theologians: An Introduction to Christian Theology Since 1918* (Malden, MA: Blackwell, 2005), 38.
7. Edwin Robertson, ed., *No Rusty Swords: Letters, Lectures & Notes from the Collected Works of Dietrich Bonhoeffer* (New York: HarperCollins, 1970), 221.
8. "Transcript: Bono remarks at the National Prayer Breakfast," *USA Today*, February 2, 2006, http://www.usatoday.com/news/washington/2006-02-02-bono-transcript_x.htm.
9. Aristotle, *Nicomachean Ethics*, translated by T. H. Irwin, 2nd Ed. (Indianapolis: Hackett, 1999), 69.

Chapter 2

1. N. T. Wright, *Surprised by Hope: Rethinking Heaven, the Resurrection, and the Mission of the Church* (New York: HarperOne, 2008), 193; italics in original.
2. Eberhard Bethge in the introduction to Dietrich Bonhoeffer, *Life Together* (San Francisco: Harper San Francisco, 1954), 11.
3. See H. Traub, "Two Recollections," *I knew Dietrich Bonhoeffer, Reminiscences by His Friends*, Wolf-Dieter Zimmermann and Ronald Gregor Smith, Eds., Kathe Gregor Smith, trans. (New York: Harper & Row, 1964), 156.
4. Jesus made this connection in John 14:31.
5. Paul Moser, "Jesus on Knowledge of God," *Christian Scholar's Review* (1999–2000): 598.
6. R. Harris, *Theological Wordbook of the Old Testament* (Chicago: Moody Press, 1980), 931.
7. "What does 'Shalom" Mean to a Christian?" (interview with John Stackhouse), http://www.youtube.com/watch?v=CsGYUkH4zZ0.
8. C. S. Lewis, *Letters to Malcom: Chiefly on Prayer* (Orlando: Houghton Mifflin Harcourt, 2002), 69.
9. Cornelius Plantinga Jr., *Not the Way It's Supposed to Be: A Breviary of Sin* (Grand Rapids: Eerdmans, 1995), 197.
10. Richard Baxter, *The Reformed Pastor* (London: Religious Tract Society, 1799), 24.
11. Henry David Thoreau, *The Essays of Henry David Thoreau*, ed. Richard Dillman (Lanham: NCUP, 1992), 44.
12. We will look at Isaiah 58 in greater detail in chapter 14.
13. Wendell Berry, "The Reactor and the Garden," *The Cultivator* col. 13, no. 3.

Chapter 3

1. Philip Yancey, *The Jesus I Never Knew* (Grand Rapids: Zondervan, 1995), 112.
2. Dr. Perkins, personal conversation with author (August 13, 2012).
3. Adam Hochschild, *Bury the Chains* (Boston: Houghton Mifflin Company, 2005), 66–68.
4. "Church apologises for slave trade," BBC News, February 8, 2006, http://news.bbc.co.uk/2/hi/uk_news/4694896.stm.

5. Hochschild, *Bury the Chains*, 67–68.
6. Ibid., 68.
7. Matthew 25:21 esv.
8. C. S. Lewis, *Surprised by Joy* (San Diego: Harvest, 1955), 226–27.
9. Isaiah 9 is perhaps the richest Old Testament chapter with regard to the coming Messiah. The text of this chapter was artistically immortalized in "The People That Walked in Darkness" and "For Unto Us a Child Is Born" from George Frederic Handel's masterful *Messiah*.
10. http://designtaxi.com/news/351168/Infographic-How-Much-Do-Americans-Spend-on-Gifts/. Accessed September 28, 2012. http://www.ibisworld.com/Common/MediaCenter/Holiday%20 Spending.pdf
11. The World Factbook, https://www.cia.gov/library/publications/ the-world-factbook/fields/2195.html. Accessed September 28, 2012.
12. Shantayanan Devarajan, Margaret J. Miller, and Eric V. Swanson, World Bank Policy Research Working Paper, "The Costs of Attaining the Millennium Development Goals." www.world bank.org/html/extdr/mdgassessment.pdf. This does not take into account the logistical and political problems with providing everyone in the world with clean drinking water, but merely a rough estimation of the financial cost.

Chapter 4

1. C. S. Lewis, *Mere Christianity* (New York: HarperCollins, 2001), 49.
2. Augustine, *The City of God*, Vol. 1, trans. Rev. Marcus Dods, M. A. (Edinburgh: T. & T. Clark, 1947), 210.
3. David Bazan, "Secret of the Easy Yoke," © 1998. Bug Music. All rights reserved. Used by permission.
4. Augustine of Hippo, *The Confessions*, ed. and trans. Philip Burton (New York: Everyman's Library, 2001), 5.
5. Thomas Aquinas, *Summa Theologica*, trans. the Fathers of the English Dominican Province. Partially reprinted in Peter Kreeft, *The Summa of the Summa* (San Francisco: Ignatius Press, 1990), I–II.2.8.
6. Albert Plé, *Duty or Pleasure? A New Appraisal of Christian Ethics*, trans. Matthew J. O'Connell (New York: Paragon House Publishers, 1987), 170.

7. G. Kittel, G. W. Bromiley, and Gerhard Friedrich, eds., *Theological Dictionary of the New Testament*, vol. 9 (Grand Rapids: Eerdmans, 1964–c1976), 370–71.

8. Ibid., 371.

9. Thomas Aquinas in Kreeft, *The Summa of the Summa*, I–II.2.8.

10. Aristotle, *The Nicomachean Ethics*, trans. T. H. Irwin, 2nd ed. (Indianapolis: Hackett, 1999), I.4.1095a17.

11. C. S. Lewis, *The Problem of Pain* (New York: HarperCollins, 1996), 116; emphasis added.

12. C. S. Lewis, *A Severe Mercy: With 18 Letters by C. S. Lewis*, ed., Sheldon Vanauken (New York: Harper & Row, 1987), 189.

13. "It is only where it finds this true joy that the soul is nourished." Augustine, *Confessions*, trans. R. S. Pine-Coffin (London: Penguin Books, 1961), 340.

14. Erin Lytle, personal e-mail correspondence, March 13, 2012.

Chapter 5

1. English Proverb, William Hardcastle Brown, ed. *Odd Derivations of Words, Phrases, Slang, Synonyms and Proverbs* (Toronto: Drexel Biddle, 1900), 102.

2. Frederick Buechner, *Whistling in the Dark: A Doubter's Dictionary* (San Francisco: HarperCollins, 1993), 74.

3. Oswald Chambers, *My Utmost for His Highest* (Uhrichsville, OH: Barbour, 1963), 252.

4. 1 Corinthians 13:13 (Latin Vulgate): *nunc autem manet fides spes caritas tria haec maior autem his est caritas . . .*

5. Bob Goff, *Love Does: Discover a Secretly Incredible Life in an Ordinary World* (Nashville: Thomas Nelson, 2012).

6. Daniel Fan, "Social Justice (Made in America): For Export Only," February 27, 2011, *Ethnic Space Blog*, http://ethnicspace.wordpress.com/2011/02/27/social-justice-made-in-america-for-export-only/.

7. www.brainyquote.com/quotes/quotes/s/saintaugus148531.html.

8. "Nelson Mandela's Speech to Trafalgar Square Crowd," February 3, 2005, www.makepovertyhistory.org/docs/mandelaspeech.doc.

9. "Portland's dark world of child sex trafficking," *Washington Times*,

July 28, 2010. http://www.washingtontimes.com/news/2010/
jul/28/portlands-dark-world-of-child-sex-trafficking/?page=all.
Accessed August 10, 2012.
10. The Oregon Historical Society, History Minutes: Oregon's
Exclusion Laws, http://www.ohs.org/education/history-minutes
-oregons-exclusion-laws.cfm.
11. Anne Morrow Lindbergh, *Gift from the Sea* (New York: Random
House, 2005), 117.
12. Eleanor Roosevelt, "In Our Hands" (1958 speech delivered on the
tenth anniversary of the Universal Declaration of Human Rights),
http://www.un.org/en/globalissues/briefingpapers/humanrights/
quotes.shtml.
13. Daniel Fan, personal e-mail correspondence, August 18, 2012.

Chapter 6

1. C. S. Lewis, *Reflections on the Psalms: The Most Celebrated
Musings on One of the Most Intriguing Books of the Bible* (San
Diego: Harvest, 1986), 32.
2. David Kinnaman, *Unchristian: What a New Generation Really
Thinks About Christianity . . . and Why It Matters* (Grand Rapids:
Baker Books, 2007), 27.
3. Eugene Peterson, *Tell It Slant: A Conversation on the Language
of Jesus in His Stories and Prayers* (Cambridge, MA: Eerdmans,
2008), 88–89.
4. Ibid., 89.
5. C. S. Lewis, *The Complete C. S. Lewis Signature Classics: The
Problem of Pain* (New York: HarperOne, 2002), 607.
6. Dietrich Bonhoeffer, *Life Together* (San Francisco: HarperOne,
1978), 11.
7. In the Old Testament, these two terms occur within four words
of each other in: Genesis 18:19; Deuteronomy 33:21; 2 Samuel
8:15; 1 Kings 10:9; Isaiah 9:7; 28:17; 32:16; 33:5; 56:1; 58:2; 59:14;
Jeremiah 4:2; 9:24; 22:3, 15; 23:5; 33:15; Ezekiel 18:5, 19, 21, 27;
33:14, 16, 19; 45:9; Amos 5:7, 24; 6:12; Psalms 33:5; 99:4; 103:6;
106:3; Job 37:23; Proverbs 21:3; 1 Chronicles 18:14; 2 Chronicles
9:8.

8. Horst Seebass, "Righteousness," *New International Dictionary of New Testament Theology,* Colin Brown, ed. (Grand Rapids: Zondervan, 1986).

9. James W. Curtis, *Tetradrachms of Roman Egypt* (New York: Durst Publications, Ltd., 1969), 4–5; J. G. Milne, *Catalogue of Alexandrian Coins* (London: Oxford University Press, 1933), xx.

10. Curtis, *Tetradrachms of Roman Egypt,* 7; Forvm Ancient Coins, "Dikaiosyne," NumisWiki: The Collaborative Numismatics Project, http://www.forumancientcoins.com/numiswiki/view .asp?key=Dikaiosyne.

11. Forvm Ancient Coins; John Melville Jones, *A Dictionary of Ancient Roman Coins* (London: Seaby, 1990), 7; Frank Thielman. "God's Righteousness as God's Fairness in Romans 1:17: An Ancient Perspective on a Significant Phrase," *Journal of the Evangelical Theological Society* 54:1 (March 2011): 41; http://www.etsjets.org/files/JETS-PDFs/54/54-1/JETS_54-1_35-48_ Thielman.pdf.

12. Tacitus, *Histories* I.4, I.5, I.13, II.8; Suetonius, "Life of Nero," in *The Lives of Twelve Caesars,* 57, http://penelope.uchicago.edu/ Thayer/E/Roman/Texts/Suetonius/12Caesars/Nero*.html#57; Edward Gibbon, *The History of the Decline and Fall of the Roman Empire* (London: Strahan and Cadell, 1776), chap. 6; all sourced from *Wikipedia,* s.v., "Nero," http://en.wikipedia.org/wiki/ Nero#cite_ref-84.

13. http://askquestions.tv/ dr-nicholas-wolterstorff-righteousness-or-justice/.

14. Gustavo Gutiérrez, *Essential Writings* (Maryknoll: Fortress Press, 1996), 301.

15. As a historical aside, my parents once started a home Bible study with a number of Dutch and American people from the Protestant church in the Hague. One Dutch couple that joined was Hans and Mies Poley—Hans was Papa ten Boom's apprentice in the book *The Hiding Place.*

Chapter 7

1. William Wilberforce as quoted by John Charles Pollock, *Wilberforce* (London: Lion Publishing, 1977), 115.

2. William Blake, *The Complete Poetry and Prose of William Blake*, David V. Erdman, ed. (Los Angeles: University of California Press, 1982), 17.
3. See chapter 9, "Compassion Can Kill."
4. Adam Hochschild, *Bury the Chains* (Boston: Mariner Books, 2004), 366.
5. "Ein Konzentrationslager für politische Gefangene In der Nähe von Dachau" (in German), *Münchner Neueste Nachrichten* (the *Munich Latest News*), the Holocaust History Project, March 21, 1933: "The Munich Chief of Police, Himmler, has issued the following press announcement: On Wednesday the first concentration camp is to be opened in Dachau with an accommodation for 5000 persons. 'All Communists and—where necessary—Reichsbanner and Social Democratic functionaries who endanger state security are to be concentrated here, as in the long run it is not possible to keep individual functionaries in the state prisons without overburdening these prisons, and on the other hand these people cannot be released because attempts have shown that they persist in their efforts to agitate and organise as soon as they are released'" (http://www.holocaust-history.org/dachau-gas -chambers/photo.cgi?02).
6. I'm going to cover a lot of history in a short time. If you haven't studied the era in history, it bears your attention. I recommend *Human Smoke* by Nicholson Baker and *Night* by Elie Wiesel as starting points.
7. Alexander Solzhenitsyn, *Solzhenitsyn: A Soul in Exile* (San Francisco: Ignatius, 2011), 195.
8. For example, Deuteronomy 10:18; 24:21; Psalm 146:9; Jeremiah 7:6; Ezekiel 22:7; Zechariah 7:10; Malachi 3:5.
9. Jenny Yang, in an e-mail to the author, August 22, 2012.
10. Ibid.
11. "A study by the Applied Research Center, which studies the intersection of immigration enforcement and the child welfare system, found that some 5,000 children in more than 20 states were put in foster care after their parents were detained or deported by immigration authorities. Experts say parents who are detained or face immigration-related prosecutions often

face obstacles communicating with family courts or access-
ing foster care systems, making it difficult to keep track of
their children or assert their rights" (http://americaswire.org/
drupal7/?q=content/foster-care-uncertain-futures-loom
-thousands-immigrant-children-2).
12. The fascinating history of sugar and its connection to the transatlantic sugar trade is told in Matthew Parker's *The Sugar Barons*
(London: Hutchinson, 2011), 349.
13. Michael Badriaki, in an e-mail to the author, August 22, 2012.
14. Robert McAfee Brown, *Elie Wiesel: Messenger to All Humanity*
(Notre Dame, IN: University of Notre Dame Press, 1983), 109.
15. Elie Wiesel's Remarks at the Dedication Ceremonies for the
United States Holocaust Memorial Museum, April 22, 1993,
United States Holocaust Memorial Museum website, http://
www.ushmm.org/research/library/faq/languages/en/06/01/
ceremony/?content=wiesel; emphasis added.
16. Ibid.

Chapter 8
1. Mark Twain, *What Is Man and Other Philosophical Writings* (Los
Angeles: University of California Press, 1997), 248.
2. Alexis de Tocqueville, *Democracy in America*, Henry Reeve, trans.
(Cambridge: University Press, 1863), 164.
3. On October 26, 2000, Sony officially launched its PlayStation
2 system in the United States, skyrocketing sales. By May
2001, one in three American households contained some kind
of PlayStation system console. By September 2001 approxi-
mately 92 million units had sold. (Playstation.com, http://
us.playstation.com/corporate/about/playstationmilestones/).
4. Marc-Olivier Herman, Broederlijk Delen, and Pieter Vermaerke,
eds., "Supporting the War Economy in the DRC: European
companies and the coltan trade: Five case studies: An IPIS
Report," International Peace Information Service (IPIS), January
2002. "At the end of 2000, the population of Kivu was suddenly
dragged into an unprecedented 'gold rush for coltan.' In a few
months' time, the price of coltan rose tenfold. In January 2000,

an international trader paid between 30 and 40 USD for a pound ˙
(lb) of unprocessed coltan ore. By December 2000, the price had
risen to 380 USD. This increase was caused by an overvaluation
of the technology market triggered by a new generation of mobile
phones (UMTS) and a rush on computer games (Sony Playstation
II), causing a sudden and steep rise in the demand for tantalum
powder. However, the coltan boom was short-lived and prices
rapidly decreased. In April 2001, coltan was priced around 150
USD/lb, in July 2001, around 100 USD/lb and in October 2001,
coltan prices were back to where they were before the 'coltan
gold rush,' i.e. around 30 USD/lb. In the meantime however,
thousands of destitute Congolese people had gone digging for the
precious ore, a few international traders had made a fortune and
millions of dollars had flowed to the parties waging war" (http://
www.grandslacs.net/doc/2343.pdf, p. 9).

5. Enough: The project to end genocide and crimes against humanity, http://enoughproject.org/. See http://vimeo.com/5345683.
The Enough Video Project entry was a collaboration of the World
Relief NEXT Project and emote360, with help from Ann Mara,
video script by Matt Smith, filming by Benjamin Edwards, and
video by Elizabeth Fischer.

6. Cornelius Plantinga, *Not the Way It's Supposed to Be: A Breviary of
Sin* (Grand Rapids: Eerdmans, 1995), 197.

7. Victor Lebow, "Price Competition in 1955," *Journal of Retailing*,
Spring 1955, http://hundredgoals.files.wordpress.com/2009/05/
journal-of-retailing.pdf, p. 3; emphasis added. Also seen in the
video "The Story of Stuff."

8. See http://www.answers.com/topic/teenager.

9. Richard Twiss, sermon at Antioch Church, June 17, 2012; emphasis added.

10. Mission Kids resources are available by subscription to families
on an individual basis, or to entire churches. The church curriculum comes with additional resources (like having your own
personalized Mission Kids website). It's a great way to jump-
start the compassion conversation with the kids in your home or
church! Visit http://missionkids.us to find out more.

11. http://www.merriam-webster.com/dictionary/fair%20trade.

12. Nathan George spoke at Antioch Church on July 22, 2012. His answer regarding fair trade can be found at http://askquestions .tv/nathan-george-how-do-you-define-fair-trade/.
13. Visit http://tradeasone.com to find out more.
14. Blaise Pascal, *Pensees* (New York: Penguin Books, 1966), 347–48.
15. This poem, "My Jesus Ain't Your Jesus," by Daniel Fan, origi-nally appeared in *Cultural Encounters: A Journal for the Theology of Culture*, vol. 5, no. 1 (Winter 2009), 109–10.

Chapter 9

1. Henry David Thoreau, *Civil Disobedience and Other Essays* (Digireads, 2005), 124.
2. www.brainyquote.com/quotes/quotes/h/hoseaballo149580.html (accessed July 20, 2012).
3. Mary Ann Yantis and Robyn Velander, "How to Recognize and Respond to Refeeding Syndrome," Nursing Center, http://www .nursingcenter.com/prodev/cearticleprint.asp?CE_ID=860811. (A starving body begins digesting its own fat and protein. If other food groups are suddenly introduced, the body can enter cardiac arrest or experience neurologic issues. This is known as "refeed-ing syndrome.")
4. World Concern, "Haiti Earthquake Facts and Figures," January 5, 2011, http://reliefweb.int/report/haiti/ haiti-earthquake-facts-and-figures.
5. Michael O. Emerson and Christian Smith, in *Divided by Faith: Evangelical Religion and the Problem of Race in America* (New York: Oxford, 2001), make the point that relationship by itself is insufficient to guarantee justice—there must also be a willing-ness of those with power in the relationship to serve and learn in the process of addressing both personal and structural injustice.
6. Bread for the World, "Global Hunger," http://www.bread.org/ hunger/global/; accessed September 19, 2012.
7. The "Global South" refers to the nations of Africa, Central and Latin America, and most of Asia. The World Bank, "World Development Indicators 2012 now

available," April 19, 2012, http://data.worldbank.org/news/
world-development-indicators-2012-now-available.

8. "According to statistics developed by *The Economist* and the
   International Monetary Fund, seven of the 10 fastest-growing
   economies into 2015 will be African nations." Africa Ascendant,
   "Business Growth in Africa," *Aon One*, September 2011, http://
   one.aon.com/business-growth-africa.

9. There are certainly humanitarian crises in which a "boots on
   the ground" organization can't provide for a specific need, and
   an outside "relief-only" organization is needed for a short while.
   A cargo plane full of blankets and drinking water landing in an
   earthquake zone would be an example of this. What we have in
   mind in this section are organizations that aim to enter a disas-
   ter/relief situation in order to *fix* it, rather than organizations that
   focus on logistics.

10. Keith Wright, in lunchtime conversation with author, July 23,
    2012.

11. Ibid.

12. A Princeton University study found that in one year (2005), 1.6 mil-
    lion United States church members took mission trips—an average
    of eight days—at a cost of $2.4 billion. Study by Robert Wuthnow,
    the Gerhard R. Andlinger professor of sociology at Princeton
    University, where he is also the chair of the department of sociol-
    ogy and director of the Princeton University Center for the Study
    of Religion. These numbers are also attested by Robert J. Priest,
    PhD, professor of mission and anthropology at Trinity Evangelical
    Divinity School in his January 2008 article in *Missiology* journal,
    "Service Learning in Short-Term Missions," 53–73.

13. Keith Wright, lunchtime conversation.

14. Paulo Freire, *Pedagogy of the Oppressed*, Myra Bergman Ramos,
    trans. (New York: Continuum, 2000), 72.

15. Philip Jenkins, Believing in the Global South, *First Things*,
    December 2006 http://www.firstthings.com/article/2007/01/
    believing-in-the-global-south-17.

16. Richard Krejcir, "Francis Schaeffer: Statistics and Reasons for
    Church Decline," http://www.intothyword.org/articles_view.asp?
    articleid=36557&contentonly=true.

17. "Catholics in crisis," *The Week*, April 30, 2010, *http://theweek .com/article/index/202388/catholics-in-crisis*.

18. Krejcir, "Francis Schaeffer."

19. See the information paper "South Pacific Commission Twenty-Third Regional Technical Meeting on Fisheries," http://www .spc.int/DigitalLibrary/Doc/FAME/Meetings/RTMF/23/IP7.pdf.

20. Brian Fikkert, David Beckmann, and Dale Hanson Bourke, "Help That Makes a Difference," *Christianity Today*, December 14, 2009, http://www.ctlibrary.com/ct/2009/december/14.54.html.

Chapter 10

1. http://www.quotationspage.com/quote/1362.html (accessed July 23, 2012).

2. Brennan Manning, *The Ragamuffin Gospel* (Sisters, OR: Multnomah, 2000), 122.

Chapter 11

1. http://www.brainyquote.com/quotes/authors/m/mother_teresa .html (accessed July 12, 2012)

2. G. K. Chesterton, *Illustrated London News*, July 16, 1910, *CW 28:563*.

3. My mom recalls taking the Cambodian refugee family living with us to Disneyland. After the nightmare of the 1970s in Cambodia and the trauma of refugee camp, watching the horrified faces of our Cambodian friends was painful. "There was no way to explain what they were seeing and thinking," she said, "in the Pirates of the Caribbean ride without feeling ashamed of the raping and terrorizing as entertainment."

4. And boys as well, though this is somewhat less common.

5. My initial thinking on some of the ideas in this chapter was influenced by a short lecture by Dr. Nicholas Wolterstorff, spring of 2011.

6. Gary Chapman, *The Five Love Languages: How to Express Heartfelt Commitment to Your Mate* (Chicago: Northfield Publishing, 1992).

Chapter 12

1. Martin Luther King Jr., Address at the 34th Annual Convention of the National Bar Association, Milwaukee, August 20, 1959.
2. Hannah Arendt, *The Life of the Mind* (Orlando: Harcourt, 1977), 180.
3. Emphasis added. The phrase "arc of the moral universe" or a similar expression occurs throughout Martin Luther King's speeches and writings. See Martin Luther King Jr., *A Testament of Hope: The Essential Writings of Martin Luther King Jr.*, ed., James Washington (San Francisco: Harper & Row, 1986), 141, 207, 230, 277, 438.
4. Paul picked up the same theme in his letter to the Galatians: "You, my brothers and sisters, were called to be free. But do not use your freedom to indulge the flesh; rather, serve one another humbly in love. For the entire law is fulfilled in keeping this one command: 'Love your neighbor as yourself'" (5:13–14).
5. The golden rule itself is credited to Jesus and is based on His words in Matthew 7:12: "In everything, do to others what you would have them do to you." This verse is discussed at length later in this chapter.
6. G. K. Chesterton, *What's Wrong with the World* (New York: Dod, Mead & Co., 1912), 48.
7. http://www.nationalww2museum.org/learn/education/for-teachers/lesson-plans/when-they-came-for-me.html.
8. "The only purpose for which power can be rightfully exercised over any member of a civilized community, against his will, is to prevent harm to others." John Stuart Mill, *On Liberty* (Grand Rapids: Baker, 1863), 23.
9. http://mlk-kpp01.stanford.edu/index.php/encyclopedia/documentsentry/ive_been_to_the_mountaintop/; emphasis added.

Chapter 13

1. http://thinkexist.com/quotation/i_think_the_first_duty_of_society_is/177361.html (accessed July 25, 2012).
2. https://www.brainyquote.com/quotes/quotes/p/plato169513.html (accessed July 6, 2012).

3. Stott wrote, "At some point during the decade following WW1, a major shift took place which historian Timothy L. Smith has termed, 'The Great Reversal.'" John Stott, *Issues Facing Christians Today*, 4th ed. (Grand Rapids: Zondervan, 2006), 28.

4. An objection might be raised that liberal Christians have also overemphasized particular concerns at the expense of other issues. Since this book is about justice, however, I am focusing only on the historical reasons for the priority shift on justice, which are most often seen in certain conservative churches.

5. U.S. Bureau of the Census, *Historical Statistics of the United States, Colonial Times to 1970*, 134. http://www2.census.gov/prod2/statcomp/documents/CT1970p1-01.pdf, accessed July 5, 2012.

6. Henry Emerson Fosdick, "Christianity's Stake in the Social Situation," in *The Hope of the World* (New York: Harper and Brothers, 1933), 25.

7. Paul M. Minus, *Walter Rauschenbusch: American Reformer* (New York: Macmillan, 1988), 84, 86.

8. Walter Rauschenbusch, *Christianizing the Social Order* (New York: Macmillian, 1914), 104.

9. *Imago Dei Blog*, http://imagodeicommunity.com/blog/. Eastern University has a similar formulation in its mission statement: "the whole gospel for the whole world through whole persons."

10. Based on the teachings of Thomas Aquinas, the term *social justice* was coined by Luigi Taparelli, an Italian Catholic priest, in his book, published between 1840 and 1843, *Theoretical Treatise on Natural Law Based on Fact*. Leila Sadeghi and Byron E. Price, *Encyclopedia of Contemporary American Social Issues*, Michael Shally-Jensen, ed. (Santa Barbara: ABC-CLIO, LLC, 2011), 711.

11. Thomas Patrick Burke, "The Origins of Social Justice: Taparelli d'Azeglio," *First Principles*, January 1, 2008, http://www.firstprinciplesjournal.com/print.aspx?article=1760&loc=b&type=cbbp.

12. Ryan Messmore, "Real Social Justice," Catholic Education Resource Center, http://www.catholiceducation.org/articles/social_justice/sj00237.htm.

Chapter 14

1. Stephen Prothero, *The American Bible* (New York: HarperOne, 2012), 232.
2. Luke Hendrix, http://askquestions.tv/luke-hendrix-what-is -worship/ (accessed August 14, 2012).
3. The passage in its entirety is being quoted from the 1984 edition of the New International Version. It is well worth your time to read this passage every day for a month because of the way it illuminates other portions of Scripture we often take for granted or assume we know.
4. John D. W. Watts, *Word Biblical Commentary: Isaiah 34–66* (Waco: Word Publishers, 1987), 274.
5. Ralph Waldo Emerson in Constance Pollock and Daniel Pollock, eds., *The Book of Uncommon Prayer* (Dallas: Word Publishing, 1996), 61.
6. Watts, *Word Biblical Commentary: Isaiah 34–66*, 277.
7. Ibid., 275.
8. 1 Peter 2:9 KJV.
9. Ernest W. Shurtleff, "Lead On, O King Eternal," *Net Hymnal*, http://www.cyberhymnal.org/htm/l/e/leadonok.htm.

Chapter 15

1. Aleksandr I. Solzhenitsyn, *The Gulag Archipelago, 1918–1956: An Experiment in Literary Investigation*, vol.1 (Boulder, CO: Westview Press, 1998), 186.
2. Reinhold Niebuhr, *Man's Nature and His Communities* (New York: Scribner, 1965), 24.
3. The NIV uses "seventy-seven." Other translations use "seventy times seven."
4. C. S. Lewis, *Out of the Silent Planet* (New York: Scribner, 1996), 137–38.
5. Lauren E. Glaze, "Correctional Population in the United States, 2010," U.S. Department of Justice, December 2011, http://bjs.ojp .usdoj.gov/content/pub/pdf/cpus10.pdf.
6. Michelle Alexander, "The New Jim Crow," *Huff Post: The Blog*, February 8, 2010, http://www.huffingtonpost.com/ michelle-alexander/the-new-jim-crow_b_454469.html.

7. Michelle Alexander, *The New Jim Crow: Mass Incarceration in the Age of Colorblindness*, repr. ed. (New York: The New Press, 2012), 16.
8. For more information about Célestin and his heart on forgiveness and reconciliation, I encourage you to read his book *Forgiving as We've Been Forgiven: Community Practices for Making Peace* (Downer's Grove, IL: IVP, 2010).
9. http://alarm-inc.org/.
10. Célestin Musekura, personal e-mail to author, August 16, 2012.
11. Ibid.

Chapter 16

1. Andrew Delbanco, *The Real American Dream: A Meditation on Hope* (Cambridge: Harvard University Press, 1999), 10.
2. Gustavo Gutiérrez, *On Job: God-Talk and the Suffering of the Innocent* (Maryknoll, NY: Orbis, 1987), 87.
3. http://www.etymonline.com/index.php?allowed_in_frame=0&search=mulato&searchmode=none.
4. http://usatoday30.usatoday.com/travel/news/2004-01-22-swa-rhyme_.html.
5. Leroy Barber, "Is gentrification of city centers affecting the churches of suburbia?" (2012 Justice Conference talk), http://vimeo.com/40606436.
6. Stuart Walton, "The World of of GK Chesterton, and what's wrong with it," *Guardian* (UK), *Books Blog*, January 8, 2010, http://www.guardian.co.uk/books/booksblog/2010/jan/08/gk-chesterton-world-whats-wrong.
7. Dallas Willard, *The Spirit of the Disciplines: Understanding How God Changes Lives* (New York: HarperCollins Publishers, 1988), 224–25.
8. Timothy Keller, *Generous Justice: How God's Grace Makes Us Just* (New York: Dutton, 2010), 93–94.

Chapter 17

1. http://www.brainyquote.com/quotes/quotes/w/williambut101244.html (accessed July 22, 2012).
2. Edward B. Kenedy, ed. *Our Presidential Candidates and Political Compendium* (F.C. Bliss & company, 1880), 19.

3. John E. Selby, *The Revolution in Virginia: 1775–1783*. (Williamsburg: Colonial Williamsburg, 2007), 158.
4. Joseph J. Ellis, *American Sphinx: The Character of Thomas Jefferson* (New York: Random House, 1998), 59–61.
5. John Chester Miller, *The Wolf by the Ears: Thomas Jefferson and Slavery* (Charlottesville: University of Virginia Press, 1991), 26–29.
6. "Assessing the Slave Trade," Trans-Atlantic Slave Trade Database: Voyages, http://www.slavevoyages.org/tast/assessment/estimates .faces.
7. International Labor Organization and United Nations, http://www.whitehouse.gov/endtrafficking, accessed 9/28/2012. Some estimates go as high as 27 million. See https://www.freetheslaves .net/SSLPage.aspx?pid=375, accessed June 20, 2012; and Kevin Bales, *Disposable People: New Slavery in the Global Economy* (Berkeley: University of California Press, 1999), 9.
8. Martin Luther King Jr., *Strength to Love*, Fortress Press ed. (Cleveland: Fortress Press, 1981), 72.
9. C. S. Lewis, "Learning in War-Time": *The Weight of Glory*, ed. Walter Hooper (New York: Touchstone, 1996), 48–49.
10. I would add that injustice does as well.
11. Bernard of Clairvaux as quoted by Josef Pieper, *Scholasticism: Personalities and Problems of Medieval Philosophy* (Chicago: St. Augustine's Press, 2001), 89.
12. Daniel Boorstin, *The Image: A Guide to Pseudo-Events in America* (1961; reprint, New York: Vintage, 1992), 57.
13. The title of Peterson's book (Downer's Grove, IL: IVP, 2000).
14. George MacDonald, *Mary Martson* (London: Sampson Low, Marston & Co., 1894), 281.
15. Nicholas Wolterstorff, *Educating for Shalom: Essays on Christian Higher Education* (Grand Rapids: Eerdmans, 2004), 24.
16. John Wooden as quoted by John C. Maxwell, *Maxwell Daily Reader* (Nashville: Thomas Nelson, 2007), 15.

Chapter 18

1. Lewis, *Mere Christianity*, 227. (See chap. 4, n. 1.)
2. Walter Brueggemann, speaking at the 2012 Justice Conference (Portland, OR), February 25, 2012.

3. Dietrich Bonhoeffer, *The Cost of Discipleship* (New York: Touchstone, 1995), 89.
4. Martin Luther, *Westminster Collection of Christian Quotes*, Martin H. Manser, ed., (Louisville: Westminster John Knox, 2001), 91.
5. This beatific vision is attributed to Saint Cyprian in the Catechism of the Catholic Church under 1028. U.S. Catholic Church, *The Catechism of the Catholic Church*, 2nd ed. (New York: DoubleDay, 1995), 290.
6. Dietrich Bonhoeffer, *Reflections on the Bible: Human Word and Word of God*, Manfred Weber, ed. (Peabody, MA: Hendrickson, 2004), 42.
7. Barnabas is the New Testament figure widely known for his encouragement—"son of encouragement" is literally what his name means.

Chapter 19

1. http://www.quotationspage.com/quote/1167.html (accessed August 1, 2012).
2. http://quotationsbook.com/quote/23667 (accessed August 1, 2012).
3. Frederick Douglass (Canandaigua, New York, August 3, 1857) in James MacGregor Burns and Stewart Burns, *The Pursuit of Rights in America* (New York: Vintage Books, 1993), contents, vii.
4. Henry Mayer, *All on Fire: William Lloyd Garrison and the Abolition of Slavery* (New York: Norton, 1998), 119–20.
5. BookBrowse, http://www.bookbrowse.com/quotes/detail/index.cfm?quote_number=156.
6. *Online Etymology Dictionary*, s.v., "passion," http://www.etymonline.com/index.php?term=passion&allowed_in_frame=0.
7. Mayer, *All on Fire*, 118.
8. Acts 17:6 ESV.

ABOUT THE AUTHOR

Ken Wytsma is the founder of The Justice Conference, one of the largest international gatherings on biblical and social justice, and the president of Kilns College in Bend, Oregon, where he teaches classes on philosophy and justice. He is also a church planter and lead pastor of Antioch, a church community known for its creativity and national intern program.

Since 2007, Ken has worked with World Relief, an international relief and development agency, as a creative advisor and strategist. He is a consultant with other nonprofits, such as Food for the Hungry, and is a leader, innovator, and social entrepreneur respected for his insight and collaborative spirit.

Ken holds an engineering degree from Clemson University and graduate degrees in both philosophy and religion. The son of a Dutch immigrant, he is a cultural translator recognized for clarifying the complex issues surrounding justice and inspiring people to live and die for bigger things. He lives at the foot of the Cascade Mountains with his wife, Tamara, and their four daughters.

kenwytsma.com

twitter: kjwytsma

ABOUT D. R. JACOBSEN

D. R. Jacobsen is a writer, editor, and teacher. He holds a bachelor's degree in English from Westmont College and a master's degree from Regent College (Christianity and the arts) and Seattle Pacific University (creative writing). He believes "the story of any one of us is in some measure the story of us all," a conviction that shapes his writing and a phrase of Frederick Buechner's that he's fond of stealing. His essays have appeared in various journals and anthologies, and he is the author of *Rookie Dad: Thoughts on First-Time Fatherhood*. He is represented by Don Jacobson of D. C. Jacobson & Associates. He and his wife have lived in California, Austria, and British Columbia, and now they make their home with their two boys in central Oregon. When not thinking about words, he enjoys mountain biking, pickup soccer, and Oregon's craft-brew scene, as well as writing terribly compelling bios.

jacobsenwriting.com

twitter: davidrjacobsen

INTERLUDE AUTHORS

JEFF JOHNSON is the resident dreamer of Themba International. He graduated from Azusa Pacific University with a degree in theology and is currently studying for his masters in divinity at Princeton Theological Seminary.

CATHY WARNER holds an MFA in Creative Writing from Seattle Pacific University, serves as Literary Editor for *Image* journal's "Good Letters" blog, and hosts writing workshops and writers on retreat. A former United Methodist pastor, her work has appeared in *Upper Room* publications and literary journals. Visit her website at www.cathywarner.com.

MICAH BOURNES, a native of Long Beach, California, is a literary artist most known for his performance poetry. His debut album, *The Man Without a Name* (released 2012) is a blend of poetry and hip hop, and it discusses issues of identity and justice. His music and poetry is displayed at www.micahbournes.com.

ALEX C. DAVIS is a writer, editor, and designer who works and plays in Portland, Oregon. He serves on the leadership team of the arts ministry at Imago Dei Community.

DANIEL FAN is a writer and activist for justice issues including indigenous rights and gender equality. He lives in Portland, Oregon, with his wife Emily Rice and their cat.

TAMARA WYTSMA lives in Bend, Oregon, with her husband Ken and four daughters.

MATT SMITH lives in Seattle, Washington, with his lovely wife Jenah. He is currently pursuing a masters degree at The Seattle School of Theology and Psychology and works full-time in coffee shops as a freelance writer.

JUDITH H. MONTGOMERY lives in the high desert of central Oregon with her husband and springer spaniel. Her first book of poetry, *Passion*, received the 2000 Oregon Book Award. *Red Jess* released in 2006, and *Pulse & Constellation* in 2007. She holds a doctorate in American literature from Syracuse University.